On the Business Side of Healthcare

COVID-19 Era and Beyond

On the Business Side of Healthcare

COVID-19 Era and Beyond

Smarter Leadership
Better Management
Best Outcome

Dr. Chris Ehiobuche &
Dr. Kwaku Ampadu-Nyarkoh

Copyright © 2024 by Christian Ehiobuche Ph.D.
Kwaku Ampadu-Nyarkoh Ph.D.

Library of Congress Control Number:		2024907634
ISBN:	Hardcover	979-8-3694-1946-5
	Softcover	979-8-3694-1947-2
	eBook	979-8-3694-1945-8

All rights reserved. No part of this book may be reproduced or transmitted in any form or by any means, electronic or mechanical, including photocopying, recording, or by any information storage and retrieval system, without permission in writing from the copyright owner.

Any people depicted in stock imagery provided by Getty Images are models, and such images are being used for illustrative purposes only.
Certain stock imagery © Getty Images.

Print information available on the last page.

Rev. date: 10/03/2024

To order additional copies of this book, contact:
Xlibris
844-714-8691
www.Xlibris.com
Orders@Xlibris.com
858396

CONTENTS

Dedication vii
Acknowledgment ix
About the Author xi
Bio xiii
Preface xv
Introduction xvii

Chapter 1   Overview of U.S. Healthcare System 1
Chapter 2   Global Healthcare Systems 16
Chapter 3   Healthcare Administration & Leadership 31
Chapter 4   Healthcare Technology & Innovation 48
Chapter 5   Healthcare Costs & Reimbursements 69
Chapter 6   COVID - 19 82
Chapter 7   Post-Pandemic Telehealth Medicine 94
Chapter 8   Post-Covid-19 Patient-providers' Landscape 110
Chapter 9   Healthcare Insurance Post-COVID-19 122
Chapter 10 Managing Patients Experience and Quality Improvement 138
Chapter 11 Leadership and Healthcare Productivity 157
Chapter 12 Healthcare Providers Post-COVID-19 Readiness 182
Chapter 13 Healthcare Organizational Leadership Post-COVID-19 190

Chapter 14 Natural Disasters, Pandemics, and Public Health
            Administration 201
Chapter 15 Environment, Sustainability, and Healthcare
            Management.. 212

References 231

DEDICATION

I dedicate this manuscript to all Physicians, Health Care Providers, and Scientists committed to helping patients survive Covid-19 and finding a permanent cure to this pandemic.

This book is also dedicated to all the survivors of COVID-19 and to all my students in the MBA-Healthcare Administration.

Lastly, I dedicate this manuscript to all Educators preparing students for a greater tomorrow.

Dedication

I dedicate this book to the following people, Nana Ampadu-Nyarkoh, my wife, Kwame Ampadu-Nyarkoh, Kwaku Ampadu-Nyarkoh, and Yaw Ampadu-Nyarkoh, my children. They have been very supportive in developing my academic and research career.

Lastly, I dedicate this book to Berkeley College and fellow professors in Management and International Business department. I appreciate their support and encouragement in building my academic and research career.

ACKNOWLEDGMENT

I am sincerely indebted to my wife, Dr. Maria Justine Birotte-Sanchez, whose contagious passion for medicine and healing brought me inevitably into the healthcare industry and for her incessant support for all my scholarly work and endeavors.

To my sons, Chinedum and Ogechi Ehiobuche, I can never be over grateful and proud of your contributions and designing all the charts and figures in this book. The enormous amount of time you both invested in helping me with literature reviews and analysis will always be remembered. Yes, your hard work paid off.

I am sincerely thankful to Professor Alphonso Ogbuehi, Dean of School of Business Stockton University, for your support and encouragement.

To all reviewers named and unnamed in this list, thank you all.

A vote of gratitude to;

Amb. Grant Ehiobuche
Dr Iheanyi Ehiobuche
Professor Lloyd Soobrain
Professor Solomon Nayanga
Dr. Zee Madueke
Tasha David
LaTasha Wells
Professor Gloria Davy
Professor Kwaku-Ampadu
Ugochukwu Okelie

Professor Margaret Binner
Dr. Glen Siaza
Professor Keith Diener
Lincoln Haley (Photgrapher)

I sincerely appreciate the immense support provided to me by my wife, Nana Ampadu-Nyarkoh. She has been the pillar behind my academic career from the beginning. My three sons, Kwame, Kwaku, and Yaw Ampadu-Nyarkoh have, together with my wife, encouraged me to pursue academic success. Thanks to all of them.

ABOUT THE AUTHOR

Dr. Chris Ehiobuche is an Assistant Professor of Business Studies, Management, Healthcare Administration, and Leadership at Stockton University Atlantic City, New Jersey. His background as a co-founder and Chief Operation Officer of Faith Family Healthcare put him in the spotlight as a serious advocate for Patient Centeredness in healthcare delivery. He has published numerous journal articles related to the future of the U.S. healthcare system. Recently, he has focused his research and writings on sustainable business practices within the healthcare industry to prevent the extinction of independent medical practices. He believes that 'Leadership and Entrepreneurship' are essential components for healthcare providers to keep their doors open. He is a passionate entrepreneur who likes to share his experience in his classrooms and through his writings.

Chris Ehiobuche holds a Ph.D. in Business and Management Sciences. He is a husband and father of two young men.

BIO

Dr. Kwaku Ampadu-Nyarkoh is a Professor of International Business and Management at Berkeley College in New York and New Jersey. Dr. Ampadu-Nyarkoh holds a Bachelor's, Master of Business Administration, and a Ph.D. degree from Rutgers University. His research has investigated international technology transfer by subsidiaries of multinational corporations with special emphasis on the pharmaceutical industry. His published journal articles are focused on corporate strategy in international business. His recent research is focused on the relationship between healthcare and the activities of multinational corporations' technology development in the pharmaceutical industry. Dr. Ampadu-Nyarkoh believes that "Innovative Leadership" is required in both healthcare management and the pharmaceutical industry to improve service delivery.

PREFACE

Step into the heart of the ever-evolving landscape where healthcare and business entwine in a dance of urgency and relevance. Brace yourself for a journey through the intricate web of challenges and opportunities that define the post-COVID era in the American healthcare system.

Behold the title, a beacon guiding us through this labyrinth: "On the Business Side of Healthcare: COVID-19 Era and Beyond." It's not just a title; it's a call to action. A call to revolutionize leadership, redefine management, and achieve nothing short of the Best Outcome. Feel the pulse of these guiding principles - "Smarter Leadership, Better Management, Best Outcome" - pulsating through the veins of innovation and strategic decision-making.

The symphony begins by acknowledging the stark reality laid bare by the pandemic: a healthcare system grappling with inequitable resource distribution. Telehealth emerges as a hero, yet its benefits remain unevenly spread across the diverse landscape of socio-economic strata. It's a tale of disparities, a narrative echoing through the corridors of health outcomes among different demographics.

As the curtain rises, the stage reveals the persistent issue of over-regulation, a complex dance of bureaucracy threatening to overshadow the resilience of the healthcare system. Striking a delicate balance becomes the act du jour, ensuring necessary regulations coexist harmoniously with the spirit of innovation.

The spotlight now shifts to the heroes of the tale - the healthcare providers. The shortage of these essential warriors is laid bare, emphasizing the need for intensified efforts to recruit and retain the skilled professionals required not just for pandemics but for the routine delivery of healthcare to all.

The narrative crescendos into a clash with pharmaceutical greed and exorbitant drug prices, demanding a reevaluation of pricing models. Access to affordable medications takes center stage, an integral act for the public health saga. The relentless reduction of reimbursement for care providers adds another layer of complexity, a challenge to ensure fair compensation and prevent burnout among the healthcare warriors.

But fear not, for there is a glimmer of hope on the horizon in the form of value-based healthcare. A commitment to this noble concept, beyond mere lip service, is the elixir needed to transform the system into one that prioritizes outcomes and patient well-being over cost-cutting measures.

In a grand finale, the complexity of the post-COVID healthcare landscape is unraveled. The call echoes louder - a concerted effort from policymakers, healthcare providers, and the community is required. Let the ongoing discussions metamorphose into tangible actions, weaving a resilient, equitable healthcare system that serves every individual, regardless of socio-economic background. This is not just a conclusion; it's an invitation to shape the future of healthcare, a future where the Best Outcome is not just a guiding principle but a reality for all.

INTRODUCTION

"Whether the event is a natural disaster, terrorism, or a pandemic, health care delivery organizations will be challenged to suddenly adjust capacity, redesign care, manage financial loss, and redeploy staff."

James A. Hamilton

COVID-19 pandemic has challenged healthcare organizations and leaders in ways that one could not imagine years ago. Along with noteworthy and ongoing emphasis on providing high quality, cost-effective, competitive care, and managers are committed to creating environments that support excellence in patient, family, vendors and community experience. This book provides footnotes on how to use decisive decision-making, adapted to novel situations and issues, ensured reliable and safe delivery of care and remain efficient and sustainable during and beyond the pandemic.

This book provides a detailed insight into the healthcare leadership and administration in post-COVID-19 conditions. The book comprises fifteen chapters, and each chapter highlights a significant element associated with healthcare leadership and administration. Each chapter discusses the critical factors linked with leadership and administration in healthcare.

Technology adoption and integration in healthcare have significantly improved the prospects of services and quality of care provided to the patients, detailed in this book. Further, insurance plans under the healthcare system in post-pandemic conditions have also been reviewed in this book. Climate change has significant impacts on public health, exaggerating the implications of COVID. These implications have also been highlighted in this manuscript.

The future of US healthcare delivery is marked by a shift towards greater accessibility, innovation, and patient-centric care. With advancements in technology, telemedicine is expected to play a prominent role, allowing patients to receive medical consultations and monitoring from the comfort of their homes. This trend not only enhances convenience but also addresses the challenge of reaching underserved rural areas.

Moreover, a focus on preventive and personalized medicine is anticipated to grow, leveraging genetic information and cutting-edge diagnostics to tailor treatments to individual patients. This approach aims to not only treat diseases but also proactively manage health risks, ultimately reducing healthcare costs and improving outcomes.

Collaboration and data sharing among healthcare providers are likely to increase, facilitated by integrated electronic health records and interoperable systems. This seamless exchange of information can lead to more coordinated and efficient care, reducing redundancies and ensuring that patients receive comprehensive and timely treatment.

Healthcare delivery is also expected to see increased emphasis on mental health services, recognizing the interconnected nature of mental and physical well-being. Integrating mental health into primary care and leveraging digital tools for mental health support are potential avenues for improvement.

However, challenges such as addressing healthcare disparities, controlling rising costs, and navigating regulatory complexities will persist. Policymakers, providers, and technology innovators will need to work collaboratively to overcome these hurdles and shape a healthcare system that prioritizes accessibility, affordability, and quality care for all.

CHAPTER 1

Overview of U.S. Healthcare System

Over the past years, the world has changed in every way possible. Our living standards means of transports, educations, and most importantly, our healthcare system. Today's health care system is not only complex, but it is also drastically different from what it used to be two centuries ago. The changes are many and represent the major shifts involved in moving from an indemnity plan, based primarily on home remedies and self-diagnosis, to a well-managed healthcare system.

Healthcare systems worldwide aim to use the latest technologies and employ the best practitioners on board to make sure that patients are getting the best possible treatment. However, there are still differences in the healthcare system of each country. These differences are mainly due to the policies regarding insurance, cost of services, and budgetary limitations. The U.S. Healthcare System has experienced a shift in its medicine model and has come a long way from what it used to be in the last century.

Before 1800, medicine in the United States was mainly considered to be a family affair. Women of the house were expected to take care of illnesses, and only on those occasions of very serious, life-threatening diseases were doctors summoned for help. The early American medical practice was a combination of home remedies, thus often termed domestic medicine. However, a few scientifically practiced procedures were still carried out by self-proclaimed doctors. They continued to practice without the kind of qualifications they must now have, traveled extensively, and experimented with various forms of treatments.

Another practice of medicine was midwifery, which included attending women in childbirth and delivering babies. This was a common profession for women since most births took place at home. Until the mid-eighteenth century, all treatments and practices in Western medicine were based on the ancient Greek principle of "four humors"—blood, phlegm, black bile, and yellow bile. It was believed that a balance among the humors was necessary to maintain and is the key to health. Hence, all diseases were thought to be caused by too much or too little of the fluids. The healing power of hot, cold, dry, and wet preparations and various plants and herbs were also highly regarded. Moreover, in case of a severe injury, people called on "bone-setters" and surgeons, most of whom had no formal training.

During the late colonial period, physicians with proper medical degrees and scientific training began showing up on the American landscape. The University of Pennsylvania, built in 1765, was the first medical college, and the Massachusetts Medical Society, incorporated in 1781, sought to license physicians. With time many medical schools continued to open by physicians who wanted to improve American medicine and raise the medical profession to the same status it enjoyed in Europe and England. With the increase in formal knowledge of medicine and scientific training, doctors became more authoritative. They began to practice medicine as small entrepreneurs by opening up clinics and small-scale hospitals while charging a fee for their services.

In the early 1800s, physicians with formal medical training in both Europe and the United States began to emphasize the idea that germs and social conditions might be the primary cause of the development and spread of various diseases, especially in cities. With the increase in infections, many municipalities began to build dispensaries that dispensed medicines to the poor and offered free physician services. These diseases eventually worsened, and epidemics of cholera, diphtheria, tuberculosis, and yellow fever engulfed the world, causing the deaths of hundreds of people. This concern led many city governments to create departments of health whose aim was to ensure hygiene and prevention of diseases. With the help of these departments, new advances in studying causes of disease such as bacteria were put to practical use. A few years later, the "germ theory" became the accepted cause for illness, and appropriate steps were taken to tackle these issues. If it weren't for the multiple epidemics and poor sanitation, the government-sponsored public health and private healthcare would not have begun to diverge systematically.

As industrialization increased and America became increasingly urbanized, hospitals first built by city governments to treat the poor began treating the not-so-poor. Doctors, who now had an increased authority and power, stopped traveling to their sickest patients and began treating them all under one roof. Patients now had to come to the hospital to seek treatment instead of calling the doctor home. Unlike hospitals in Europe, where patients were treated in large wards, American patients who could pay were treated in smaller, often private rooms.

After the Civil War (1865), hospitals became either public or private. More medical schools and institutions began to devote funds to medical research. The need to train physicians more extensively led to the change in Johns Hopkins University's medical school requirements. According to this requirement, all medical students were now mandated to arrive with a four-year degree and spend another four years becoming physicians.

In 1846, the American Medical Association (AMA) was established so that the doctors worldwide had an organization to resolve their issues. With time, the AMA had great influence over the politics and practice of medicine, and the regulation of drugs was one of their early victories.

Just after the Civil War, the profession of nursing began to surface as a profession. This led to the establishment of three training schools for nurses. During its initial period, nursing was considered a gender-based and female stereotyped "nurturing" occupation. However, over the next 100 years, nursing became more professionalized and less gender-biased.

By the late twentieth century, more nurses began to receive advanced degrees and play a greater role in the administration of health care.

As the nineteenth century ended, advancements were in full swing. Researches, discoveries, and inventions in the field of biology, chemistry, and related medical sciences meant that the great diseases—tuberculosis, yellow fever, diphtheria, cholera, and others—were practically eliminated with the development of diagnostic tests and vaccines. Extensive public health projects were initiated—these projects aimed at fighting causes of disease and preventing them from spreading. As a result, there was a noticeable increase in the levels of public health.

By the early part of the twentieth century, doctors had more authority, enjoyed a higher status, and were better paid than ever before. Associations, such as the AMA and the American Hospital Association (AHA), founded in 1899, became stronger and more influential. Moreover, employers and labor unions began to offer a range of benefits to workers, including paid medical care. National health insurance, such as provided by many European nations, became associated with socialism, and the concept became unpopular in the United States. This opened the door for private health insurance to cover the rising costs of medical care.

Even though private health insurance emerged before World War I, it was not until well after the war and toward the end of the 1920s that the first large medical insurance company, Blue Cross, was established. People began to use medical plans that the insurance companies provided as the rise in healthcare costs began to become unaffordable for the working class.

The 1930s saw a further increase in healthcare costs and health insurance plans. At this time, doctors were paid by a system called "fee-for-service." New insurance plans, such as Blue Cross and Blue Shield, allowed its members to pay both the costs of hospitalization and for treatment by physicians. The AHA in the 1930s took an active role in supporting group hospitalization plans. During World War II, a medical plan started by Henry J. Kaiser for his employees featured a pre-paid program that paved the way for Health Maintenance Organizations (HMOs) 40 years later.

The post-World War II era saw great expansions in the workforce accompanied by advancements in medical science and medical care and increasing healthcare costs. The Baby Boom generation, the name given to the large numbers of children born just after World War II, received ever-higher levels of medical and preventive care during the 1950s as compared to the parents' generation. Advances in medicine and diagnostic techniques, such as x rays, life-saving drugs, such as penicillin, and vaccinations against diseases, such as polio, began to create an ever-deepening scientific culture that included laboratory technicians, therapists, widening roles for nurses, and increasing specialization among physicians.

These post-World War II technological advances professionalized the roles of non-physician therapists and technicians, including respiratory therapists, physical therapists, x-ray technicians, and laboratory technicians. However, the improvements in technology and increasingly sophisticated treatments and therapies also pushed up the cost of healthcare during the same period.

During this period, the U.S. government research and health institutions and programs, such as the National Institutes of Health and the Centers for Disease Control, were also established to increase the researches being done. In the 1960s, social programs to aid in the medical care of the aged (Medicare) and poor (Medicaid) were initiated. However, before the founding of these institutions, the U.S. government had founded other health programs and institutions, such as the Indian Health Service, the U.S. Public Health Service, the Food and Drug Administration. It established an executive cabinet-level agency, the Department of Health and Human Services as well.

From the end of World War II until the late 1980s, most doctors were still independent and compensated through fee-for-service. They aimed to keep it that ways, and through the powerful AMA and other organizations, they fought off political attempts at creating a nationalized, universal coverage medical systems, such as those in Canada, the United Kingdom, and Europe.

While doctors tried their best to fight off the creation of universal coverage medical systems, they failed to notice the growth of Health

Maintenance Organizations (HMOs). By the mid-1980s, HMOs began to dominate both the organization of health care and reimbursement to physicians. In the 1990s, HMOs and their varieties successfully revolutionized the organization of health care in the United States. They provoked controversy among recipients of healthcare as well as doctors, who came to find themselves in less control of their practices. Fee-for-service began to fade as doctors increasingly found themselves working for corporations that made profits from pre-paid healthcare by reducing the costs of healthcare, carefully restricting services, and focusing on preventive healthcare.

Fee-for-service began to be slowly replaced by "capitation," a system that paid doctors a set fee from which they had to care for all of their patients, the sick and the well. This system, also termed as "managed care," produced changes in the consumers' role in healthcare. It placed greater emphasis on preventive medicine, consumer choice, and being accountable for one's own health and healthcare. Furthermore, communications advancements such as the Internet and the World Wide Web in the 1990s added to the health information available to consumers. During this time, consumer interest also grew in "alternative medicine," such as acupuncture, herbal preparations, and vitamin therapies. These interests could be seen as a reaction against the medical-industrial complex.

With the increase in communication and technology, telemedicine was introduced. This practice allows physicians to use a system utilizing the Internet by which patients could be diagnosed and often treated by physicians at a distance. This practice is expected to help in keeping the physician and patients connected even if they are at a distance. In the present scenario where most of the places in the world are in a state of lockdown, this practice is helping people seek treatment without having to risk their health and visit the hospital.

Twenty-first-century technology promises to continue changing the nature, complexity, and costs of healthcare. As knowledge increases about the genetic bases of disease, the healthcare system will make greater use of gene therapies, developing ways to prevent genetically caused diseases. Similarly, it also aims to treat and prevent diseases that were previously considered fatal.

Just as the impact of new technologies, such as x rays, antibiotics, vaccines, and surgical advances changed early and mid-twentieth-century medicine socially and scientifically, scientific and medical innovations, as well as social movements and economic realities, will continue to shape twenty-first-century medicine and health care. One of the few ways it has begun to happen is with the help of healthcare delivery facilities that the US is now using to make sure that healthcare is reaching its residents in every possible form. Some of the healthcare delivery facilities are mentioned in figure 1.1:

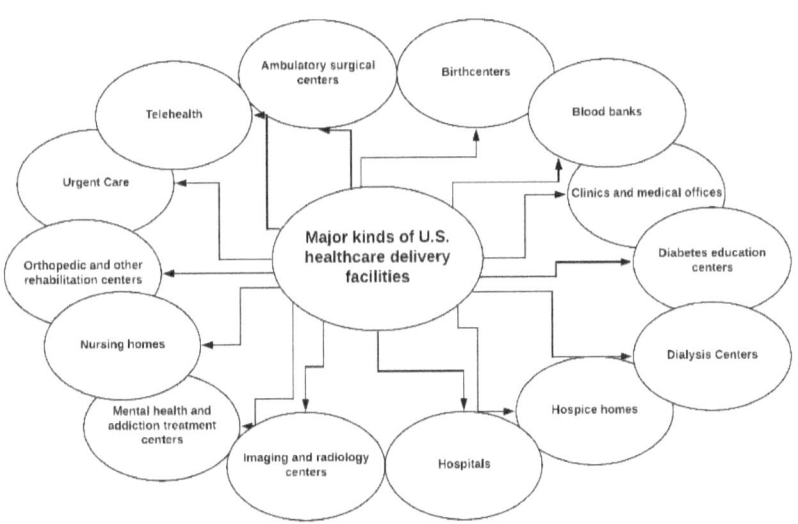

Figure 1.1: Major Kinds of U.S. healthcare Delivery Facilities

Figure 1.1 illustrates the major kinds of healthcare delivery facilities in the U.S. These include blood banks, clinics, and medical offices, diabetes education centers, dialysis centers, hospice homes, hospitals, imaging and radiology centers, mental health and addiction treatment centers, nursing homes, orthopedic and rehabilitation centers, urgent care, telehealth, ambulatory surgical centers, and birth-centers.

These healthcare centers comprise of an array of clinicians, specialists, hospitals and other healthcare facilities, purchasers of health care services, and insurance plans. These facilities operate in various configurations of networks, groups, and independent practices. Some of these healthcare facilities operate in the private sector, while others operate in the public sector. Collaborations, communication, or systems planning in these entities is almost incidental to their operations.

According to the Commonwealth Fund, which regularly ranks the health systems of a handful of developed countries, the best countries for health care are the United Kingdom, the Netherlands, and Australia. The present U.S. health system is a complex mix of public and private, for-profit and nonprofit insurers and health care providers. The federal government provides funding for the national Medicare program for adults age 65 and older and some people with disabilities as well as for various programs for veterans and low-income people, including Medicaid and the Children's Health Insurance Program. Private insurance is the dominant form of coverage and is provided primarily by employers. Both public and private insurers set their own benefits packages and cost-sharing structures within federal and state regulations. However, it is only because of the Affordable Care Act that the number of insurers has decreased to 8.5 percent from 16 percent in 2010[1].

Along with the increase in the number of insurers over the past years, the threat to the healthcare system has also increased. These threats are making it difficult for physicians to keep doing their jobs with consistent motivation and resilience. One of the main threats to the healthcare system is Physicians Burnout. This term was first coined in 1974 by clinical psychologist Herbert Freudenberger, PhD, who noticed this phenomenon while working at a volunteer health clinic in New York City's East Village. His colleagues were experiencing high levels of depletion and psychosomatic symptoms. After careful observation of these symptoms, he defined burnout as "excessive demands on energy, strength, or resources" experienced in the workplace leading to frustration, fatigue, malaise, inefficiency, and cynicism.

Over the years, burnout has become a huge problem in the United States, and its repercussions are known to trickle down to patients in the form of poor care. After controlling for covariates like age and sex, researchers have shown that more than half of American physicians' experience burnout which is more than double that of their peers in other occupations. Causes of burnout include excessive work hours—with the average U.S. physician working 51 hours a week. Excess bureaucracy demanded by the rigmarole of Medicare, Medicaid, and private insurance companies also contributes to burnout. Sadly, for every 1 hour a physician spends seeing a patient, there are 2 hours of associated "paperwork."

Possible solutions to burnout include improved leadership that stresses self-care, alternative incentives such as time off, and greater flexibility in allowing physicians to schedule their own hours. Furthermore, according to some studies, burned-out surgeons tend to commit more errors, and burned-out physicians are more likely to quit their jobs—which exacerbates another major problem threatening healthcare: the physician shortage.

The problem of the physician shortage in the United States is only getting worse. The Association of American Medical Colleges projects a deficit of 46,100 to 90,400 physicians by 2025. Moreover, the U.S. population is expected to grow to 347.3 million in 2025, compared with 316.5 million in 2013—a nearly 10% increase—with the elderly population expanding by 46%[2]. To meet demand, medical schools have been educating more physicians. However, Medicare is capped in how many residency slots it can finance.

This means that the existing population of physicians is expected to keep working so that there are enough physicians to accommodate the increasing population of patients. Although some fear that physicians practicing in their twilight years could be dangerous, the prospect of a mandatory age for retirement scares many. Making physicians retire at a certain age could cull those who still have the skills needed to practice and hasten the physician shortage.

Ever since 1965, the number of practicing physicians age 65 years and older has almost quadrupled. In 2015, 23% of physicians were older than 65 years[3]. Although cognitive decline is a highly prevalent variable among individuals, people aged 40-75 years have cognitive declines that average greater than 20%[4].

Apart from these issues, there are flaws in the healthcare system that tend to increase the issues that both physicians and patients face. Some of these issues are:

1. A Lack of Insurance Coverage.

One of the main issues in the healthcare system of the U.S. is the fact that health care and health insurance are not equivalent. This means that getting more people insured will not necessarily improve health outcomes. The literature on insurance demonstrates that having insurance lowers mortality and is equivalent to a public-health intervention. More than 27 million people in the U.S., which is nearly 10 percent of the population, were uninsured in 2016[5]. This is because they are not able to afford coverage, live in a state that didn't expand Medicaid, or are undocumented. Those aren't problems that people in places like the United Kingdom have to worry about.

2. Administrative Inefficiency.

According to the Commonwealth Fund's most recent report, in the United States, doctors and patients tend to spend a lot of time on billing and insurance claims as compared to other countries that rely on private health insurers, like the Netherlands that has minimized some of these problems by standardizing basic benefit packages, which can both reduce the administrative burden for providers and ensure that patients face predictable copayments. In other words, while insurance coverage, in general, is great, it's not ideal that different insurance plans cover different treatments and procedures, forcing doctors to spend precious hours coordinating with insurance companies. In contrast, they can spend the same time providing care.

3. Underperforming Primary Care.

In 2014 the Commonwealth Fund found that many primary-care physicians struggle to receive relevant clinical information from specialists and hospitals, complicating efforts to provide seamless, coordinated care. On top of a lack of investment in primary care, there is also a lack of investment in social services, which are important determinants of health. This also includes things like home visiting, better housing, and healthy subsidized food that could extend the work of doctors and do a lot to improve chronic disease outcomes. The American health care system has not only undergone drastic changes within two generations, but it is still continuing to evolve. However, these advancements need to be in favor of both the physician and the patient, as the healthcare system will collapse if either of them is unavailable. As our population continues to age, as health care costs continue to increase, as treatments become costlier, and as increasing numbers of people are without health care coverage, the threat to the healthcare system also increases. Therefore, necessary changes in the healthcare system that are in favor of all should be implemented at the earliest[6].

The healthcare system in the U.S. has encountered a shift in its medicine model and has come a long way from what it used to be in the last century. Early medical practice was usually called domestic medicine as it was based on a combination of home remedies. With increasing industrialization and urbanization, the challenges of the healthcare system are also increasing. The U.S. healthcare system needs to develop and implement a competency framework to overcome the prevailing challenges[7]. Advancing communication and technology has introduced the concept of telemedicine which might accelerate U.S. healthcare services. Since the healthcare system is still evolving, the U.S. government can help in redefining the concepts of quality-oriented care for the improvement and promotion of health.

In the wake of the COVID-19 pandemic, the American healthcare system is grappling with a multitude of challenges, further unveiling deep-rooted issues that demand urgent attention. One glaring concern is the inequitable distribution of resources, exposing a stark contrast in healthcare accessibility between different socioeconomic groups. While telehealth services have emerged as a positive development, providing remote consultations and broader access, the benefits are not uniformly distributed.

Health disparities have been exacerbated, laying bare the existing inequalities in healthcare outcomes among various demographic groups. This calls for a comprehensive approach to address the root causes of these disparities, ranging from social determinants of health to systemic barriers that hinder equitable care.

Over-regulation has been a persistent issue, adding layers of complexity and bureaucracy to an already intricate system. Striking a balance between necessary regulations and fostering innovation is crucial for a healthcare system that can adapt to evolving challenges efficiently.

The shortage of care providers is another pressing concern. The pandemic has underscored the need for a robust healthcare workforce, and efforts must be intensified to recruit and retain skilled professionals. Adequate staffing is essential not only for managing crises like pandemics but also for ensuring routine healthcare services are readily available to all.

Pharmaceutical greed and exorbitant drug prices have long been a contentious issue, and the post-COVID era demands a reevaluation of pricing models. Access to affordable medications is integral to public health, and addressing this aspect is crucial for a more equitable and sustainable healthcare system.

Furthermore, the relentless reduction of reimbursement for care providers and hospitals adds strain to an already burdened system. Ensuring fair compensation for healthcare services is essential to maintain the quality of care and prevent burnout among healthcare professionals.

The concept of value-based healthcare, while well-intentioned, often receives mere lip service from insurance providers. A sincere commitment to implementing and sustaining value-based care models is imperative for fostering a healthcare system that prioritizes outcomes and patient well-being over mere cost-cutting measures.

The post-COVID-19 American healthcare landscape is a complex tapestry of challenges and opportunities. Addressing these issues requires a concerted effort from policymakers, healthcare providers, and the community to build a system that is resilient, equitable, and truly focused on improving health outcomes for all. The ongoing discussions about potential reforms and improvements must translate into tangible actions to create a healthcare system that serves the needs of every individual, regardless of their socio-economic background.

Strategic Vision: Effective leadership goes beyond just day-to-day operations. It requires crafting a comprehensive and sustainable vision for healthcare. This involves setting long-term goals that prioritize preventive care, innovation, and community health. By having a clear direction, healthcare organizations can navigate challenges and work towards a healthier future.

Resource Allocation: Smart management is all about making the most of available resources. Whether it's human capital or financial investments, effective leaders ensure efficient allocation. By investing in technology, training programs, and preventive measures, healthcare becomes not only cost-effective but also sustainable in the long run.

Innovation and Technology: Keeping up with technological advancements is crucial for improving patient care and streamlining processes. Leaders should foster a culture of innovation, encouraging the integration of digital health solutions and data-driven decision-making. This approach not only enhances efficiency but also keeps healthcare on the cutting edge of progress.

Employee Engagement: The backbone of any healthcare system is its staff. Better management involves creating a positive and supportive work environment, offering ongoing training, and acknowledging the contributions of healthcare professionals. This, in turn, leads to higher job satisfaction and retention rates, ultimately benefiting the entire healthcare ecosystem.

Community Involvement: Sustainable healthcare isn't a solo endeavor. Leaders should actively engage with local communities to understand their unique needs. By promoting health education and establishing preventive care initiatives, healthcare becomes more community-centric and responsive to the diverse needs of its population.

Adaptability and Resilience: The healthcare landscape is ever-evolving. Effective leadership requires adaptability and resilience in the face of dynamic changes in technology, policies, and global health challenges. This adaptability allows the healthcare system to navigate uncertainties and respond proactively to emerging needs.

Data-Driven Decision-Making: In the age of information, utilizing data analytics is paramount. Leaders and managers should leverage data to identify trends, allocate resources efficiently, and implement evidence-based practices. This data-driven approach enhances decision-making processes and ultimately improves patient outcomes.

Regulatory Compliance: Staying on top of healthcare regulations is non-negotiable. Smart management ensures that the organization operates within legal frameworks, mitigating risks and building trust among stakeholders. Adhering to regulations is not just a legal obligation but a foundation for a well-functioning and trustworthy healthcare system.

Collaboration: Healthcare involves a network of entities – hospitals, clinics, research institutions. Effective leaders foster collaboration among these entities, creating a cohesive approach that improves overall efficiency and encourages the sharing of best practices. This collaborative spirit contributes to a more integrated and effective healthcare delivery system.

Environmental Responsibility: Sustainability in healthcare isn't only about human health but also about the planet. Leaders can play a role by implementing eco-friendly practices, reducing waste, and promoting energy-efficient solutions. This environmental responsibility aligns healthcare with broader efforts towards a healthier planet.

In essence, the combination of visionary leadership and effective management is the key to transforming healthcare into a sustainable, efficient, and patient-centered system. It's not just about treating illnesses; it's about creating a healthcare ecosystem that thrives in the long term, benefiting both individuals and the community at large.

CHAPTER 2

Global Healthcare Systems

The increasing attention towards human welfare over the years has led to many advancements in the healthcare industry. This is mainly due to the fact that there are many more diseases now than there were a couple of centuries ago. The global health system focuses on global issues such as health care financing, governance, and human resources for health. Objects of analysis in the global health system are generally countries and institutions, while the engagement in such issues is often at the national or subnational level. This engagement at the global level aims at addressing global health issues and diseases such as those depicted in figure 2.1.

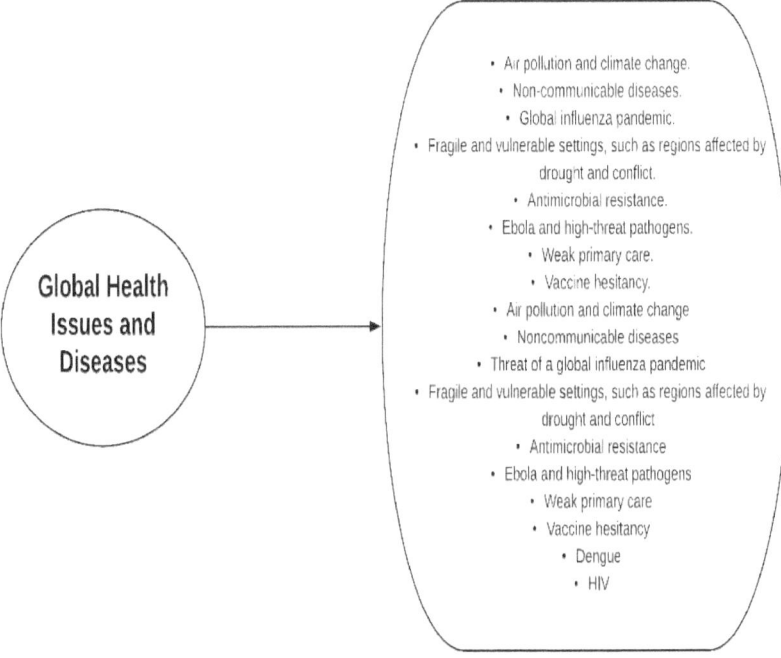

Figure 2.1: Global Health Issues and Diseases

Figure 2.1 illustrates the global health issues and diseases that have been prevailing currently and the factors leading to these diseases and health issues. These factors include air pollution and climate change, antimicrobial resistance, weak primary care, vaccine hesitancy, fragile and vulnerable settings such as areas that have been affected by drought, and the emergence of Ebola and high-threat pathogens like HIV and dengue. The prevailing health issues and diseases associated with these factors include non-communicable diseases and the global influenza pandemic.

On a global scale, the rate of mortalities associated with non-communicable diseases is increasing[1]. Moreover, the rate of deaths due to infectious diseases is also increasing, such as tuberculosis, malaria, and vaccine-preventable diseases. Climate changes are recognized as a significant reason behind the spread of the emergence of Ebola and high-threat pathogens like HIV and dengue as well as non-communicable diseases.

In addition, it has also brought attention to the differences in healthcare systems across countries. According to the WHO, average global life expectancy is rising steadily, which suggests that the quality of healthcare also tends to increase. The rankings of health systems in the world show that only high-income countries are better off when it comes to the providence of healthcare. However, in a study called Mirror, Mirror 2017- International Comparison Reflects Flaws and Opportunities for Better U.S. Health Care, the Commonwealth Fund assessed the performance of healthcare systems in 11 countries based on 72 indicators[2]. This study aimed to find out how efficient healthcare in the United States is. The results of the survey ranked the U.S. last, even though it is one of the developed countries in the world. In fact, the United States is the only one of the 33 developed countries that does not have universal health care.

In the United States, about 67.2 percent of residents are covered under private health insurance. Employer-based health insurance continues to be the most prevalent, with 56 percent receiving coverage through work. Moreover, 19.3 percent of the population was covered by Medicaid, while Medicare covered 17.2 percent in 2017. The fact that the U.S. does not offer universal coverage is one of the many reasons why it is last on this list. Nevertheless, 91.2 percent of the population was covered for all or part of 2017 under a health insurance plan due to the American Health Care Act.

Healthcare in the United States is expensive, with the maximum out-of-pocket limit reaching up to $7,150 for an individual and $14,700 for a family in 2017. These amounts do not include the monthly premiums each individual is responsible for paying. If an individual is covered under Medicaid, then they do not have any out-of-pocket expenses for covered medical services. Medicare Part A has a deductible of $1,340 per year, and Medicare Part B has an annual deductible of $183. Without a Medicare Supplement or Medicare Advantage plan, Medicare beneficiaries do not have an out-of-pocket maximum, so they could end up paying a lot more for their medical expenses.

On the Business Side of Healthcare

The healthcare of the U.S. is quite different as compared to that of other countries. In Sweden and Norway, residents have universal coverage. The majority of the residents in both countries are covered by the public health insurance available through the government. There is also limited private medical insurance available for the residents to purchase if they choose to. Currently, about 1 in 12 residents in Sweden has opted for private health insurance coverage. Though Sweden and Norway both have universal coverage available to their residents, healthcare is not free. Residents pay copays for office visits and hospital stay, but there is a spending cap per year. In Norway, the annual limit of expenditure is 2,000 Norwegian krone, roughly $220.61 in U.S. currency. Swedish residents have an annual limit of 1,100 Swedish krona, roughly $120.99. Once these caps are met in 12 months, both countries cover health expenses at 100 percent.

Taxes largely fund the health systems in Norway and Sweden. The majority of the hospitals in Norway and Sweden are owned and operated by the government. In the United States, about 21 percent of the hospitals are federal or state government hospitals. Most physicians work for public health systems in Sweden and Norway. In contrast, in the United States, the majority of physicians work for private organizations.

Both Norway and Sweden have a decentralized health care system. The goal of both countries is to move healthcare away from the central government. They transfer authority to the local governments; however, the federal government does have overall managerial authority. Sweden has local municipalities which are responsible for deciding what is covered under the public health system. The biggest issue Swedish and Norwegian residents face when it comes to health care is receiving care in a timely manner. Sweden passed a law in 2005 which guarantees its residents receive health care when they need it. Swedish residents are guaranteed a primary doctor's visit within seven days and a specialist or operation within 90 days of seeking treatment. Norway is also improving at reducing their wait times, with the average sitting at 60 days to start treatment.

Norway and Sweden have a better overall health system than the United States. However, it is not perfect in either country. The greatest difference in the health care systems of the United States versus Norway and Sweden is the cost for the residents. The out-of-pocket spending for healthcare is much lower in Norway and Sweden than it is in the United States. Both countries also offer universal healthcare coverage, whereas, in the United States, there is still a high number of uninsured residents — about 12.2 percent in 2017.

Apart from the European healthcare systems, the Canadian system of universal health care has long been viewed as an alternative, superior model for the U.S. to follow. Canada's single-payer system is mostly publicly funded, while the U.S. has a multi-payer, heavily private system. Much of the appeal of the Canadian system comes from the fact that it seems to do more for less. Canada provides universal access to health care for its citizens, while nearly one in five non-elderly Americans is uninsured. In Canada, coverage is not tied to your job or dependent on your income; rich and poor are in the same system and enjoy equal access. Yet last year, Canada spent far less of its GDP on health care than did the U.S. — 10.4% compared with 17.8% in the U.S. — which was the highest percentage of any nation in the world, according to the World Health Organization. For all that, Canada scored better than the U.S. on two commonly cited health outcome measures — infant mortality and life expectancy.

Not just this, the U.S. healthcare system also has led to a socialism state in which the government had to raise taxes on all citizens to pay for these services. Moreover, in order to make sure all citizens pay taxes, the government is forced to control the distribution of goods and services as the controlled movement of commodities would turn the United States into a socialist state. According to a study, U.S. doctors spend four times as much as Canadians dealing with insurance companies[3]. This means that the administrative costs and wastage of time are higher in the U.S. healthcare system. Furthermore, with the help of easy access to health care, some people will seek care with conditions that don't require medical attention. These kinds of individuals will burden the system unnecessarily. The government may adopt rationing of medical services as seen in countries like France, Canada, among others.

The healthcare system of underdeveloped countries has also grabbed much attention in the past years, just like the healthcare system of developed countries. However, the reasons are quite different. Over the years, it has become especially important to emphasize health care systems in low- and middle-income countries because of the substantial external funding provided for disease-specific programs, especially for drugs and medical supplies, and the relative underfunding of the broader health care infrastructures in these countries[4].

Recent analyses have drawn attention to the weaknesses of health care systems in low- and middle-income countries. For example, in the 75 countries that account for more than 95% of maternal and child deaths, the median proportion of births attended by a skilled health worker is only 62% (range, 10 to 100%). Women without money or coverage for this service are much less likely to receive it than are women with the means to pay for it[5]. Lack of financial protection for the costs of healthcare means that approximately 100 million people are pushed below the poverty line each year by payments for health care. Many more will not seek care because they lack the necessary funds[6].

In response to such deficiencies in the health care system, a number of countries and their partners in development have been introducing new approaches to financing, organizing, and delivering health care. A major problem in low- and middle-income countries is the lack of financial support for those who need health care, deterring service use and burdening household budgets.

Almost 50% of health care financing in low-income countries comes from out-of-pocket payments, as compared with 30% in middle-income countries and 14% in high-income countries. When payments from general government expenditures, social (public) health insurance and prepaid private insurance are combined, only 38% of health care financing in low-income countries is combined in funding pools, which allow the risks of health care costs to be shared across the population groups, as compared with approximately 60% in middle-income countries and 80% in high-income countries.

The Philippines and Vietnam, for instance, have sought to expand financial protection by encouraging voluntary enrollment in social health insurance programs. In contrast, other countries, such as Thailand, have used funds from general taxation that are channeled to ministries of health or local health authorities. The recent report from the High-Level Expert Group on Universal Health Coverage, which was charged by the Indian Planning Commission to develop a blueprint for achieving universal coverage in India by 2020, recommended channeling considerably increased funding from general tax revenue to large public providers through a public purchaser at the state level. The report is clear in its rejection of contributory insurance arrangements[7].

In Africa, Rwanda is frequently referred to as a country that has achieved remarkably high voluntary insurance coverage[8]. However, the depth of coverage (i.e., the number of services covered) is limited, and there is still insufficient financial protection for the poorest groups. Ghana, another African country cited for its efforts to expand health care coverage, introduced a national health insurance program in which enrollment is compulsory for the formal sector and voluntary for the informal sector and in which coverage is free for the poorest members of the population.

However, problems in making premiums affordable and in maintaining voluntary enrollment led the ruling party to propose one-time payment rather than annual payment from those outside the formal sector[9]. General taxation (through a value-added tax) is already the main financing source for Ghana's national health insurance. Still, the introduction of a one-time payment would clearly signal a decrease in the importance attached to contributory insurance.

Given the limited tax base in low- and middle-income countries and the limited ability of many households to pay for health care, whether directly or through contributory insurance, progress toward improved financial protection will inevitably be gradual. Countries need to and do draw on a mix of financing sources. Their key concern should be to determine which financing arrangements, given their particular economic, social, and political environment, will best protect the most vulnerable segment of the population and ensure both breadth of coverage (the number of people protected) and reasonable depth of coverage.

To deal with the inequalities in healthcare systems and to make sure that each individual has a chance to avail better treatment options, many NGOs are offering medical services around the world.

With the passage of time, the role of NGOs in the healthcare system has only evolved. Some of those roles are mentioned in figure 2.2 below.

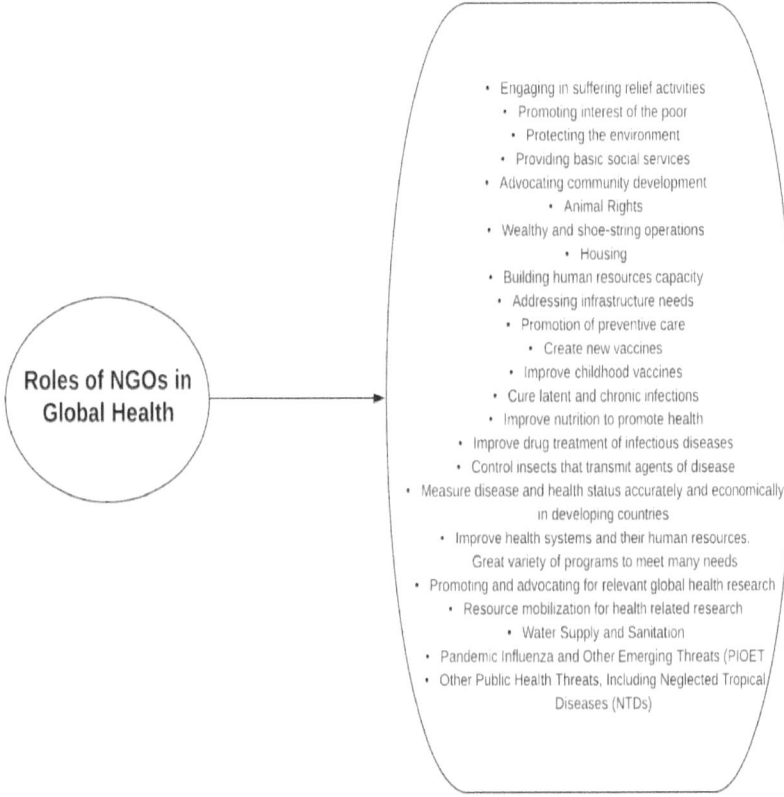

Figure 2.2: Roles of NGOs in Global Health

Figure 2.2 enlists the roles of NGOs in global health. NGOs are required to engage efficiently in suffering relief activities, promoting interest of the poor, protecting the environment, providing basic social services, advocating community development, animal rights protection, wealthy and shoe-string operations, housing, building human resources capacity, addressing the infrastructure needs, promotion of preventive care, creation of new vacancies, and improving childhood vaccines. NGOs are also required to participate in health programs that improve nutrition to promote health, improve drug treatment for infectious diseases, control the insects that transmit agents of disease, and measure disease and health status economically and accurately in developing countries.

NGOs must facilitate in improving health systems and their human resources, improvement of water supply and sanitation, and resource mobilization for health-related research. NGOs are also accustomed to participate in programs such as Pandemic Influenza and Other Emerging threats (PIOET), and certain other similar Public Health Threats such as Neglected Tropical Diseases (NTDs).

These organizations are changing communities through prevention, prenatal care, disease control, vaccinations, and mobile education and understanding of their health issues. These organizations span from big cities to the most rural parts of the world to bring healthcare to children and adults. Some of these organizations are listed in figure 2.3 below:

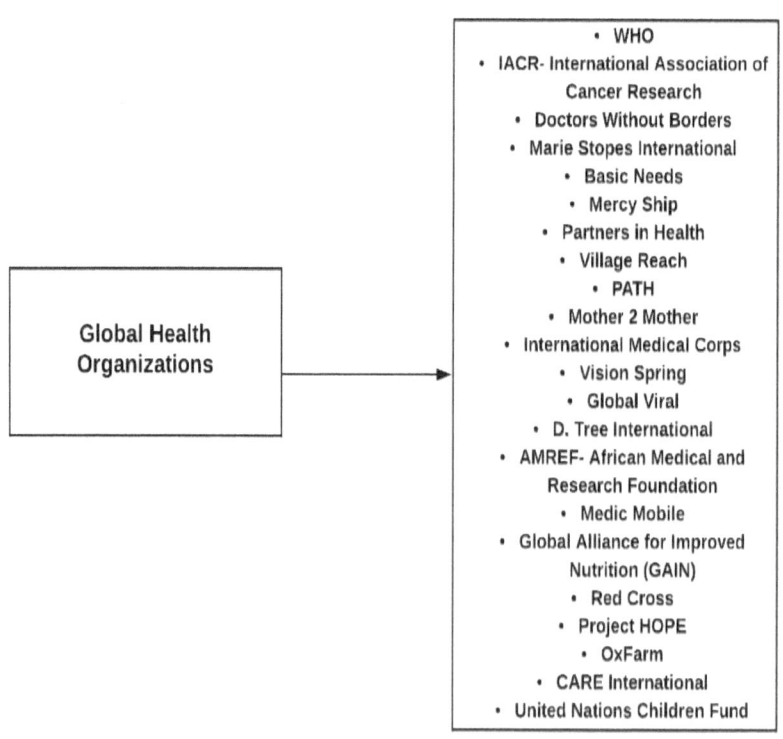

Figure 2.3: Global Heath Agencies

Figure 2.3 enlists the health agencies that have been operating at a global scale for public health protection. These include World Health Organization, International Association of Cancer Research (IACR), Doctors without borders, Marie Stopes International, Mercy ship, Basic Needs, village reach, Partners in Health, Mother 2 Mother, PATH, Global Viral, Medic Mobile, International Medical Corps, Global Alliance for Improved Nutrition, United Nations for Children Fund, Project HOPE, Red Cross, CARE International, Oxfam, and African Medical and Research Foundation.

Global health organizations aim to protect public health and empower healthcare practitioners to participate in public health safety. Moreover, these organizations are funded by the government and other non-governmental entities to ensure and promote health.

1. Global Alliance for Improved Nutrition (GAIN)

The Global Alliance for Improved Nutrition (GAIN) is an alliance driven by the vision of a world without malnutrition. Created in 2002 at a Special Session of the U.N. General Assembly on Children, GAIN supports public-private partnerships to increase access to the missing nutrients in diets necessary for people, communities and economies to be stronger and healthier.

In less than a decade, GAIN has been able to scale its operations by working in partnership with governments and international agencies, and through projects involving more than 600 companies and civil society organizations in more than 30 countries, reaching an estimated 667 million people with nutritionally enhanced food products. About half of the beneficiaries are women and children. GAIN's goal is to reach 1 billion people by 2015 with nutritious foods that have a sustainable nutritional impact.

2. Health Leads

Health Leads believes that a different kind of healthcare system is possible for America – one that addresses all patients' basic resource needs as a standard part of quality care. They believe that one day, all healthcare providers will be able to prescribe solutions that improve health, not just manage the disease. The organization seeks to align the forces necessary for this change, using Health Leads' work in partner hospitals and health centers to make a broader case for integrating basic resources into healthcare delivery. At the same time, America is poised for a healthcare transformation due to market-driven imperatives focused on improving patient health and reducing costs.

When patients and their families seek medical care, they often face critical challenges in their lives at the same time – they have little food, have no job, and struggle to keep up with bills for gas and electricity. Not surprisingly, these challenges affect their health. Health Leads enables healthcare providers to prescribe basic resources like food and heat just as they do medication and refer patients to a program just as they do any other specialty. They recruit and train college students—Health Leads Advocates – to fill these prescriptions by working side by side with patients to connect them with the basic resources they need to be healthy.

3. Medic Mobile

Medic Mobile began when a few students at Stanford and Lewis & Clark started using a free software application called FrontlineSMS to coordinate community health workers at St Gabriel's Hospital. They weren't software developers or medical doctors—just passionate, thoughtful people who enjoyed tinkering and realized that they could use technology to improve health care in very challenging settings. Building on early successes in Malawi, they've since helped more than fifty organizations use technology to improve health services in more than twenty countries.

Their broader toolkit now includes software the team has developed as well as open-source software created by other organizations. They've stayed true to the idea that the greatest health impact per dollar invested comes from making use of tools that are already available rather than developing something new for each project. As a tech company that's constantly fired up about health impact, they're proud to have supported some outstanding health care providers. One hundred percent of the impact comes from helping our partners access mobile technology that can improve the services they provide.

4. African Medical and Research Foundation (AMREF)

AMREF has over 54 years of experience in health development. In 1957, three surgeons founded the Flying Doctors Service of East Africa, laying the foundation for what is now one of the continent's leading health development and research organizations. Today, AMREF implements its projects through country programs in Kenya, Ethiopia, Uganda, Tanzania, Senegal, South Sudan and South Africa. Training and consulting support are provided to an additional 30 African countries. AMREF believes that by focusing on the health of women and children, the health of the whole community can be improved. They are concerned with skilled care of mothers before, during and after childbirth, prevention and treatment of cervical cancer, and proper management of childhood illnesses. Their main areas of intervention are maternal and child health, HIV and Tuberculosis, safe water and sanitation, malaria, and essential clinical care.

5. D-Tree International

Millions of people die unnecessarily each year due to a lack of health care. Many of these are children living in poverty who die from malaria, pneumonia and diarrheal disease because they could not get effective medical treatment. Adults with chronic diseases such as diabetes and heart disease are unable to receive the continuous care needed to live a healthy life. A major reason for these unnecessary deaths is the shortage of doctors and nurses in developing countries, especially in rural areas where the poorest people live. Yet, most of these problems can be easily treated by other types of health workers if they are given the tools they need to effectively diagnose and treat these patients. D-Tree International aims to bring accurate and effective diagnosis and treatment to the world's poor through the introduction of easy to use software incorporating electronic protocols that guide the health worker step by step to the correct diagnosis and treatment for each patient. This use of clinical standards of care has been shown to be an effective way to improve the quality of the care provided to patients.

The World Health Organization (WHO) has also made its efforts to make sure that individuals all over the world are healthy. The World Health Organization (WHO) plays an essential role in the global governance of health and disease; due to its core global functions of establishing, monitoring and enforcing international norms and standards, and coordinating multiple actors toward common goals. WHO is a public health body representing the world's needs. At a global scale, the work WHO conducts is different from that of national and regional public health bodies. One of the main purposes of WHO is to monitor diseases throughout the world. This is essential not only as part of its mandate but also for the measurement of performance with regard to how well the MDGs are being met. The work WHO conducts is multidimensional. While concentrating on mapping global health trends and disease eradication, it is probably the best-placed organization to ensure that the poorest countries receive the support they need. Another key role of WHO is to provide a body of technical expertise through the production, dissemination, and implementation of evidence-based guidelines. This is especially important because, in a globalizing world, it is becoming increasingly clear that national health policy measures may not be as effective as they once were; in fact, WHO issues nearly 200 recommendations and policy statements every year.

Healthcare systems all over the world vary due to the differences in economic status and cultures. While issues concerning both of these may take some time to resolve, health issues cannot. This means that policies should be implemented on a global level so that each individual has access to proper healthcare no matter where they live, what culture they follow or what their economic status is. The right to healthcare and proper treatment is one of the basic rights of humans and should be given priority by all.

Global health is a tangled web, and its threads are intricately woven into the fabric of the US health system. The state of global health today is both a challenge and an opportunity for the United States. The interconnectedness of our world means that diseases and health crises know no borders. Ignoring global health issues is akin to leaving a leaky boat unattended—it might stay afloat for a while, but eventually, we all sink.

The current landscape showcases the urgency of addressing global health with a proactive stance. From infectious diseases spreading rapidly across continents to the threat of antimicrobial resistance, the challenges are real and looming. The COVID-19 pandemic has been a harsh reminder that our health is only as strong as the weakest link in the global chain.

Looking ahead, the future of global health demands collaboration, innovation, and a commitment to equity. The US health system cannot thrive in isolation; it needs a global environment that fosters health and well-being. Investing in global health not only protects Americans from the spillover effects of international health crises but also promotes stability and economic prosperity.

Neglecting global health would be a shortsighted move, akin to dismantling the first line of defense against emerging threats. It's in our best interest to be proactive, to strengthen healthcare systems worldwide, and to tackle the root causes of health disparities on a global scale.

The impact on the US health system is profound. Neglecting global health means ignoring the potential breeding grounds for new diseases, neglecting research opportunities, and turning a blind eye to the health of the global workforce. As diseases evolve and borders become more porous, an investment in global health is an investment in the resilience and sustainability of the US health system.

In the current and future state of global health is inseparable from the well-being of the United States. To safeguard our own health, we must be active participants in the global health community, addressing challenges collectively and ensuring a healthier, safer future for all.

Smarter leadership is the key to unlocking the full potential of global health and steering us toward a brighter future. In the complex and interconnected world of healthcare, visionary leaders can make all the difference.

First and foremost, smarter leadership involves recognizing the interdependence of nations when it comes to health. Leaders need to embrace a global perspective, understanding that diseases don't respect borders and that collaboration is essential. This means fostering international partnerships, sharing resources, and collectively addressing health challenges that affect us all.

Intelligent leadership in global health involves strategic and sustainable investments. Allocating resources efficiently, prioritizing research and development, and supporting healthcare infrastructure worldwide are crucial steps. Smarter leaders understand that a stitch in time saves nine, and investing in preventive measures and early interventions can prevent global health crises before they escalate.

In addition, effective leaders in global health must champion innovation. Embracing technological advancements, promoting research, and leveraging data-driven solutions can revolutionize healthcare on a global scale. This not only accelerates the development of treatments and vaccines but also enhances the efficiency and accessibility of healthcare systems worldwide.

Equally important is a commitment to addressing health disparities. Smarter leaders recognize that a healthy world is an equitable world. This involves not only providing aid to less fortunate nations but also actively working to eliminate the root causes of health inequalities, such as poverty, lack of education, and inadequate healthcare infrastructure.

Ultimately, the future of global health rests on the shoulders of leaders who understand the intricacies of the global landscape and are willing to collaborate, innovate, invest wisely, and champion equity. Smarter leadership can undoubtedly brighten the path forward, ensuring a healthier, more resilient world for generations to come.

CHAPTER 3

Healthcare Administration & Leadership

In the intricate tapestry of healthcare, the analogy to a master weaver is not just poetic; it encapsulates the essence of the interconnected lives and intricate systems at play. The threads woven into this intricate fabric symbolize the diverse elements of healthcare—from medical practitioners and facilities to policies and patient experiences. Smarter leadership and effective management emerge as the guiding hands that delicately intertwine these threads, creating a resilient and harmonious structure.

Much like a symphony's conductor, healthcare leaders must navigate the complexities of the system, ensuring that each component plays its part seamlessly. The symphony of healthcare is not solely about curing illnesses; it's about orchestrating a holistic approach that considers prevention, accessibility, and quality of care. A skilled leader acts as the conductor, harmonizing the different elements into a melodious whole that resonates with improved health outcomes, patient satisfaction, and overall well-being.

The pursuit of better healthcare delivery and outcomes goes beyond mere ambition; it's a moral imperative. The conviction that every individual deserves a crescendo of well-being echoes the fundamental principle that healthcare is a human right. Intelligent leadership in healthcare translates this conviction into actionable strategies, driving innovations, fostering collaboration, and dismantling barriers that hinder the symphony of well-being.

In this symphony of life and health, the baton of intelligent leadership becomes the catalyst for transformative potential. Leaders have the power to redefine the very fabric of our collective well-being. Through visionary guidance, strategic decision-making, and a commitment to inclusivity, healthcare leaders can elevate the symphony to new heights, creating a future where the melody of health and happiness resonates for every individual, weaving a tapestry of well-being that stands the test of time.

It is often said that people are led, and resources are managed. Therefore, a good leader should be able to do both, and a clear understanding of this critical yet meaningful difference is the beginning of leadership wisdom that opens the way to being successful. Throughout human history, leadership has been of great importance. Today more than ever, effective leadership is what organizations need in order to survive through today's dynamic world where the business environment is consistently changing and driven by economic instability. Both global and domestic advances in technology have changed markets and brought about fierce competition call to have objectives met most adequately. Studies show that organizations who have realized that effective leadership will provide them with a competitive superiority over rivals have experienced profound transformation in their overall functions.

The health care industry is a huge business. It is one of the most dynamic sectors which is driven by the economic situation. Every person in the world needs it, and governments are judged on it as almost everyone is interested in how it is delivered. It is known that better health promotes economic growth, which in turn catalyzes the equitable distribution of wealth and leads to healthier populations. In such a sensitive sector, leadership and continuity of leadership are of great significance for the provision of effective services along with effective management of the same.

Organizing and managing healthcare delivery to meet higher standardized quality levels is a complex undertaking. Be it at the national level, local levels or at the level of individual interaction between a healthcare professional and patient, best knowledge of both management and leadership principles are required to navigate and successfully solve problems of cost, quality, and access to care across the continuum of care in our society. Leaders are indeed the catalysts for organizational, group, and individual greatness. No great leaders of our time have been successful and prosperous without first understanding the principles of leadership. Although complex in its composition, successful health organizations need effective leadership and management to enable their functioning as a single unit for effective better achievements.

Leadership is both an art and a science. It is synchronized both as innate skills and acquired knowledge that defines successful and effective leaders. As an art, leadership is characterized by skills that help in the maintenance of relationships, interpersonal skills, timing and tempo, power, and intuition. While referring to leadership in the technical acumen, skills calling for principles along with expertise, professionalism, punctuality and accountability are needed. However, these are not the only qualities that are required (see figure 3.1).

Healthcare administrative and leadership skills such as those depicted in figure 3.1 are competency oriented and correspond to the skills adopted by ideal health leaders. The challenging scenarios currently presented to healthcare after the COVID-19 pandemic require more competent and professionally dynamic healthcare leaders that can address the range of challenges in their setting and lead a team towards success.

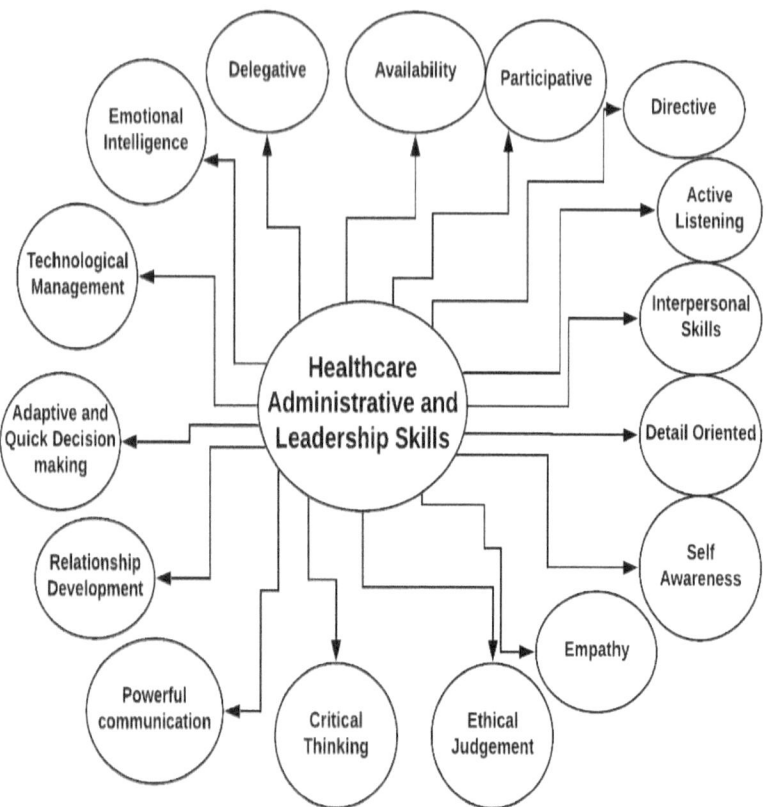

Figure 3.1: Healthcare Administrative and Leadership Skills

Figure 3.1 represents the healthcare administrative and leadership skills, which include active listening, interpersonal skills, detail-oriented information, self-awareness, empathy, ethical judgment, critical thinking, powerful communication, relationship development, adaptive and quick decision making, technological management, emotional intelligence, delegation, availability, participative and directive skills.

Additionally, possessing the ability to transform into the most compatible leadership style in situations is also a necessary and helpful skill. It promotes taking action for a healthcare administration position. The most widely adopted leadership styles include transformational, laissez-faire, servant, charisma, and situational. Generally, healthcare leadership styles are adopted to comply with the principles of patient-centered care and quality care delivery practices.

There are at least a hundred definitions of leadership differing from each other as it is about leadership styles, functional leadership, situational leadership, bureaucratic leadership, charismatic leadership, servant leadership, follower leadership, group-centered leadership, and so on. Therefore, it is easier to recognize the style of leadership than defining it. According to James MacGregor Burns, *"Leadership over human beings is exercised when persons with certain motives and purposes mobilize, in competition or conflict with others, institutional, political, psychological, and other resources to arouse, engage, and satisfy the motives of followers"* (MacGregor 1978: 69 cited in Winston 2012).

Leadership encompasses influencing the activities of a group and coping with change either on the structure or functioning of the organization for shared achievements. It begins to exist when someone (the leader) has been given the power to exercise influence over others (the followers) in a given organization. No matter whether the influence is wide-ranging or narrowly focused within formal organizations, the emphasis is put on the espoused value, directions in which the future of the group is directed, and how everyday tasks are accomplished. One of the most important roles of a leader is to set the organization vision and make it meaningful largely through clear language, actions and stories. He should provide a clear framework of understanding of the established vision and build interdisciplinary collaboration, cohesive and adaptive work teams. The more followers clearly understand and know what they have to do, the more they adhere to the vision for better achievements.

Leadership at the unit and hospital levels is essential to ensure excellence in practice, as well as adequate clinical governance. It is about promoting the intellectual stimulation of individual staff members regardless of the setting by communicating a clear vision, motivating a team to achieve a common goal, communicating effectively with others, creating and sustaining the critical elements of a healthy work environment and implementing change and innovation. From this point of view, effective leadership can be seen as getting things done without excessive "pressure" from the manager. As management and leadership cannot be separated, successful health care leaders are those that can both empower people and effectively manage available recourses.

In the health care sector, the term 'leadership' is closely associated and often used interchangeably with 'management'. So much so that leadership and management are often used as overlapping concepts. However, they represent two facets of how organizations, groups or individuals set about creating change. Although management and leadership may represent two distinct disciplinary and practice areas, distinguishing between the two concepts in practice may be difficult. In certain instances, management functions can provide leadership, while leadership activities can contribute to managing. Additionally, managers and leaders are expected to function effectively in different situations, not limited by their traditional roles, reflecting the view that they (managers and leaders) are expected to be all things to all people. This view is consistent with that of Bass and Avolio, who opined that effective leadership is a reflection of an optimal mix of different styles, including management and leadership practices.

To be successful, an organization has to combine efficient management strategies with the best of leadership processes. Leadership has to do with setting a vision for people, inspiring them and setting organizational values and strategic direction. In contrast, management involves directing people and resources to achieve organizational values and strategic direction established and propagated by leadership. A lack of either leadership or management makes it more difficult for an organization to experience change or progress.

According to WHO, *"Good leadership and management in a healthcare organization are about providing direction to, and gaining commitment from, partners and staff, facilitating change and achieving better health services through efficient, creative and responsible deployment of people and other resources."*

However, the position of a leader has its fair share of struggles as well. The difficulty when considering leadership in health is that healthcare is actually one of the most complex, costly and challenged sectors of our contemporary societies. This complexity is often a result of constraints relating to different disease areas, multidirectional goals, and multidisciplinary staff. It is composed of numerous working and departments of different specialties with intricate, nonlinear interactions between them; within large organizations such as healthcare systems with numerous professional groups of different background bound to do work together, there might surely be a conflict between them.

The leader has the responsibility to coordinate all the staff members to vibrate at the same wave to capitalize on that diversity and efficiently utilize resources when designing management processes and while encouraging personnel to work towards common goals.

Healthcare and administrative leadership challenges encompass the whole healthcare system within an organization. These challenges are detail-oriented and require competencies and skills that are dynamic and evidence-based. Such healthcare and administrative challenges can affect the quality of services provided in the organization and the patient's experience. Some of these challenges are mentioned in figure 3.2.

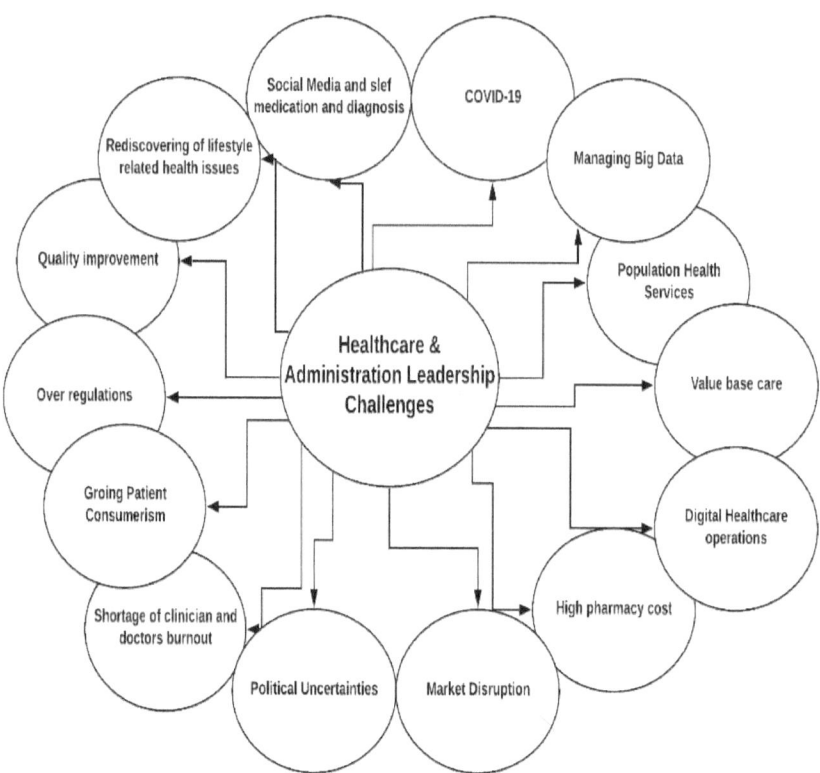

Figure 3.2: Healthcare & Administration Leadership Challenges

Figure 3.2 represents the healthcare and administrative leadership challenges. These include management of big data, population health services, value base care, digital healthcare operations, high pharmacy cost, market disruption, market disruption, political uncertainties, shortage of clinician and doctors' burnout, growing patient consumerism, over-regulations, quality improvement, rediscovering of lifestyle-related health issues, social media, self-medication and diagnosis, and COVID-19.

These challenges have affected the quality of care and services provided by the health protection agencies. In addition to these challenges, medical and technological advancement, healthcare rising costs, ethical challenges, and healthcare regulatory issues also impact the pace of services provided to the service users. There is a significant need for investigation of resolving strategies for these challenges.

The Institute of Medicine (IOM) has defined high – quality care as being safe, effective, patient-centered, timely, efficient, and equitable. The IOM has recommended that quality improvements be addressed on four levels: that of the patient, of health-delivery Microsystems (teams or units), of organizations that house such systems (hospitals, clinics, health systems etc.), and of the regulatory and financial environment in which those systems operate. Effective leadership is needed on all four levels to meet these aims and support a quality-driven healthcare system. Much of the literature agrees that leadership is important at any level of an organization. Good leadership is an important tool in the decision-making process as it enhances the success of the organization in meeting its goals. Even though some decisions are easily solved, whereas others may call for critical analysis, each decision made by a leader, whatever the circumstances, have consequences for human resources and the organization itself. It is subsequently worthwhile for individuals to be interested and trained in leadership in other to become well equipped to make the right decision at the right time.

As in any organization, we found three main managerial levels: Lower (First-line) management, top management and middle management, and effective leadership must be embedded at every organizational level, be it at the strategic level, the service level or the frontline level to ensure that the multitude of decisions made peripherally on a daily basis in large healthcare systems adds up to some concerted action aligned with the organization's goals. Any lack of effective leadership and a clear chain of command can lead to anarchy as significant decisions involving the whole organization can be made at the frontline with no regard for the organization's overall strategy.

Today's world is too complex that, whether in a commercial business or health care, no one can pretend to know everything and do it all at the same time. As long as people are part of the equation of health systems, either as workforce members or patients, leaders need to interact with other people to create leadership teams to successfully meet the common goals. However, despite all the facts that leadership is a cornerstone of every successful healthcare organization, there is a danger that certain managers will see leadership – or possibly have already seen it – as the latest panacea, the magic solution to all of their managerial problems. These managers will be tempted to believe that things are simply taken for granted, just as the last managerial panacea they discovered. The success of every organization, however, remains a crude struggle since none form of leadership can replace hard and devoted work that is put in by healthcare professionals.

Even though healthcare professionals all over the world acquire the same knowledge, there are many differences in their services. This difference is mainly due to the different management models that the healthcare industry uses. These models are carefully designed, and each has its own benefits. These are:

1. The Beveridge Model: Single-payer National Health Service

Sir William Beveridge first developed the Beveridge Model in 1948. Established in the United Kingdom and spread throughout many areas of Northern Europe and the world, this system is often centralized through the establishment of a national health service. The government acts as the single-payer, eliminating competition in the market and generally keeping prices low. Funding health care through income taxes allows for health care to be free at the point of service. After an appointment or operation, the patient does not have to pay any out-of-pocket fees because of their contribution through taxes. Under this system, a large majority of health staff is composed of government employees. A central tenant of this model is health as a human right. Thus, universal coverage is guaranteed by the government, and anyone who is a citizen has the same access to care.

With the government as the sole payer in this healthcare system, costs can be kept low, and benefits are standardized across the country. However, a common criticism of this system is the tendency toward long waiting lists. Because everyone is guaranteed access to health services, over-utilization of the system may lead to increasing costs. There are fears that the adoption of a single-payer national health service in the US would lead to an increase in demand for all procedures, even medically unnecessary ones, because citizens would not pay upfront costs for these services. However, other analysts argue against this problem, stating that current American practices waste a similar amount of money covering the uninsured.

Another practical concern is the government's response to a crisis. In the case of a precarious national emergency, such as war or a health crisis, funding for health services may decline as public revenue decreases, exacerbating the financial burden inherent in a large influx of patients. Such a situation would require careful allocation of emergency funding before the crisis.

2. The Bismarck Model: Social Health Insurance Model

A more decentralized form of healthcare, the Bismarck model, was created near the end of the 19th century by Otto von Bismarck. Employers and employees fund health insurance in this model – those who are employed have access to "sickness funds" created by compulsory payroll dedications. In addition, private insurance plans cover every employed person, regardless of pre-existing conditions.

Health providers are generally private institutions, though the Social Health Insurance funds are considered public. In some countries, there is a single insurer (France, Korea); other countries may have multiple competing insurers (Germany, Czech Republic) or multiple non-competing insurers (Japan). Regardless of the number of insurers, the government tightly controls prices while insurers do not make a profit. These measures allow the government to exercise a similar amount of control over prices for health services seen in the Beveridge model.

The requirement of employment for health insurance provides benefits and causes problems. These measures ensure that employed people will have the healthcare needed to continue working and ensure a productive workforce. Because it was not initially established to provide universal health coverage, the Bismarck model focuses resources on those who can contribute financially. With a shift in mindset from health as a privilege for employed citizens to the right for all citizens, the model faces a number of concerns, such as how to care for those unable to work or those who may not be able to afford contributions. More immediate practical concerns include how to contend with aging populations, with an uneven number of retired citizens compared to employed citizens, and how to stay competitive in attracting international companies that may prefer locations without these required payroll dedications.

3. The National Health Insurance Model: Single-payer National Health Insurance

The National Health Insurance model incorporates aspects of both the Bismarck and Beveridge models. Like the Beveridge model, the government acts as the single-payer for medical procedures. Like the Bismarck model, providers are private. Universal insurance does not make a profit or deny claims. There has been a tendency in recent years for countries with Beveridge-type health care systems to incorporate Bismarck characteristics or vice versa, leading to the health care policies in a number of countries like Hungary and Germany to trend towards the mixed model. In some countries like Canada, private insurance contracting is permitted for those who would prefer them.

The balance between public insurance and private practice allows hospitals to maintain independence while also reducing internal complications with insurance policies. Financial barriers to treatment are generally low, and patients usually are able to choose their healthcare providers.

Like the Beveridge model, this system covers most procedures regardless of income level. The model also may reduce the costs involved with the administration of health insurance, as the government processes all claims and reduces the amount of duplication of services. Perhaps the largest complaint is that these systems can suffer from long waiting lists for treatment. Waitlists are not limited to elective surgeries or other non-emergency procedures, as patients waiting to be seen in some fields like neurosurgery often may face long delays until they can see a physician. In a study by Viberg et al. from 2013, a majority of countries, including Australia, Canada, and Italy, consider waiting times a serious health policy issue. Waiting times in Canada for hip replacements can be from 42 to 178 days, depending on the province. Aging population demographics and overutilization of health resources in the non-urgent situation are also problems for the long-term stability of this model.

4. The Out-of-Pocket Model: Market-driven Health Care

In less developed areas with too few resources to create mass medical care, patients must pay for their procedures out-of-pocket. Without enough money, the poor are unable to afford appropriate health care. Unfortunately, this situation is common in most countries since only the wealthiest countries have robust health care systems. Disparities in wealth lead to disparities in health outcomes in these areas.

In the United States, many aspects of health care are driven by income level. Adults in the US are less likely to see a regular physician. They are more likely to have untreated conditions than adults in Canada, while at the same time rating their care as either extremely high or low in quality more often than Canadians. The latter are more moderate in their responses. Disparities in care due to socioeconomic status and ethnicity are found in all countries. Still, they tend to be more pronounced in the United States than in areas like Canada. The number of uninsured individuals ranges for different states, from as low as 3.6% in Massachusetts to as high as 20.6% in Texas[1]. As of 2015, the percent of uninsured persons is 13.0% in the United States[2].

The debate over increasing coverage and minimizing costs still rages in Congress – any developments may drastically change these numbers.

This means that no matter what model a country may follow, it is necessary for them to implement strategic management policies to make sure that their model is running smoothly and to the best of its ability. Strategic management also provides several benefits for healthcare organizations to become more proactive with strategy[3]. These are:

1. It allows organizations to be agile. A good strategic management approach ensures that communication and feedback on performance against strategic goals occur on a regular cadence. By having a strategic management framework, your organization has "pivot-ability"[4]. In other terms, when your environment changes (new market entrants, new regulations, etc.), strategic management allows organizations to hit the pause button and review current strategic initiatives for impact and relevancy.
2. It encourages continual dialogue on strategy. Many organizations have a strategic planning process. However, once the strategy is developed, future dialogue on environment changes, competitor actions, and industry trends tends to happen once every three to five years. By focusing on strategic management, executives can move to an annual process that requires continual reflection and scanning of the industry and review of performance.
3. It focuses on performance and results. Performance reviews against strategy become either a monthly, quarterly, or yearly process. A key component for many strategic management approaches is action planning for variances between goals and performance. These goals are inextricably tied to the achievement of strategic ends. Monthly senior executive meetings become the forum for review of performance tools, such as scorecards, that will highlight performance gaps and trends.
4. It engages the entire organization. Older models for strategic planning consist of a variety of processes carried out by functions or business units that are in isolation. This model does not foster collaboration or communication between functions, and strategy can become disconnected from those responsible for execution. To assist with the integration of strategy, organizations have established a project management office (PMO) or strategy management office to coordinate responsibilities of strategic management and make connection points between functional groups.

The health care sector is complex, characterized by constant changes and reforms. Strong and competent management and leadership workforces are thus required to navigate the sector through the complex web of interacting factors and lead reforms for effective and efficient health care delivery. An added challenge to leadership development is that leadership is spread across health management and clinical workforces. In contrast, some clinical leaders may work in management roles; for others, leadership is exercised from a clinical position. The need for competent management and leadership workforces has fueled an upsurge in interest in health management and leadership, as reflected in the large number of studies examining the concept across different countries since the turn of the century.

Healthcare services quality significantly relies on leadership and administration. The leadership style adopted by healthcare professionals corresponds to their integral values adopted within the system. Supportive leadership helps professionals in the system grow personally and professionally while also improving the paradigms of care within healthcare. In the healthcare sector, leadership and continuity of leadership are of great significance for the provision of effective services along with effective management of the same[5].

Leaders are indeed the catalysts for organizational, group, and individual greatness. No great leaders of our time have been successful and prosperous without first understanding the principles of leadership. Although complex in its composition, successful health organizations need effective leadership and management to enable their functioning as a single unit for effective better achievements. Today's world is too complex that, whether in a commercial business or health care, no one can pretend to know everything and do it all at the same time. As long as people are part of the equation of health systems, either as workforce members or patients, leaders need to interact with other people to create leadership teams to successfully meet the common goals[6].

Leadership Role in Bridging Race, Racism and Social Justice in Healthcare

Addressing race, racism, and social justice in healthcare requires strong leadership that goes beyond mere acknowledgment of the issues.

A leader in healthcare should be committed to creating an inclusive and equitable environment for both patients and staff. Here's how leadership can play a pivotal role in bridging these gaps:

1. **Promoting Diversity and Inclusion:**
    - Leaders should actively promote diversity within the healthcare workforce. This involves recruiting and retaining individuals from diverse racial and ethnic backgrounds.
    - Fostering an inclusive culture where everyone feels valued and respected is crucial. This can be achieved through training programs, open dialogue, and creating policies that actively combat discrimination.

2. **Education and Training:**
    - Leaders should invest in ongoing education and training for healthcare professionals on cultural competence, implicit bias, and the historical context of racism in healthcare.
    - Implementing regular diversity and inclusion workshops can help sensitize staff to the challenges faced by patients from different racial backgrounds.

3. **Policy Development:**
    - Leadership plays a key role in shaping and enforcing policies that address racial disparities in healthcare. This includes developing and implementing anti-racism policies and protocols.
    - Regularly reviewing and updating these policies ensures that the organization remains responsive to emerging issues and adapts to evolving societal norms.

4. **Community Engagement:**
    - Leaders should actively engage with the communities they serve. This involves listening to the concerns and needs of diverse populations and incorporating community feedback into healthcare strategies.

- Establishing partnerships with community organizations and leaders can enhance trust and facilitate collaborative efforts to address healthcare disparities.

5. **Data Collection and Analysis:**
   - Leadership should prioritize the collection and analysis of demographic data to identify disparities in healthcare outcomes. This information is crucial for implementing targeted interventions and measuring progress over time.
   - Transparency in reporting outcomes related to racial disparities is essential for accountability and building trust with both the healthcare workforce and the community.

6. **Advocacy:**
   - Effective leaders in healthcare should advocate for policies and practices that address systemic racism at a broader societal level. This involves using their influence to bring attention to racial disparities in healthcare and pushing for legislative changes.

7. **Cultural Competence in Patient Care:**
   - Leaders can drive initiatives to ensure that healthcare providers receive training in cultural competence, enabling them to deliver patient-centered care that considers the unique needs of individuals from diverse backgrounds.

In summary, leadership in healthcare should be proactive in addressing race, racism, and social justice by fostering a culture of inclusivity, advocating for policy changes, engaging with communities, and continually educating and training healthcare professionals. The goal is to create a healthcare system that is truly equitable for all, regardless of race or ethnicity.

CHAPTER 4

Healthcare Technology & Innovation

As technology continues to improve every day, new developments are constantly infiltrating our lives and changing the way we live. Whether it's the way we shop, how we communicate with friends, the job we do, or the way we travel, technology has managed to transform each aspect of our behavior. However, we must not forget that there are many factors that have driven innovation and technology to become advanced (see Figure 4.1).

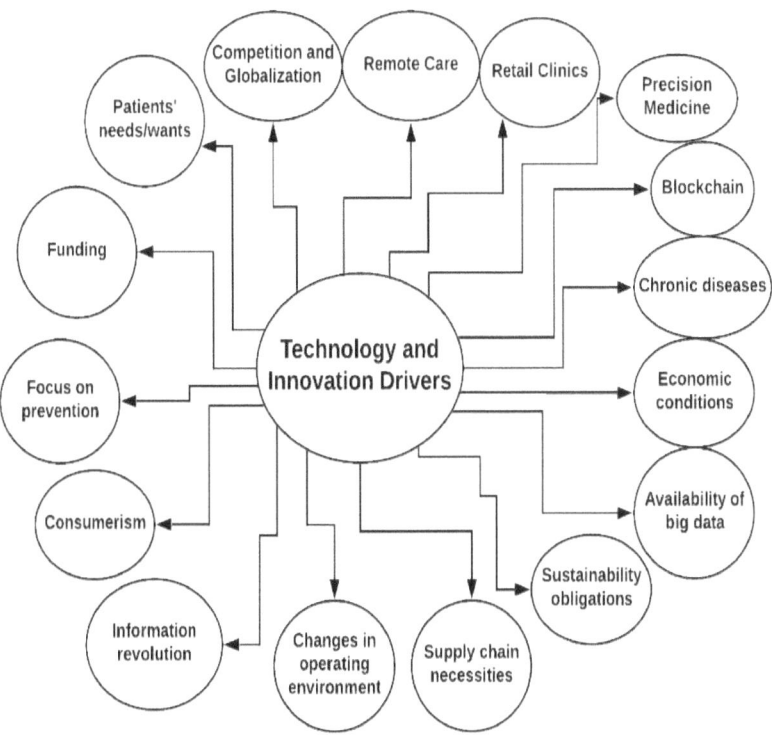

Figure 4.1: Technology and Innovation Drivers

Figure 4.1 represents the essential technology and innovation drivers. The identified potential drivers are precision medicine, blockchain, chronic diseases, economic conditions, availability of big data, sustainability obligations, supply chain necessities, changes in operating environment, information revolution, consumerism, focus on prevention, funding, patient needs, competition and globalization, remote care, and retail clinics.

Technology is the key driver towards advancement and the heart of enabling businesses to evolve and sustain the competitive advantage. In the context of healthcare, drivers to technology and innovation intend to improve healthcare services and the quality of patient care. Moreover, these drivers make the healthcare systems dynamic and robust.

One of the most useful inventions in the modern world is the Internet. Today most of what we do is linked to the Internet, from buying our air tickets to booking an appointment with our physician. According to the Pew Internet and American Life Project, in a 2004 survey of 8 million seniors who use the Internet, only 66% said they searched healthcare information online[1]. In 2009, 24 million Americans reported the same.

It goes without saying that today more and more people are using the Internet to research their medical issues. This means not only looking up symptoms but exploring treatments and medicines on the web. While it is never a good idea to skip out on the doctor completely, the Internet has helped in gaining access to the latest treatment options and made patients more empowered to make decisions about what to do next. However, the internet is just one of the innovations that has changed the fate of the healthcare industry (see Figure 4.2). Innovation refers to the implementation of particular new ideas for a good cause. Technology and innovation drivers, depicted in figure 4.1, are integral to the wide range of systems in developed countries. These technology drivers set the foundation of high-quality services and help in sustaining the economy of the state. By linking the technology and innovation drivers (figure 4.1) with healthcare innovation (figure 4.2), it can be observed that healthcare makes a profound contribution in providing services and stabilizing the economy of the state. Current healthcare innovations are robust, up-to-date, and widely adopted by primary, secondary and tertiary care centers.

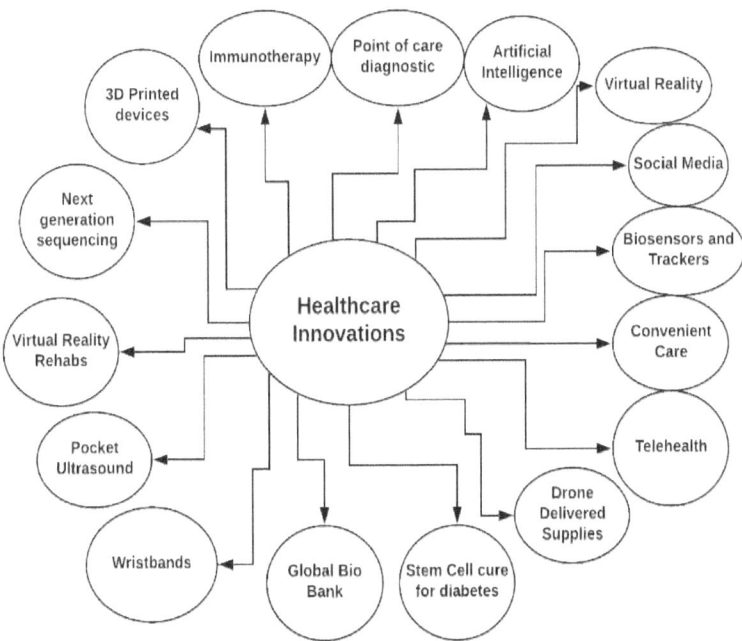

Figure 4.2: Healthcare Innovations

Figure 4.2 enlists the healthcare innovations that have improved healthcare services in the past few years. The most prominent innovations include social media, biosensors and trackers, convenient care, telehealth, drone delivered supplies, stem cell cure for diabetes global biobank, wristbands, pocket ultrasound, virtual reality rehabs, next-generation sequencing, 3D printed devices, immunotherapy, point of care diagnostic, and artificial intelligence.

The integration of healthcare innovations has led to technological advancements and improved the services of healthcare providers. These innovations and technological advancements have also reduced the costs needed for the treatment of patients. Furthermore, innovations in the treatment and management of non-communicable diseases have led to a reduction in deaths such as those associated with cancer and diabetes.

Moreover, breakthroughs in information gathering, research, treatments, and communications have given medical providers new tools to work with and fresh ways to practice medicine. Some of the tools that have changed the way medicine was practiced are:

1. mHealth.

mHealth (mobile health) is a general term for the use of mobile phones and other wireless technology in medical care. The most common application of mHealth is the use of mobile devices to educate consumers about preventive healthcare services. However, mHealth is also used for disease surveillance, treatment support, epidemic outbreak tracking, and chronic disease management. Mobile health is the advancement that has freed healthcare devices of wires and cords and has enabled physicians and patients alike to check on healthcare processes on the go. An R&R Market Research report estimated that the global mHealth market reached $20.7 billion in 2019. These statistics indicate that mHealth is only becoming bigger and more prevalent as smartphones and tablets continue to allow healthcare providers to access and send information more freely. Physicians and service providers can also use mHealth tools for orders, documentation, and simply to reach more information when with patients.

However, mHealth is not only about wireless connectivity. It has also become a tool that allows patients to become active players in their treatment by connecting communication with biometrics. For consumers, a major benefit of mHealth is its convenience. Wearable devices and other mobile technology allow users to continuously track and manage certain health data without having to see their healthcare provider. There is also a plethora of apps to choose from. As of 2017, there were 325,000 mHealth apps available for download from app stores, according to digital health consulting firm research2guidance[2].

Health can also help bridge gaps in care by allowing patients to communicate with their physician or care team and vice versa without meeting face to face. Secure messaging, for example, allows physicians to alert parents when their child is out of surgery. It also allows healthcare providers to communicate with each other about patients -- for example, letting a nurse know when a patient has arrived for an appointment. Some mobile health apps, such as the Apple Health App, can integrate with a patient's electronic health record, allowing users to access their health data on their iPhone or iPad.

2. Telemedicine/Telehealth.

Telemedicine refers to the practice of caring for patients remotely when the provider and patient are not physically present with each other. Modern technology has enabled doctors to consult patients by using HIPAA-compliant video-conferencing tools. Studies consistently show the benefit of telehealth, especially in rural settings that do not have access to the same resources metropolitan areas may have. A large-scale study published in CHEST Journal shows patients in an intensive care unit equipped with telehealth services were discharged from the ICU 20 percent more quickly and saw a 26 percent lower mortality rate than patients in a regular ICU. At the same time, telemedicine is not necessarily a new development, it is a growing field, and its scope of possibility is expanding.

The cost benefits of telehealth can't be ignored either. For example, Indianapolis-based health insurer WellPoint rolled out a video consultation program in February 2013 where patients can receive a full assessment through a video chat with a physician. Claims are automatically generated, but the fees are reduced to factor out traditional office costs. Setting the actual healthcare cost aside, these telemedicine clinics will also reduce time out of office costs for employees and employers by eliminating the need to leave work to go to a primary care office.

3. Portal Technology.

A patient portal is a secure online website that gives patients convenient, 24-hour access to personal health information from anywhere with an Internet connection. Using a secure username and password, patients can view health information such as recent doctor visits, discharge summaries, and medications. Patient portals are becoming popular with the passage of time in the healthcare industry. According to the national coordinator for health information technology, 64% of the hospitals gave their access to view, download, and transmit their health data in 2014. 51% had the ability to secure messages with their patients[3].

With the help of the portal, patients are increasingly becoming active players in their own healthcare. Portal technology allows physicians and patients to access medical records and interact online. It has also allowed patients to become more closely involved in their treatment and better educated about their care. In addition to increasing access and availability of medical information, portal technology can be a source of empowerment and responsibility for patients.

4. Self-service Kiosks.

Similar to portal technology, self-service kiosks can help expedite processes like hospital registration. Automated kiosks can assist patients with paying co-pays, checking identification, signing paperwork, and other registration requirements. There are also tablet variations that allow the same technology to be used in outpatient and bedside settings. However, hospitals need to be cautious when integrating it to ensure human-to-human communication is not entirely eliminated.

Implementing self-service kiosks in hospitals can reduce costs for the facility. Self-check-ins save the hospital from using paper, filing the forms, and allows them to quickly look up information on that patient without having to sort through piles and cabinets of paperwork. Additionally, with self-service kiosks, nurses spend less time doing the bulk of the hospital's administrative duties and more time providing care for patients. Moreover, the need to fill out paper forms is also replaced with an easy-to-operate digitized system. Usually, the administrative staff has to manually record the patient's information and find the appropriate medical department that will tend to the patient's healthcare needs. This process can be eliminated as self-service kiosks make it easier to check-in and verify patient information by simply swiping an identification card.

5. Remote Monitoring Tools.

Many hospitals nowadays rely on remote patient monitoring (RPM) and telehealth solutions to reduce readmissions and to improve outcomes. When deemed ready, some patients are sent home with wearable tools that track metrics such as blood pressure, weight, and oxygen saturation. Combined with videoconferencing, the technology offers a way to keep tabs from afar.

Such continuity of care helps save time and avoid confusion (another provider's electronic health record platform could be from a different vendor and lack timely context, for example). And if concerns are detected virtually in the days ahead, the original providers can bring patients back for expedited consultations and treatment, potentially preventing complications. The technology appears to have a willing audience: At the end of 2012, 2.8 million patients worldwide were using a home monitoring system, according to a Research and Markets report[4]. Moreover, a 2019 survey conducted by a wearable solutions provider found that two-thirds of patients 40 and older would utilize a health monitoring device if it meant they could reduce the number of times they had to physically visit a doctor or hospital.

An article by Kaiser Health News, National Public Radio, and Minnesota Public Radio discussed the effects a home monitoring system had on readmission rates for heart disease patients at Duluth, Minn.-based Essentia Health. The national average rate of readmissions for patients with heart disease is 25 percent, but after Essentia Health implemented a home monitoring system, the rates of readmission for their heart disease patients fell to a mere two percent. And now that hospitals are being financially penalized for readmissions, home monitoring systems may offer a solution to avoid those penalties.

6. Sensors and Wearable Technology.

Wearable technologies can be innovative solutions for healthcare problems. Wearable technologies enable the continuous monitoring of human physical activities and behaviors, as well as physiological and biochemical parameters during daily life. The most commonly measured data include vital signs such as heart rate, blood pressure, and body temperature, as well as blood oxygen saturation, posture, and physical activities through the use of electrocardiogram (ECG), ballistocardiogram (BCG), and other devices.

Potentially, wearable photo or video devices could provide additional clinical information. Wearable devices can be attached to shoes, eyeglasses, earrings, clothing, gloves, and watches. Wearable devices also may evolve to be skin-attachable devices. Sensors can be embedded into the environment, such as chairs, car seats, and mattresses. A smartphone is typically used to collect information and transmit it to a remote server for storage and analysis. Some devices have been developed for healthcare professionals to monitor walking patterns, including the accelerometer, multi-angle video recorders, and gyroscopes. Other devices have been developed for health consumers, including on-wrist activity trackers (such as Fitbit) and mobile phone apps and add-ons. Wearable devices and data analysis algorithms are often used together to perform gait assessment tasks in different scenarios.

The wearable medical device market is growing at a compound annual growth rate of 16.4 percent a year, according to a Transparency Market Research report. Wearable medical devices and sensors are simply another way to collect data, which is one of the aims and purposes of healthcare. Sensors and wearable technology could be as simple as an alert sent to a care provider when a patient falls down or a bandage that can detect skin pH levels to tell if a cut is getting infected.

7. Wireless Communication.

Wireless communication in healthcare has rapidly advanced and changed the working environment. It is reshaping the way patients are handled, and information is being recorded, stored, and shared.

While wireless medical devices have been around for some time, they were primarily used to help providers with assessments and to monitor critical patient data. Now, facilities and organizations are becoming connected, allowing for greater access and management. This cross-device communication allows for quicker analysis and sharing of data with providers. It also carries its own set of rules and regulations.

While instant messaging and walkie-talkies aren't new technologies themselves, they have only recently been introduced into the hospital setting, replacing devices like beepers and overhead pagers. Healthcare organizations are adapting to wireless communication systems to retrieve, store, share, and send data. Healthcare professionals now enter data on wirelessly-connected laptops or tablets and monitoring patients and patient data via cell phones or wireless video cameras. Tele-medicine happens across a variety of wireless devices handling communication between patients and healthcare providers. Radios, smartphones, telephones, computers, and IoT (Internet of Things) are connecting patients and providers in new ways.

Systems like Vocera Messaging offer platforms for users to send secure messages like lab tests and alerts to one another using smartphones, web-based consoles, or third-party clinical systems. These messaging systems can expedite the communication process while still tracking and logging sent and received information in a secure manner.

8. Real-time Locating Services.

In healthcare, a Real-Time Location System (RTLS) is a system used to provide immediate or real-time tracking and management of medical equipment, staff, and patients within all types of patient care environments. While the technology differs from using location data captured by satellite trilateration, it can be thought of as a type of "indoor GPS" for hospitals. However, more so than just locating assets, accurate locating technology that easily integrates with other Healthcare IT solutions enables facilities to improve workflow, reduce costs and increase clinical quality. RTLS solutions comprise various tags and badges, technology platforms (Wi-Fi, Infrared, Bluetooth Low Energy, Low Frequency, ultrasound, and others), hardware infrastructure (readers & exciters), and other components (servers, middleware & end-user software).

RTLS solutions typically include location sensors that are attached to various assets, be it a patient, a staff member, or a piece of equipment. Utilizing a unique ID, the system can locate the tags and give you real-time information about its positioning within the facility. At the most basic level, these services can ensure equipment and supplies aren't leaving the building, and for high-cost equipment and supplies of which hospitals may only have one or a few, being able to track their location can help verify its utilization.

9. Pharmacogenomics/Genome Sequencing.

Personalized medicine continues to edge closer to the forefront of the healthcare industry. Tailoring treatment plans to individuals and anticipating the onset of certain diseases offers promising benefits for healthcare efficiency and diagnostic accuracy. Pharmacogenomics, in particular, has helped reduce the billions of dollars in excess healthcare spending due to adverse drug events, misdiagnoses, readmissions, and other unnecessary costs.

Before a full-fledged system of pharmacogenomics comes to fruition, the healthcare industry needs a tool that can aggregate and analyze all the big data and digital health information. The ability to actually compare that information is going to be valuable as we move forward, making sure the medications we are taking are going to work for us. Tools for big data analysis for pharmacogenomics are still being developed, but data analytics and data aggregation for population health may be the next big advancement on the horizon.

10. The Electronic Health Record (EHR)

An electronic health record (EHR) is a digital version of a patient's paper chart. EHRs are real-time, patient-centered records that make information available instantly and securely to authorized users. While an EHR does contain the medical and treatment histories of patients, an EHR system is built to go beyond standard clinical data collected in a provider's office and can be inclusive of a broader view of a patient's care. EHRs are a vital part of health IT and can:

- Contain a patient's medical history, diagnoses, medications, treatment plans, immunization dates, allergies, radiology images, and laboratory and test results
- Allow access to evidence-based tools that providers can use to make decisions about a patient's care
- Automate and streamline provider workflow

One of the key features of an EHR is that health information can be created and managed by authorized providers in a digital format capable of being shared with other providers across more than one health care organization. EHRs are built to share information with other health care providers and organizations – such as laboratories, specialists, medical imaging facilities, pharmacies, emergency facilities, and school and workplace clinics – so they contain information from all clinicians involved in a patient's care.

In 2009, only 16 percent of U.S. hospitals were using an EHR. By 2013, about 80 percent of hospitals eligible for CMS' meaningful use incentives program had incorporated an EHR into their organizations. For a long time, we had such disparate systems, meaning you had one system that did pharmacy, one did orders, one that did documentation. Integrating these systems into a single platform, or at least a more structured platform, has allowed more integrated and efficient care for patients. While the EHR has already created big strides in the centralization and efficiency of patient information, it can also be used as a data and population health tool for the future.

The benefits of an EHR can be categorized as follows:

a. **Potential Productivity and Financial Improvement**

One of the main benefits of EHR is the increase in productivity and finances that has been observed in the form of fewer chart pulls, efficient handling of telephone messages and medication refills, improved billing and coding of visits, improvement in the quality of care, increased preventive care services due to easier preventive care and reduced transcription costs. In addition, it was also observed that due to the use of EHR secondary actions such as population management and proactive patient reminders; reimbursement from payers, participation in pay-for-performance programs, point-of-care decision support, access to patient information, chronic disease management, and integration of evidence-based clinical guidelines was significantly improved.

b. **Job Satisfaction Improvement**

Another benefit of EHR that has been observed is the increase in job satisfaction among the employees. The employees who used EHR in their day-to-day activities at work reported that they now experienced fewer repetitive and tedious tasks, less chart chasing, improved intraoffice communication, easier access to patient information on call and in the hospital, easier compliance with regulations, and high-quality care.

c. **Customer Satisfaction Improvement**

EHR has not only benefitted the healthcare industry it has also benefitted the customers. Many of them have reported that with the use of EHHR, they are able to quickly access their records, spend less time on telephone messages and medication refills, have more access to care and patient education material.

The impact of these tools on the healthcare system is almost magical. Now that patients know what is happening with them, they are more satisfied and are also healing at a faster rate than before. Some of the prominent impacts of technology in Healthcare are mentioned in figure 4.3 below.

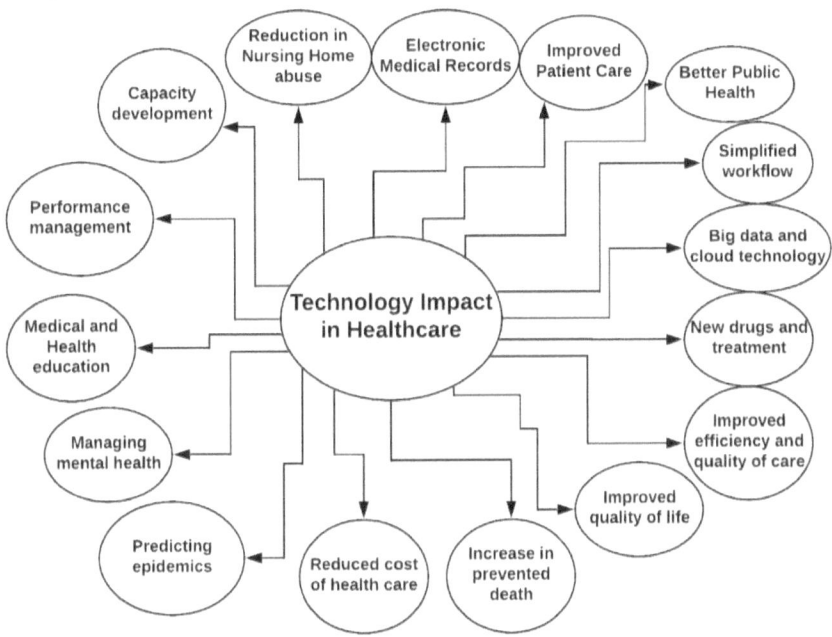

Figure 4.3: Technology Impact in Healthcare

Figure 4.3 enlists the impacts caused by technology on healthcare. Technology has improved patient care, simplified the workflow, integrated big data and cloud technology, led to new drugs and treatments development, improved the efficiency and quality of care, improved the patients' quality of life, decreased the rate of mortality, better prediction of epidemics, improved mental health management, promoted medical and health education, improved the systems for performance management, promoted capacity development, led to a reduction in nursing homes and led to the integration of electronic health records.

Improvement of quality of life and prevention of deaths is the most significant impact of technology on healthcare. It has been ensured via the integration of effective evidence-based healthcare models and evidence-based care approaches. With the positive transformations in healthcare, patient satisfaction is also increased.

All these tools are a part of Health Information Technology which is the multitude of technology tools used by physicians, nurses, health administrators, patients, insurance companies, government entities, and others to compile, store, analyze and share health information. Health IT tools include electronic health records (EHR), personal health records, electronic prescription services, health-related smartphone apps, and more. However, it is not similar to Health Informatics which includes acquisition, storage, retrieval, and use of healthcare information to foster better collaboration among a patient's various healthcare providers.

Health informatics plays a critical role in the push toward healthcare reform. Health informatics is an evolving specialization that links information technology, communications, and healthcare to improve the quality and safety of patient care. Health informatics applies informatics concepts, theories, and practices to real-life situations to achieve better health outcomes. This includes collecting, storing, analyzing, and presenting data in a digital format.

Even though technological advancements today are able to aid in the treatment of almost all diseases, there are some factors that may act as barriers and hinder the implementation and adaptation of technology. Some of them are mentioned in figure 4.4 below.

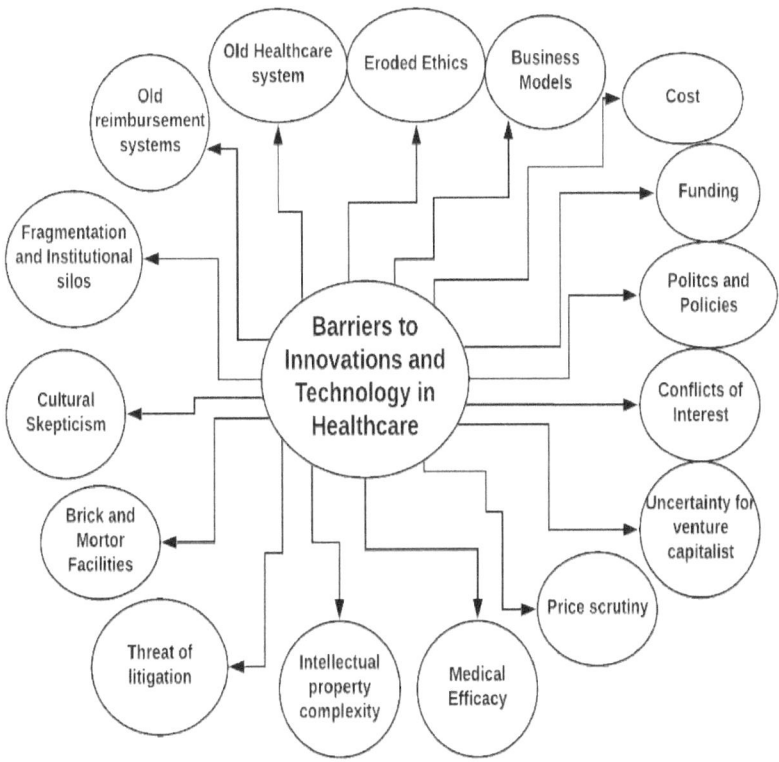

Figure 4.4: Barriers to Innovations and Technology in Healthcare

Figure 4.4 identifies the barriers to innovation and technology in healthcare. Major barriers include funding, politics and policies, conflict of interest, uncertainty for a venture capitalist, price scrutiny, medical efficacy, intellectual property complexity, the threat to litigation, brick and mortar facilities, cultural skepticism, fragmentation, and institutional silos, old reimbursement systems, eroded ethics, business problems, and cost.

The identified barriers are recognized as the significant cause of comprise in healthcare delivery services and the quality of care provided by the healthcare practitioners. Barriers to innovation and technology also reduce the efficiency of implementation of evidence-based care approaches. Moreover, it prevents healthcare practitioners from complying with standard care practices.

In addition to inventing new tools to better healthcare management, technology has also helped medicines become better, more effective, and more efficient along with reducing chances of error. For prescribers and pharmacists, IT can enable the storage of structured patient records, facilitate the electronic prescribing, dispensing, and administration of medicines, automate the handling of medicines in the supply chain and provide tools for monitoring the efficacy and safety of medicines in use. IT can, therefore, improve patient safety, enable professionals to provide high-quality care, and help patients make the most of their medicines.

Pharmacists are already using IT systems to support their daily work. When considering the IT requirements for emerging working practices, pharmacists should consider what functions could be provided by systems that they already use. For example, all pharmacies use pharmacy management systems for medication records, dispensing, labeling, ordering, and stock control. However, many pharmacies do not use all of the available functionality of their system, for example, modules to handle patient-centered services, such as medicines use reviews or prescription interventions.

Pharmacists should also make the most of the services that are available in their locality, for example, electronic prescription service release 2. Adoption and use of EPS release 2 in areas where it is available has the potential to make dispensing and reimbursement processes more efficient for community pharmacists, and the nomination process may help pharmacists to secure prescription business.

Access to patient record systems will assist pharmacists with professional decision-making in providing patient-centered services. For example, the summary care record is now available in many areas. It is beneficial for hospital pharmacists for medicines reconciliation. In the future, it may be used by community pharmacists, for example, with MURs and emergency supplies. As pharmacists deliver more patient-focused services in the future, they will increasingly use national and local patient record services to do so.

Healthcare services in the present have drastically changed in comparison to their state a couple of decades ago. Technology has been the main driver of this change. Today, multiple tools and systems are being introduced to not just make healthcare efficient but also accessible to all irrespective of where the patient is and what condition they are in.

Doctors are in touch with their patients more than they ever did, mainly because both doctors and patients are not required to travel or wait for prolonged hours for treatment. Moreover, with every piece of information being available digitally, there are fewer chances of error which indicates higher efficiency. As technology continues to evolve, the healthcare sector is presumed to become more well-organized and equipped to handle more patients in lesser time and with the help of lesser resources.

Technology is the key driver towards advancement and the heart of enabling businesses to evolve and sustain the competitive advantage. In the context of healthcare, drivers to technology and innovation intend to improve healthcare services and the quality of patient care. Moreover, these drivers make the healthcare systems dynamic and robust. Improvement of quality of life and prevention of deaths is the most significant impact of technology on healthcare. It has been ensured via the integration of effective evidence-based healthcare models and evidence-based care approaches. With the positive transformations in healthcare, patient satisfaction is also increased.

Healthcare services in the present have drastically changed in comparison to their state a couple of decades ago. Technology has been the main driver of this change. Today, multiple tools and systems are being introduced to not just make healthcare efficient but also accessible to all irrespective of where the patient is and what condition they are in.

AI and the future of healthcare

The future of AI in healthcare is like a rollercoaster of awesomeness! Picture this: personalized medicine, super-smart diagnostics, and treatment plans tailored just for you. AI is like the Sherlock Holmes of the medical world, sniffing out patterns and predicting health issues before they even throw a party in your body.

Imagine having your own virtual health assistant, a medical sidekick, if you will. It knows your health history, monitors your vitals, and nudges you to make those healthy choices. It's like having a health-conscious buddy in your pocket, minus the judgment. AI is set to revolutionize patient care by making it more proactive and personalized.

Then there's the superhero of early detection. AI algorithms can analyze tons of medical data at lightning speed, spotting anomalies that might go unnoticed by mere mortal doctors. This means catching diseases in their infancy, when they're like tiny troublemakers rather than full-blown villains.

But wait, there's more! AI is making waves in drug discovery, turning the whole process into a speedier, more efficient quest. It's like having a lab assistant with a PhD in efficiency. This means new medications hitting the shelves faster, and who doesn't want that?

Telemedicine is also getting a futuristic facelift. AI is stepping in to enhance virtual consultations, providing real-time insights and even assisting in surgical procedures remotely. It's like having a medical hologram from the future, right in your living room.

Of course, privacy concerns and ethical questions are on the horizon, but with great power comes great responsibility, and the healthcare world is gearing up for this AI-powered revolution responsibly. The future is looking bright, my friend, with AI playing a pivotal role in making healthcare smarter, more accessible, and downright amazing!

Pros:

1. **Efficient Diagnostics:** AI can analyze vast amounts of medical data in seconds, aiding in quicker and more accurate diagnostics. This means faster identification of diseases and better-informed treatment decisions.
2. **Personalized Medicine:** With AI, treatments can be tailored to individual patients based on their genetic makeup, lifestyle, and specific health data. This could lead to more effective and personalized healthcare plans.

3. **Predictive Analytics:** AI algorithms can predict disease outbreaks, patient deterioration, and trends in public health. This allows for proactive measures and resource allocation, improving overall healthcare management.
4. **Workflow Optimization:** Automation of routine tasks like data entry and administrative work allows healthcare professionals to focus on patient care. This efficiency can potentially reduce wait times and improve the overall patient experience.
5. **Remote Patient Monitoring:** AI can enable continuous monitoring of patients, especially those with chronic conditions, at home. This helps in early detection of potential issues and reduces the need for frequent hospital visits.
6. **Drug Discovery:** AI accelerates the drug discovery process by analyzing vast datasets to identify potential drug candidates and predict their efficacy. This can significantly shorten the time and cost involved in bringing new drugs to market.

Cons:

1. **Privacy Concerns:** The use of AI in healthcare involves handling sensitive patient data. Ensuring the privacy and security of this information is a major challenge and a potential drawback.
2. **Ethical Dilemmas:** AI decision-making may raise ethical questions, especially when it comes to critical healthcare choices. The responsibility and accountability for AI decisions need to be clearly defined.
3. **Data Quality:** AI systems heavily rely on large datasets for training. If the data used is biased or of low quality, it can result in biased algorithms and inaccurate predictions.
4. **Integration Challenges:** Implementing AI in existing healthcare systems can be challenging. Integrating new technologies with legacy systems, training healthcare professionals, and ensuring a smooth transition pose significant hurdles.
5. **Job Displacement:** Automation of certain tasks may lead to concerns about job displacement for certain roles in healthcare.

Striking a balance between automation and human involvement is crucial.
6. **Over-reliance on Technology:** There's a risk of over-reliance on AI, where healthcare professionals may depend too heavily on machine-generated insights, potentially overlooking their own clinical judgment.

In conclusion, while the future of AI in healthcare is brimming with potential, addressing the associated challenges is crucial. Striking the right balance between technological advancement and ethical considerations will be key to maximizing the benefits of AI in healthcare while minimizing potential drawbacks. Exciting times ahead!

CHAPTER 5

Healthcare Costs & Reimbursements

When humankind started to form tribes, they began to exchange their services. Each person of the tribe would do something and exchange it for another good or service with consent. This included salt, fur, skin, rice, wheat, utensils, and weapons, etc., and was also known as a barter exchange or commodity money. However, with time man realized that always exchanging goods and services was not enough. As human civilization continued to progress, commodity money changed into metallic money, and metals like gold, silver, and copper started to be used as money to buy and sell goods and services. One of the main reasons why these metals were used was because they could be easily handled, and their quantity could be easily ascertained.

Metallic money continued to be the main form of money throughout the major portion of recorded history until it became dangerous to carry gold and silver coins from place to place. This led to the invention of paper money and marked a very important stage in the evolution of money. While people continued to use paper money all over the world, credit money was given equal importance. People kept a part of their cash as deposits with banks, which they could withdraw whenever they wanted to through cheques. Nowadays, plastic money in the form of credit cards and debit cards is extensively used by most people in the world, and it is expected that soon the need to carry cash will be completely eradicated.

There is no doubt that money has played a vital role in the history of humanity. Judas betrayed Jesus for money (30 coins of silver), and most of us continue to work despite horrible managers and intense office politics only for the money. All in all, money has driven humankind in ways that were never imagined. Today, money is at the core of each and everything we do. From the tiniest thing in our house to the things that are key to our survival, money is the only thing that can make it happen.

'Health is wealth' is one of the most common phrases we all have grown up listening to. Maybe this is why when it comes to health, people are ready to spend millions to feel better and regain their lost health. While a lot of countries in the world have made sure that healthcare does not cost a leg, the United States has failed to do so.

The United States healthcare system is known to be the most expensive one in the world. It reached $3.5 trillion in 2017 ($10,739 per person), making up 17.9% of the country's gross domestic product (GDP), and is expected to reach 19.7% GDP (or $5.7 trillion) by 2026[2]. The unsustainable levels of healthcare costs have jeopardized America's international competitiveness, burdened U.S. families, and weakened the economy at both federal and state levels.

The factors that have driven healthcare costs are numerous, multifaceted, interconnected, evolving, and often fluctuating in their unique impact on the citizens during any given period. In addition, many factors may also vary by region and state, while some are just primarily inherent (see figure 5.1)

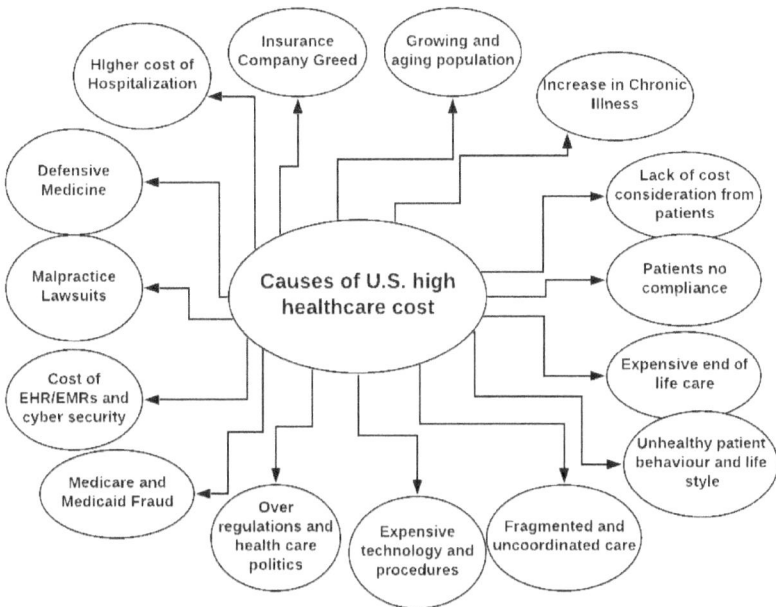

Figure 5.1: Causes of U.S. high healthcare cost

Figure 5.1 enlists the probable causes of high healthcare costs in the U.S. The prominent causes include an increase in chronic illnesses, lack of cost consideration from patients, noncompliance of patients, expensive end of life care, unhealthy patient behavior and lifestyle, fragmented and uncoordinated care, expensive technology and care, over regulations and healthcare politics, Medicare and Medicaid fraud, cost of HER/EMRs and cybersecurity, malpractice lawsuits, defensive medicine, higher cost of hospitalization, insurance company greed, and growing and aging population.

High healthcare costs have several negative impacts. When healthcare spending is high, the capacity of service users to spend on other goods and services is compromised. Moreover, high healthcare costs also reduce the access of low socioeconomic population to healthcare services, deplete their retirement savings, and often bankrupts the consumers.

According to a 2017 research which was published in the Journal of the American Medical Association (JAMA)[1], the expenditure on healthcare was reported to increase by $933.5 billion from 1996 to 2013. This study looked at five factors that were key drivers of healthcare spending. These factors were population growth, population aging, disease prevalence or incidence, utilization of service, and service price and its intensity.

The population growth and aging, as expected, were found to be significant factors that were responsible for driving healthcare spending. The increase in the population of the United States from 1996 to 2013 accounted for about 23.1% increase in spending, thus amounting to $269.5 billion. On the other hand, aging accounted for an 11.6% increase and totaled to $135.7 billion[3]. The study revealed that the U.S. is basically just spending more money on more people due to population growth. Another fact that contributed to the same was the increase in the number of people qualifying for Medicare and Medicaid, both of which are the U.S.'s major payers in healthcare expenditure.

In 2017, around 57.6 million people were enrolled in Medicare, and this number is expected to increase substantially to around 73.7 million people in the next ten years. Similarly, about 72.7 million people were on Medicaid in 2017, and this figure is also expected to rise to 81.3 million in the next decade. The ultimate reality of population growth is that as more money will continue to be spent on healthcare for more people, and as Americans keep living longer, getting older, and sicker, healthcare spending is expected to only continue to rise more and more.

Apart from population growth and aging, the study also revealed that pricing and intensity also increase as a primary driver of healthcare spending from 1996-2013. In fact, this factor resulted in about a 50% increase in spending and totaled to about $583.5 billion. In simple words, Americans were charged extra for their healthcare products and services, along with a surge in the amount of technically complex, advanced services that can address care needs.

Ongoing data also confirmed that the United States still continues to pay higher prices for healthcare products and services than most countries in the world. It was also reported that as the intensity of care continues to increase, so will the overall costs. Some experts have agreed that addressing the price is a fundamental starting point if the U.S. is hoping to get healthcare costs under control. However, doing so is a formidable task, as the underlying components driving price are both complex and numerous.

In 2012, the Bipartisan Policy Center (BPC), which was established by former Senate Majority Leaders Howard Baker, Bob Dole, Tom Daschle, and George Mitchell, co-created the Health Care Cost Containment Initiative. The fundamental aim of the initiative was to explore and evaluate strategies that contain health care cost growth on a system-wide basis, along with the enhancement of healthcare quality and value. The BPC also commissioned a study titled, "What is Driving U.S. Health Care Spending? America's Unsustainable Health Care Cost Growth." The finding of this paper noted that *"at a basic level, our health spending is the product of the price of health care services and the utilization of those services."*

Since healthcare is not affordable for all citizens, health insurance plans were introduced to make healthcare accessible to all. Many Americans today are able to seek the treatment they are in need of with the help of insurance plans and its premiums. Most Americans who are younger than 65 extensively rely on employer-subsidized policies in order to cover the medical costs, even as the cost of those policies jump each year.

Having access to medical insurance has been a hot-button political issue for many years. Ever since 2014, the Patient Protection and Affordable Care Act (ACA) has made it compulsory for everyone to carry insurance. However, the so-called mandate is being rolled back with the dismissal of the tax penalty for not having a policy.

Individuals who do not get coverage at their job buy insurance through federally subsidized insurance exchanges that are part of the ACA, which is also known as Obamacare. However, even though the Congressional Budget Office (CBO) has estimated that the government will pay $685 billion in ACA subsidies in 2018, there are about 29 million people who are still continuing to go uninsured. According to Congressional Budget Office (CBO), in 2018, about 89% of Americans had health insurance, and this number is estimated to escalate as the federal government lifts a tax penalty for not carrying a policy. This has made it critical for each individual to know what they are paying for. Here are a few things that you need to know about your healthcare insurance:

1. Health Insurance Premiums

A health insurance premium is a monthly payment that is made to an insurance company to buy a policy. They are the primary source of profits for all insurance providers. In order to make a profit, providers need to take in more money in premium payments than they pay out in the benefits. Moreover, unlike copays and deductibles, premiums must be paid whether an insured person has medical expenses or not.

For the majority of American families, healthcare premiums are one of the greatest health care costs. According to a study by Kaiser Family Foundation, premiums for family coverage through employer-sponsored plans rose 55% between 2007 and 2017. Where employers generally pay a substantial amount of their workers' premiums, most workers tend to pay premium costs (31 percent). In 2017 alone, the average family premium for Employer-Sponsored Insurance (ESI) coverage was $17,581.

The employer portion of worker healthcare premiums is exempted from the federal and state income taxes, and the employee portion is usually being deducted before withholding and is excluded from taxable income. Lower wage workers also generally pay a greater percentage of their health insurance premium. It was reported that those who are employed at small firms pay 39% of the premium for family coverage as compared to 28% for workers at large companies.

2. Health Insurance Deductibles

A health insurance deductible is the number of medical costs that the insured individual must pay before the insurance coverage begins.

Deductible amounts may vary by plan but are generally stipulated as an annual maximum figure. The deductible is renewed annually; hence each year, policyholders tend to face a fresh deductible even if they have paid the full deductible in the previous year. For instance, an individual with a $1,500 deductible will have to pay for the first $1,500 of care he or she may receive each year.

An insurance policy with a high deductible also usually comes with a lower monthly premium. Some plans may also have separate deductibles for specific services. Under some policies, there will be certain services, such as a trip to an emergency room or a routine doctor's visit, that may not require a deductible payment at all. The Obamacare law has exempted certain procedures, such as annual physicals and immunizations, from the deductible amount.

The ESI plans covered around 151 million people in 2017, with over half the population being non-elderly. 81% of the policies also contained an annual deductible requirement, for which the average deductible for a single coverage policy reached around $1,505. The deductible was 55% higher than the amount in 2009. Furthermore, from 2012 and 2017, the percentage of workers with an annual deductible of $1,000 or more increased from 31% to 51%.

3. Health Insurance Copays

A copay is basically a fixed charge that is paid by an insured individual when they visit a doctor, be it a specialist, urgent care or the emergency room, or in many cases, even purchasing a prescription drug. It may vary by policy, and copays might also increase dramatically for those who have HMO and PPO policies and are receiving treatment from medical practices outside their policies' provider networks.

A few years ago, most of the health insurance plans allowed policyholders to pick their own doctors, hospitals, and clinics. However, as costs continued to rise, insurers started looking for ways to trim their expenses. Hence they began to cut deals with doctors, physician groups, hospitals, and myriad other healthcare providers that were offering lower rates, thus allowing the insurers to pass the savings to policyholders. Insurers also use copays coinsurance to split costs with their policyholders.

The copay system may save money; however, it has added to the complexity of healthcare. Policyholders typically need to consider two sets of fees: those that are set for providers in their approved networks and those that are outside the networks. Generally, fees are much lower if you only see approved providers.

Unlike deductibles, copays are complicated as they are fees imposed each time you visit a medical provider. The fees may vary, and you may find yourself paying one fee to visit a family practice doctor, another to a specialist, and another to an emergency room or clinic. In addition, copays are also charged for tests, prescription drugs, physical therapy, and various other covered expenses.

This means that copay costs can rise sharply for those with costly medical emergencies or chronic conditions that are costly to treat. Therefore, to limit what patients have to pay, most policies have annual as well as lifetime caps on out-of-pocket payments. Obamacare sought to address some of these costs by creating exemptions and requiring insurers to offer preventative-care procedures without sharing the cost. The exempted services include annual checkups, immunizations, well-woman visits, and certain diagnostic exams.

Even though copays are a predictable part of the healthcare-cost equation, they are dwindling, reducing as a portion of what insured people are paying for care. According to the Kaiser Family Foundation, rising deductibles are the biggest culprits when it comes to out-of-pocket healthcare spending for employer-sponsored plans. They have increased from an average of $303 a year in 2006 to $1,200 a year by 2016. Enrollee spending on deductibles also rose from $151 to $417 during the period, and this was a 176 percent increase. However, the amount spent on copays actually decreased by 38%, from $225 in 2006 to $140 in 2016[4].

Premiums, deductibles, co-pays, and co-insurance are all costs that need to be borne by the consumer of an insurance plan. Employees who are enrolled in ESI plans generally have their premium costs deducted from their paychecks on a pre-tax basis. While Medicare recipients have their premiums deducted from their Social Security checks. On the other hand, self-insured individuals pay their premiums to their insurance companies directly, and other out-of-pocket costs must be paid to healthcare providers at the time of service or during billing. Any taxpayer who enrolls in a high-deductible health plan (HDHP) can open a Health Savings Account (HSA). Funds that are contributed to an HSA are not subject to federal income taxes if they are used for qualified medical expenses. This includes co-pays, deductibles, co-insurance, and many other costs such as dental, ophthalmic, and chiropractic care. Individuals with healthcare insurance should also be aware of the different reimbursement plans and decide for themselves which one would suit their needs. Some of these are mentioned in figure 5.2 below:

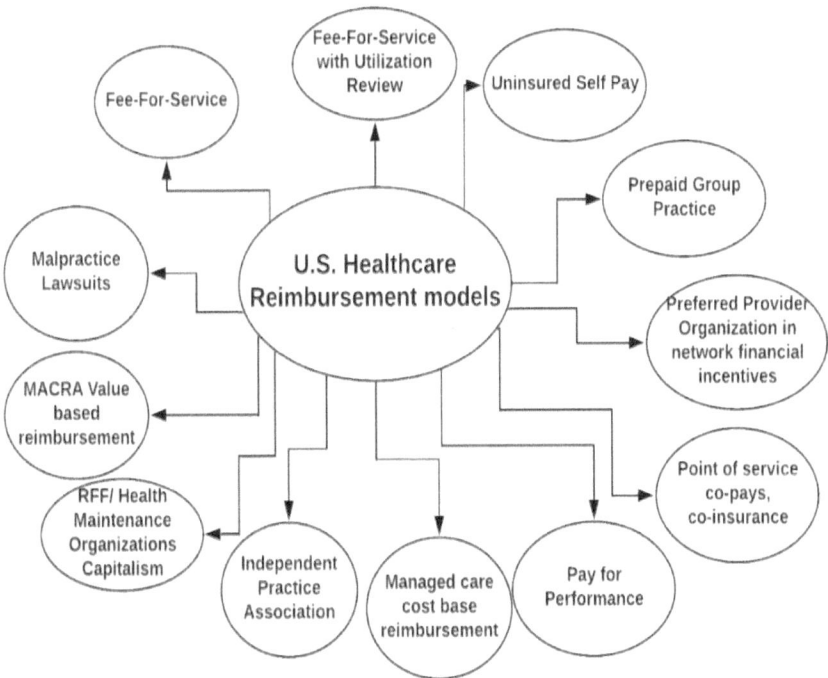

Figure 5.2: U.S. Healthcare Reimbursement Models

Figure 5.2 represents the U.S. healthcare reimbursement models that have been integrated into healthcare services. These include Prepaid

Group Practice, Preferred Provider Organization in network financial incentives, Point of Service Co-Pays, co-insurance, Pay for Performance, managed care cost base reimbursement, independent practice association, RFF/Health maintenance organizations capitalism, MACRA value-based reimbursement, malpractice lawsuits, Free-for-Service, Free-For-Service with Utilization review, and Uninsured Self Pay.

Healthcare reimbursement models promote and emphasize cost-effective decisions regarding the medical care of patients. These reimbursement models, therefore, help in improving the quality and efficiency of services provided to the patient. Healthcare reimbursement models reduce the healthcare cost that helps both service providers and service users.

The most common forms of reimbursement plans are Capitation, Pay per Service, and Value-based payments.

1. Capitation Payment Model

Capitation payments are payments that are agreed upon in a capitated contract between the health insurance company and medical provider. These are fixed, pre-arranged monthly payments which are received by a physician, clinic, or hospital per patient enrolled in a health plan, or sometimes per capita. The monthly payment is calculated a year in advance. It remains fixed for the same year, regardless of how often the patient needs their services.

Rates for capitation of payments are developed using local costs and average utilization of needed services. This is why they can vary from one region of the state to another. Many plans also establish risk pools as a percentage of the capitation payment, and money in a risk pool is withheld from the physician until the end of the fiscal year. If the health plan does well in terms of finances, the medical provider receives this money. If the health plan does poorly, the money is kept in order to pay the deficit expenses.

2. Fee-for-Service Model

The fee-for-service system is a source of many inefficiencies. It does not encourage innovation and practice redesign that improves patient access and care at a reduced cost. For instance, a primary care office (PCP) may want to have some services delivered by a member of the care team other than a physician, such as a nurse or a dietician, who is qualified to deliver high-quality, appropriate services in some situations.

The per-hour costs of these alternative providers are less than what a physician may charge, and retaining their skills frees up physician time for the patients who are in dire need of their distinctive skills and expertise, creating improved access. Inopportunely, the fee-for-service system may not be able to pay for visits with a dietician or a nurse, even though they are also well qualified to deliver the care. The FFS reimbursement rules entail that the care needs to be delivered by a physician. Yet better use of lower-cost staff results in better provider, staff, and patient contentment at lower costs. Moreover, providing patients access to care via electronic patient portals, secure email, and telephonic nurse are effective methods of creating efficient, convenient, and appropriate care for routine conditions which do not require an exam, such as urinary tract infection.

Unfortunately, fee-for-service does not recognize or pay for these virtual interactions even though patients may prefer to have a virtual "exam" without the trouble of an office visit. Without a source of profits to underwrite the additional cost of providing this "non-billable" service, providers are discouraged from offering it.

Many providers also recognize that U.S. health care in its current form is quite inefficient, overly expensive, and unsustainable. However, under a fee-for-service model, they have a little financial incentive to transmute the way medicine is practiced. They are not only rewarded for economizing; they are also penalized if they provide fewer services or lower-cost services. Even though MCOs work hard to manage care and costs, their impact is restricted since they are not the ones to make the day-to-day diagnostic and treatment decisions that determine costs.

In the typical fee-for-service arrangement, providers usually make these decisions. In contrast, MCOs have only limited ways to influence them.

3. Value-based Payment Models

Value-based payment structures are gaining popularity for many reasons.

a. Financial incentives can be designed to reward behavior and promote practice changes needed to successfully implement more efficient and effective models of care.
b. Financial incentives can help providers pay for investments in technology, process improvements, staff training, and culture changes needed for practice transformation.
c. Value-based payment promotes the delivery of the right care in the timeliest and cost-effective settings. Patient portals, secure emails, and nurse triage can be installed without an adverse impact on the provider's revenue. Routine care issues which may not require an exam can be handled more quickly and conveniently for the patients, and early intervention may also prevent a costlier level of the visit or an adverse event.
d. The use of alternative members of the care team turns out to be practical. In many cases, nurses, medical assistants, pharmacists, dieticians, patient navigators, and others are able to deliver certain kinds of care or assistance more proficiently and effectively.
e. Providers are compensated based on the value they produce, even if the volume of services is decreased. This model can align incentives to encourage dissimilar providers to collaborate and achieve objectives.

Cost savings can be easily shared with nursing homes, behavioral health providers, specialists, hospitals, home, and community-based providers, and others who are creating value for the beneficiary and even the system as a whole. A well-structured model also draws attention to the full continuum of healthcare services. This includes long-term services and supports (LTSS) and behavioral health services, which have traditionally been of little interest to providers not directly involved in providing these services. Coordinating the full range of services is a key focus for CMS' Medicare Medicaid Alignment Initiative (MMAI). The high-costs, complex dually eligible individuals have historically suffered suboptimal outcomes due to inadequate coordination among primary care providers, LTSS, and hospital providers.

The healthcare system of the US is undoubtedly too expensive to be afforded by a working-class citizen. However, the initiation of insurance plans and their various payment plans have made it possible for each individual to customize their plan and opt for the one that best suits their need. While most people are managing their lives with the current healthcare services, it is better if the government introduces policies to make it affordable for people who do not have health insurance so that all citizens are able to get the treatment that they need.

Impact of Unpaid duties (overload of paper work)

CHAPTER 6

COVID - 19

The second decade of the century started a little mellow, with most people having mixed feelings about the ending of a decade. While some bid goodbye to their past and made new plans to kickstart the ending of the decade, everybody failed to notice the increasing numbers of patients that were being infected by a novel respiratory infection. This infection named Corona Virus or COVID – 19 was characterized by respiratory symptoms such as coughing, sore throat, as well as shortness of breath, along with fever. Various other symptoms may also be experienced. It includes a runny nose, consistent headaches, muscle and/or joint pains, nausea, diarrhea, vomiting, loss of sense of smell, altered sense of taste, loss of appetite, and fatigue[1].This infection originated in Wuhan, China. By the end of 2019, the whole world was dancing on its fingers. As the number of fatalities began to grow rapidly, so did the concern of people. This infection was spreading like wildfire, as contact with infected humans, air, and even with surfaces that may have the microbes were causing this infection. There was nothing humankind could do to stop it. With no vaccine or treatment available, there was nothing that could help fight it. In order to keep everyone safe, it was decided that it is best if human interactions are limited and people spend more time in their houses.

This decision led to a change that many did not expect. A worldwide lockdown was implemented in March 2020. Individuals across the country were locked inside their homes, with little to nothing to do with the huge amount of time that they now had on their hands. Restaurants, hotels, shopping malls, air travel, and even educational institutions were closed.

This change led to many new trends and also instigated new habits in people who perceived this time to be one of change. People began to cook the dishes they had been wanting to, renovate their houses, read more, and exercise often along with managing their work from home. There are many countries that are still under lockdown as the cases in that area are not decreasing. As scientists are still working on creating vaccines and treatment for this infection, there are a few things that are advised to do in order to avoid contracting the infection. This includes maintenance of good hygiene, physical distancing, avoidance of public gatherings, isolation if necessary, and use of masks at all times when you step outside. While these practices may not serve as a course of treatment, they do ensure a decrease in the chances of getting infected[2]. In the current situation, most industries have suffered. Both employees and employers are figuring out better ways to work from home while making sure the line between both of them is not blurring at any point. Not just that, leadership styles have also evolved during the pandemic (see figure 6.1).

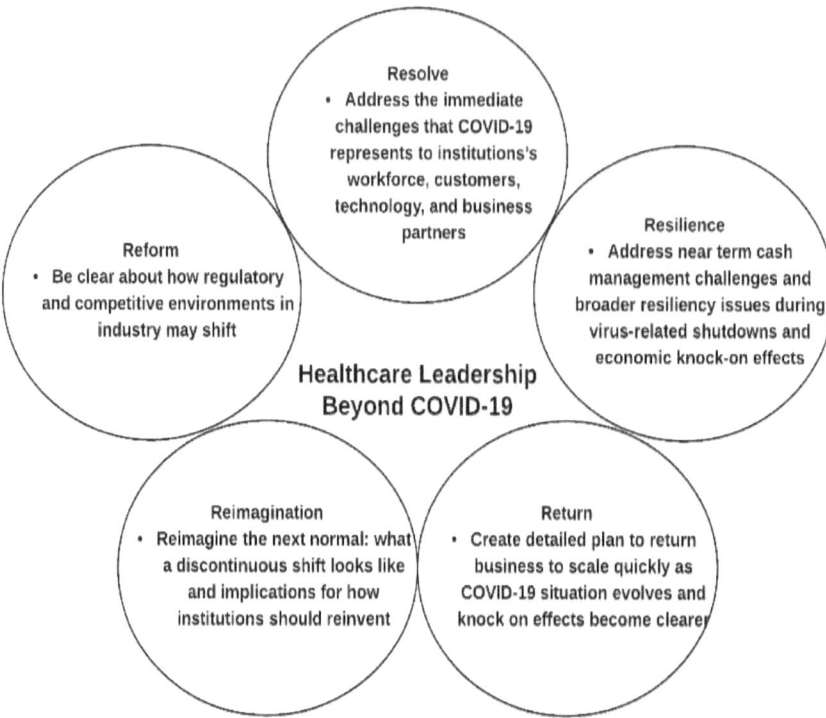

Figure 6.1: Healthcare Leadership Beyond COVID-19

Figure 6.1 represents the factors associated with healthcare leadership beyond COVID-19. Prominent leadership aspects include resilience, return, re-imagination, reform, and resolve. Resilience in leadership addressed the near-term cash management challenges and border resiliency issues during pandemic-associated lockdowns and economic knock-on effects. Furthermore, it also led to the development of a detailed plan to return the business to scale quickly as the pandemic situation evolved. As depicted in figure 6.1, healthcare leadership beyond COVID-19 works through effective and competent leadership skills. It reimagined the next normal and assessed what a discontinuous shift looks like and implications for how institutions should reinvent. Healthcare leadership beyond COVID-19 provides reforms and be clear about how competitive and regulatory environments in the industry may shift. This healthcare leadership also addresses and resolves the immediate challenges that are represented by COVID-19 to customers, the workforce, business partners, and technology.

Further contemplation in leadership aspects also led to the development of strategies for the coming months. Reforms have also been developed and issued about how regulatory and competitive environments in the industry may shift. The resolving strategies addressed the immediate challenges that are represented by COVID-19 to the workforce, institutions, customers, business partners, and technology[3]. Healthcare is one of the industries that has witnessed a considerable change due to the pandemic. In times of unprecedented global health challenges and large-scale shocks strike, resilience is the virtue that is in great demand. It is needed by all, including individuals, organizations, and even society, to survive and thrive in the face of combat against the virus and associated economic and societal shocks. In dealing with a global health crisis, resilience does not only require psychological readiness but also organizational support and system-level preparation. Researches have shown that occupational contexts can play a vital role in enabling both individuals and organizations in order to build resilience and develop effective coping strategies. Some of these strategies need to be implemented beyond the scope of COVID 19.

Healthcare leadership is presented with several challenges, and COVID-19 puts significant pressure on young leaders. Therefore, it is the need of the hour to recognize the strategic actions healthcare leaders can take to overcome the challenges contributed by COVID-19. There is a need for the identification of survival strategies for both leaders and followers in healthcare after adverse effects of the pandemic. Some survival strategies have been depicted in the figure below.

Figure 6.2 represents the survival strategies beyond COVID-19. These strategies are based on how to handle patient compliance, to mobilize resources, to maintain stable supply chain management, to revive financial status, to maintain morale while working remotely, to protect employees, to set up cross-functional response team, to stay close to customers, to practice plan with the top team with in-depth tabletop exercise, to handle the new norms with insurance companies, to improve telehealth and other health innovations, to navigate new regulations and healthcare standards, and to handle system capacity.

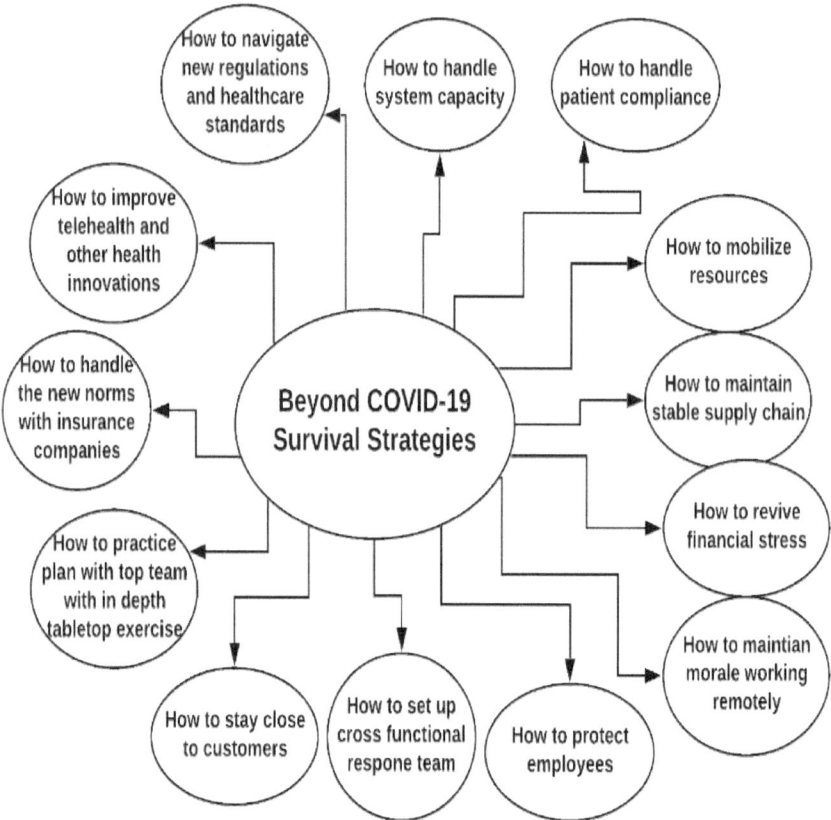

Figure 6.2: Beyond COVID-19 Survival Strategies

Survival strategies beyond COVID-19 significantly needed to be implemented at the national and international level to address the healthcare challenges. The most important areas that need focus include operations rebuilding, revenue recovery, acceleration of digital solution adoption, and rethinking the organization. The pandemic has a diverse impact on healthcare services due to transformations in healthcare reforms and policies.

The COVID-19 pandemic has changed how healthcare is delivered in the United States and has also affected the operations of healthcare facilities. Its effects may include an increase in patients seeking care for respiratory illness, which could be COVID-19, deferment and delay in non-COVID-19 care, disruptions in supply chains, fluctuations in occupancy of facilities, absenteeism due to illness, or caregiving responsibilities, along with increases in mental health concerns[4]. In response to the challenges posed in order to prevent infection by COVID-19, CDC has developed a set of infection prevention as well as control recommendations for COVID-19 in healthcare settings. These recommendations provide detailed guidance for the care of patients who are suspected or confirmed to be infected with COVID-19 in healthcare settings. It has also developed a guideline for the care of patients who are not suspected or confirmed to have COVID-19. It is necessary for all health care facilities to be familiar with these recommendations and guidelines along with ensuring that their staff is equipped with the necessary tools and training that can help inefficiently following the guidance as part of a comprehensive strategy to manage operations during the COVID-19 pandemic.

Healthcare facilities are required to provide care for all patients in the safest way possible. Be it the patients who need home-based care, outpatient care, urgent care, emergency room care, inpatient care, or even intensive care. It is recommended for healthcare facilities to operate effectively during the COVID-19 pandemic and adjust the way they deliver healthcare services in order to reduce the need to provide in-person care. It is also necessary to follow infection prevention and control recommendations tailored to their respective setting along with ensuring the providence of necessary in-person clinical services for health conditions other than COVID-19 in the safest way possible to curtail disease transmission to patients. All of these can be implemented by using the following:

a. **Using Telehealth Services**

Given the limitations that the pandemic has imposed on us, telehealth services need to be optimized when available and appropriate. The federal government has also made telehealth services easier to implement and access since it believes that telehealth could be used to deliver services such as screening of patients who may have symptoms of COVID-19, provision of urgent care for non-COVID-19 conditions, along with identification of higher acuity care needs, creating access to primary care providers and specialists, including mental and behavioral healthcare providers, for persistent health conditions and management of medication[5].

Moreover, telehealth can also be used to help individuals participate in physical therapy, occupational therapy, and other modalities for optimal health. It can also help healthcare professionals monitor clinical signs of certain medical conditions remotely, such as blood pressure and blood glucose levels, especially for the patients who have difficulty accessing care, especially for the ones who are residing in rural settings, older adults, or those with limited mobility.

Telehealth not only helps in proper treatment but also helps healthcare professionals' follow-up with patients even after they have been discharged from the healthcare facility and provide advanced care planning and counseling to patients and caregivers in case a life-threatening event or medical crisis occurs. They are also able to provide non-emergent care to residents in long-term care facilities. Telehealth can also help healthcare professionals learn from the best they have by providing education and training through peer-to-peer professional medical consultations, which are not locally available, particularly in rural areas.

In present times, healthcare professionals who are using telehealth are able to instruct patients who think they may have contracted COVID-19 to use the available advice lines, patient portals, online self-assessment tools and to call and speak to the staff instead of coming in person. It is also helping healthcare professionals develop protocols for staff to triage and evaluate patients quickly.

The algorithms of telehealth are also able to help determine and identify which patients can be managed by telephone and should be advised to stay home and which patients are in need to be sent in for emergency care, in-person visits, and follow up with a lab for COVID-19 diagnostic testing or other testing services. It is also helping healthcare professionals assess the patient's ability to safely self-isolate and monitor their symptoms at home, along with the careful evaluation of the risk of the virus spreading to others living in the same environment.

Telehealth also helps the caregivers of the patients by providing them clear instructions regarding home care, including when and how they can access the healthcare system for in-person care or urgent/emergent conditions. However, the staff makes sure that they, too, are monitoring patients at home with the help of daily check-ins using telephone calls, texts, patient portals, or any other means. In some cases, the healthcare facilities are also arranging local public health resources, including home health services and community organizations, in order to assist with support services and aid in the delivery of food, medication, and other goods for the patients who are isolating at home.

b.   Universal Source Control

In order to prevent transmission of COVID-19 by symptomatic and pre-symptomatic individuals, healthcare facilities are using source control for all those who enter a healthcare facility (e.g., staff, patients, visitors). Source control is the use of masks and gloves, which may help in preventing transmission from infected individuals, which may or may not show the symptoms of COVID-19. However, cloth face coverings are not considered personal protective equipment (PPE), and healthcare professionals who are dealing with infected individuals need to use personal protective equipment (PPE). For both the visitors and patients, a cloth face covering is considered appropriate. If a visitor or patient has arrived at the healthcare facility without a cloth face covering, a face mask may be provided to them immediately if supplies are available. Moreover, it is also advised that cloth face coverings or masks should not be placed on children, who are under the age of 2 or on anyone who has trouble breathing, is unconscious, disabled, or otherwise unable to take off the mask themselves[6].

Apart from using technology and deploying all positive measures, healthcare facilities are advised to pay attention to their preparedness to rapidly detect and respond to an increase of COVID-19 cases locally.

However, this needs to be done in a way that ensures that care is being provided in the safest way possible and telehealth services are being used when available and appropriate. They are also recommended to gradually begin expanding in-person clinical care services and prioritize at-risk populations. This includes the individuals who are the most at-risk for complications from delayed care and those who do not have access to telehealth services.

Given the fact that COVID-19 has the potential to asymptomatically transmit healthcare professionals who are providing in-person care to patients that are not suspected or confirmed to have COVID-19 are strongly advised to follow the recommended infection control practices specific to COVID-19 in order to prevent transmission of the infection. Moreover, there are specific considerations and precautions for the care of patients that are not suspected or confirmed to have COVID-19 as well. Other than that, healthcare facilities are advised to place visual alerts, such as signs and posters in appropriate languages that are easy to understand for people from all walks of life. These signs should be placed at entrances and in strategic places. They should encourage and guide people regarding hand hygiene, respiratory hygiene, such as using cloth face coverings and cough etiquettes.

In cases it is absolutely necessary to visit the healthcare facility, it is advised to maintain physical distance as much as possible and make sure that visitors are being assessed for fever and other COVID-19 symptoms before they enter the facility. When visitors are in the facility, they need to be strictly instructed to wear a facemask, perform frequent hand hygiene, and limit their visit to the patient's room or other areas that are designated by the facility. It is also recommended to use video conferencing if it is something that can be discussed using the same.

For the safety of healthcare professionals, it is advised to increase workstation spacing and decrease the number of individuals that are allowed in common areas such as breakrooms and elevators. It is also advised that healthcare practitioners should limit visitors to the facility to only those who are crucial for the patient's physical or emotional well-being and care. Instead, they should contact patients who are at an increased risk of contracting a severe illness from COVID-19 related complications to make sure they are adhering to current medications and therapeutic regimens. They should also confirm if they have access to sufficient medication refills and instruct the patient or their caregiver to notify their provider by phone if they are sick.

If the symptoms are serious and an in-person visit is necessary, then the patients are requested to call before they leave home so that the staff is able to make the necessary safety arrangement and are ready to receive them and treat them while using appropriate infection control practices and personal protective equipment. For caregivers who are accompanying patients, their safety measures should be followed, and waiting rooms should allow individuals to be at least 6 feet apart. If a certain facility does not have a waiting area, then the use of partitions or signs to create designated areas or waiting lines should be ensured. In addition, it is also advised to reduce crowding by either setting up triage booths to screen patients safely or by asking patients to remain outside in their vehicles or a designated outdoor waiting area till they are called into the facility for their appointment.

As the pandemic continues to prevail, the healthcare system of America needs to create a sustainable balance between the need to provide necessary clinical services and treatments while minimizing risk to patients and healthcare professionals. The US healthcare system, which strives to become the best in the world, is under deep stress due to the coronavirus outbreak, with medical professionals expecting hundreds and thousands of patients in need of urgent care in the coming days. So much so that the Trump administration has now marshaled all its resources to handle this alarming situation. It has also sought the help of retired doctors to help treat the growing number of patients while the Army Corps of Engineers is busy building makeshift hospitals across the country on a war footing.

The health situation in New York, which is home to some of the best hospitals, is even worse. Despite having a large concentration of doctors, specialists, and hospital beds, it is under deep stress, with many hospitals resorting to what they call rationing care. Health officials fear a similar situation is set to occur in various metropolitan cities across America as COVID-19 continues to spread like wildfire. Since the impacts of

COVID-19 tend to vary among different communities, the healthcare system of America needs to consider the local levels of COVID-19 transmission while making decisions about providing medical services for health conditions other than COVID-19.

The pandemic is set to transform the global health community's acceptance and use of digital health technologies that are an alternative to the traditional practices of medicine. As healthcare system of America and even others around the world are now becoming overwhelmed as they respond to COVID-19 while continuing to make sure that health care services are being provided and leaders are adopting technologies that a few months ago were on the sidelines of most healthcare systems. An increasing amount of doctors, patients, and home care providers are turning towards telemedicine in order to reduce exposure to COVID-19. They are discovering these virtual consultations that are proving to be rather effective for triaging care, sharing critical guidance, and also for providing emotional support.

Dashboards for logistic management systems are now improving the effective deployment of essential resources ranging from hospital beds to PPE to, eventually, vaccines. More advanced technologies, including AI, are also being introduced to provide insights into complex questions regarding the individual behaviors impact transmission and identifying which policies are effective for certain groups[7]. The phrase, *"you can't put the genie back in the bottle once it is out,"* fits the current situation. This means that once humankind has the deployed technology in healthcare, its use will only expand as we continue to solve the consistent challenges of the present and future as well. The use of technology will also help in tackling other problems that preoccupied us prior to COVID-19 — such as shortage of health personnel, inadequate budgets, and weak health systems. In addition, there is a high probability that these technologies may help in getting closer to the shared goal of universal health coverage.

However, in the present times, the whole of humankind needs to stay resilient and collectively 'bounce back'. For it is only when we stand strong in the face of this pandemic that we will be able to combat it and also launch 'new norms' for organizations and societies. To repeat the inspirational words of Winston Churchill, *"Success is not final, failure is not fatal; it is, in fact, the courage to continue that counts,"* we are in dire need of the courage, readiness, and ability to build and strengthen resilience and rebuild our confidence and trust in global health systems.

Lessons from COVID -19

CHAPTER 7
Post-Pandemic Telehealth Medicine

The COVID 19 pandemic has changed almost everything. Humans have learned new skills, developed unique ways to perform their usual tasks, and most importantly, they have discovered their capabilities and flaws that they previously had no time to pay attention to. The nature of work has also changed; jobs that were assumed only to be executed in an office are now being done from homes. Professionals all around the world are now more than ever aware of ways to get their work done without having to meet virtually.

The healthcare industry has also been greatly affected by the pandemic. Apart from highlighting the flaws in healthcare systems, it has compelled it to deploy ways to ensure that each individual is receiving the care they need without putting their lives in danger. This led to the use of a technology that has made it possible for people to seek healthcare without having to risk their lives and visit a hospital: telehealth.

Telehealth is essentially the use of telecommunication technologies for the purpose of health education, health administration, and, most importantly, clinical care. It utilizes modalities such as video conferencing, remote patient monitoring, and streaming of media. Live video conferencing typically involves a two-way audiovisual connection between the care provider and the patient. Whereas remote patient monitoring utilizes electronic tools to record health data on patients that a practitioner can review in a different location (see figure 7.1).

Telehealth and its oriented services have reduced the demands for hospital beds' supply. This has been ensured by keeping low-risk patients at home. Telehealth has also improved the care delivery system by providing service providers with timely access to the medical records of their patients. Figure 7.1 depicts the wide range of tools used in telehealth.

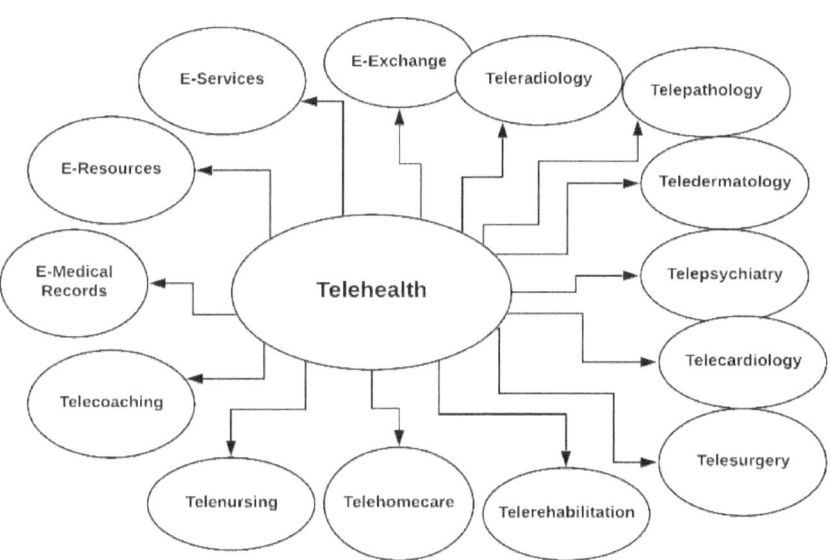

Figure 7.1: Telehealth

Figure 7.1 represents the telehealth-oriented services that are provided to service users. These include telepathology, telepsychiatry, telecardiology, telesurgery, telerehabilitation, telehomecare, telenursing, telecoaching, E-medical records, e-resources, e-services, and e-exchange. The definition of these concepts is presented below:

E-services: Refer to the electronic tools and digital media used for different purposes, such as telehealth.

E-exchange: An electronic exchange serves as a trading platform in which matching of buy and sell orders, order entry and forwarding, price determination is performed by a computer.

Telecardiology: Advanced medical practice that employs telecommunication for the remote diagnosis and treatment of cardiologic diseases such as arrhythmias, coronary artery diseases, and congestive heart failure.

Telesurgery: Corresponds to the surgical procedure carried out at a distance through computer technology and robotics.

Telepathology: A medical practice that employs telecommunication to conduct diagnosis, education, and research via facilitating the transfer of image-rich pathology data between distant locations.

Telepsychiatry: The use of telecommunication technology for the delivery of psychiatric assessment and care, particularly via videoconferencing.

Telerehabilitation: Provision of rehabilitation services through communication and information technology to provide services of assessment, prevention, treatment, education, and counseling.

Tele homecare: Provides healthcare services to the patients at home by enabling interaction of video, voice and health-related data via telecommunication technology.

Telenursing: Uses communication and information technology to provide nursing services to distant service users.

Tele coaching: The use of communication and information technology to help and encourage service users to solve issues, achieve goals, and improve the quality of life.

E-medical records: Refers to an electronic or digital collection of medical information of the patient, which may include the patient health history such as allergies, diagnoses, immunizations, tests and treatment plans.

E-resources: These are the materials in digital format that can be accessed electronically. These include e-books, e-journals, and web pages.

Tele dermatology: Dermatology services provided to the distant patients with communications technology.

Telehealth services have been substantially integrated as tools for healthcare delivery in the post-COVID era. Telehealth services are also helping the service users to access the treatments on a timely basis. COVID-19 pandemic has significantly affected the population in developing countries, and their population requires robust tools to access effective healthcare services, which can be ensured by telehealth.

The COVID-19 pandemic has impacted society and has especially transformed the U.S. healthcare system. The use of telehealth services that meet patients' needs during the COVID 19 pandemic has been extraordinary. The shift to a virtual clinician and patient interaction as the main modality of healthcare has impacted not only the 0.6% of Americans with confirmed COVID-19 infections but also every other person who is coming in contact with the healthcare system in one way or the other. Starting from mid-March through April 2020, the growth in the use of telehealth went from being 5% or less of all U.S. face-to-face office-based medical visits per week to almost 80% and higher. While 25 percent of major providers had a structured video-based telehealth program at the beginning of this year, that number increased to over 90% by mid-April. It is very clear that until new vaccines, treatments, and herd immunity are not entrenched, the vast majority of COVID-19 and non-COVID-19 triage and care, which is about 900+ million face-to-face provider visits in 2019 -- will continue to be fully or partially electronic.

Over half of all U.S. hospitals are now using telemedicine, and this trend is only expected to rise. In fact, in a recent survey, it was found

90 percent of healthcare executives have already begun developing or implementing a telemedicine program in their respective organizations[1]. Even healthcare providers in smaller and independent practices are starting to adopt telehealth to compete with local retail clinics and stop losing their patients.

The use of telehealth has been a part of the healthcare industry for several decades, but its use markedly increased with the advent of the COVID-19 outbreak. Since it offers the capacity to provide care from a distance, it fills a critical need: physical distancing. Due to this factor, the consumer adoption of telehealth has skyrocketed, from 11 percent in 2019 to 46 percent of consumers now using telehealth as a replacement for canceled healthcare visits[3]. This has led to a precipitous increase in the appoints, and healthcare providers see 50 to 175 times2 3 4 the number of patients using telehealth than they did before. Before the outbreak of COVID-19, the total annual revenues of U.S. telehealth players were estimated to be around $3 billion, with the largest vendors mainly focusing on the "virtual urgent care" segment. This included helping consumers get on-demand instant telehealth visits with physicians across the world. However, due to COVID 19, the consumer and provider adoption of telehealth has accelerated, and telehealth has extended beyond virtual urgent care, thus creating the possibility of virtualizing up to $250 billion of current U.S. healthcare[4].

This shift is inevitable and will require adaptation of new ways of working for a broad set of providers, step-change improvements in information exchange, and broadening access and incorporation of technology. The potential effect is improved convenience and access to care, better patient outcomes, and a more effective overall healthcare system. Healthcare players may also consider moves that support such a shift and improve their future position.

The federal government has ordained to increase the use of telehealth during the pandemic, so have the governments of Washington D.C. and 18 other states. They recently passed new laws and amended existing laws to allow doctors and patients to connect using technology, including phone calls. As states are closing non-essential services and often issuing stay-in-place orders, state lawmakers are trying their best to remove barriers to telehealth that can aid in reducing the pressure on clinics. According to the Center for Connected Health Policy (CCHP) in California, the states have been easing Medicaid rules, including permitting telehealth to serve as the vehicle of a doctor-patient relationship. Some states have also waived rules to allow residents access to mental health care from the comfort of their homes.

Efforts to expand telehealth have taken an array of forms in different states of America. Texas Governor Greg Abbott has issued a disaster declaration which allows state healthcare providers to use telemedicine to treat patients. Similarly, Massachusetts governor Charlie Baker has ordered state health plans and commercial insurers to cover telehealth services, and authorities in West Virginia have issued declarations to boost the use of audiovisual telehealth for specific services, including mental health and medical care that is offered in rural clinics. The U.S. Drug Enforcement Agency has issued guidelines regarding how care providers can prescribe controlled drugs using telemedicine. Moreover, the American Medical Association has published information on the use of telemedicine in practice[5].

Even though most states are now passing laws regarding telehealth, there is no denying the fact that, like anything else, it too has some disadvantages. However, these advantages tend to outweigh the disadvantages. Adopting up-to-date telehealth initiatives can help healthcare practitioners achieve several benefits. This includes lower healthcare costs, an increase in efficiency and revenue, better access to healthcare services, and ultimately happier, healthier patients. Some more advantages of telehealth are:

- **More Convenient and Accessible Patient Care**

In today's healthcare world, convenience is key, and people prefer getting things done with ease. According to a Cisco global survey, 74% of patients prefer easy access to healthcare services over in-person interactions with providers. Therefore, adding virtual care to your practice with offer your patients simple, on-demand care without the usual waste of time and cost of most in-person visits. Patients who reside in remote locations, are homebound, or just can't take off time from work can now access health care virtually. With the help of video conferencing, smartphone apps, and online management systems, more patients are able to connect with providers than before.

- **Telehealth Cost Effectiveness & Healthcare Savings**

Remote analysis, monitoring services, and electronic data storage have helped in significantly reducing healthcare service costs, thereby saving money for patients and insurance companies. Telehealth also decreases unnecessary non-urgent E.R. visits and transportation expenses for regular checkups and appointments.

Recently, the American Hospital Association has reported that a telemedicine program saved 11% in costs and tripled ROI for its investors. Beyond these general cost-savings, telehealth can also help boost revenue by turning on-call hours into billable time, attracting new patients, reducing no-shows and overhead for physicians who decide to switch to a flexible work-from-home model.

- **Extended Specialist and Referring Physician Access**

With the use of telehealth, patients in rural or remote areas can benefit from quicker and convenient specialist access without having to travel much. It has been estimated that in the U.S. alone, for every 100,000 rural patients, there are about forty-three specialists available. These patients have no other choice than to endure longer appointment commutes and also have trouble accessing lifesaving consultations for specific diseases or chronic care plans. Telemedicine also offers better access to specialists in various parts of the world, regardless of location.

- **Increased Patient Engagement**

When patients are aware of and committed to their own healthcare goals, it leads to a decrease in costs and improvement in health status. Engaging your patients via telemedicine can help them maintain appointments and care schedules with a tap of a finger. Increased engagement initiative of telehealth can also help curb obesity rates and tobacco use by encouraging patients to make healthy lifestyle choices. In addition, virtual visits reassure patients that their providers are available and involved in their care, thereby making it much easier for them to reach out to their healthcare provider with questions, report early warning signs, and make a follow-up appointment to make sure that they're on track.

- **Better Patient Care Quality**

Telemedicine offers patient-centered approaches, including improved timeliness of care which is critical to quality patient care. Patients can also address healthcare issues quickly with real-time urgent care consultations and learn about various options within a few minutes. A new study shows that telehealth patients score lower for depression, anxiety, and stress, and 38% fewer hospital admissions have also been reported[6].

While telehealth is promising to grow rapidly over the next decade and has clear benefits, it poses certain technical and practical problems for all providers of healthcare.

- **Technical Training and Equipment**

The implementation of telehealth includes restructuring I.T. staff responsibilities, and purchasing equipment takes time and costs money. Training is crucial to building an efficient telehealth program. Physicians, practice managers, and other medical staff need to be trained on the new systems to make sure that there is a solid ROI. In addition, staffing requirements may also decrease as telehealth helps in monitoring multiple patients at the same time.

- **Reduced Care Continuity**

In situations where patients are using on-demand telemedicine services which connect them to a random healthcare provider, the care continuity begins to suffer. The patient's primary care provider may not have access to records from other visits and end up with an incomplete history of the patient. The shuffling of service providers increases the risk of a doctor not knowing a patient's history or have notes about their care routines.

Since reduced care continuity can also decrease care quality, consumer telemedicine providers must apply sound data solutions that can help maintain adequate and accessible patient records. As more healthcare providers begin to adopt telehealth solutions with their own patients, care continuity will most likely increase, thus lessening the chances of patients ending up at a retail clinic and urgent care centers when they need immediate care.

- **Fewer In-Person Consultations**

Many providers tend to be worried about the technical problems that are associated with telemedicine and could lead to possible patient mismanagement. Many providers and patients alike still prefer a "personal touch" and believe that not all procedures, even simple checkups, can be performed digitally. Nevertheless, in cases where patients cannot get in to see their doctors in person, and for many cases that don't require a physical exam, telehealth can prove to be a good alternate.

- **Tricky Policies and Reimbursement Rules**

Over the years, healthcare laws, reimbursement policies, and privacy protection rules strive to keep up with the fast-growing industry. While most significant developments have been made to telehealth reimbursement over the past couple of years, it is still a common stumbling block for the providers who are interested in using telehealth in their organizations.

On the Business Side of Healthcare
Telehealth and Preventive Medicine

Apart from presenting healthcare providers with a safer option to practice medicine during such times, telehealth has impacted the existing practices of medicine by merging with it. Recently the Centers for Medicare & Medicaid Services have broadened their access to the Medicare telehealth services under Coronavirus Preparedness and Response Supplemental Appropriations Act along with Section 1135 waiver authority. Clinical preventive medicine services are among the particular set of services that CMS has identified under the broadened access for its beneficiaries.

However, the role of preventive medicine physicians is beyond that. Even though telehealth use is markedly different between the COVID-19 and pre-COVID-19 periods, there are many unknowns about its nature, scope, and even impact. Over the last several months, telehealth strategies have undoubtedly shifted in response to change in the incidence and prevalence of COVID 19. This has also increased the experiences gained regarding practicality, effectiveness, and convenience of telehealth services in care delivery for different patient populations. During the pandemic, preventive medicine has played a vital role in the advancement of telehealth strategies. Preventive medicine training has equipped to take the lead on several activities in this domain. These activities vary from advocacy to secure funding for the expansion of telehealth services with the help of Telehealth Innovation and Improvement Act of 2019 to help the local hospitals and health systems to take advantage of the new CMS rules and an array of waivers of federal requirements and to identify the policy topics that should be addressed to facilitate widespread adoption of telehealth services.

With the help of preventive medicine, it is possible to rapidly inform actionable COVID-19 Era telehealth implementation strategies across the nation. Such efforts have helped in dramatically expanding our understanding of the impact that the COVID-19 shift to telehealth has on individuals, communities, healthcare providers, and healthcare systems. It has also provided actionable evidence, help surmount barriers, and implement facilitators so that this technological adaptation can lead to improved patient-centered outcomes during both the COVID-19 surge and post surge periods, particularly for vulnerable populations.

Telehealth has also impacted the Urgent Care medicine. Over the past years' growth and development of Urgent Care Medicine have been pretty much driven by frustration over long waits in the emergency room and lack of availability of primary care appointments. A growth spout for the Urgent Care industry began in the mid-1990s and is continuing today. However, with the onset of COVID 19, there has been some change to the way it operated. The public's desire for instant access to medical care along with ensuring safety has fueled this monumental growth. It has compelled Urgent Care medicine and telehealth to join hands and making quick access to treatment even more convenient for consumers.

The Cleveland Clinic partnered with the American Well in 2015 to add a 24-hour online statewide telemedicine service. Express Care Online allowed patients to see a medical professional for urgent care via computer or smartphone at any time of day or even night. Patients only pay a $49 fee by credit card at the time of service and access the service through a free app. Providers then evaluate, diagnose, treat an ailment, and, if needed, also prescribe medication. These services aimed at helping people with acute health symptoms, including cough, urinary tract infections, abdominal pain, diarrhea, fever, headaches etc.

Clinics that are devoted solely to the practice of urgent care medicine have incorporated telemedicine as a way to reduce costs, increase market share, and generate more revenue per provider. In the present scenario, the chief goal of the entire healthcare system is to deploy ways to keep people out of emergency rooms when it isn't necessary for them to be there. Even though, in some cases, it is obvious that a patient needs to be seen immediately and that too in a fully equipped setting. In other situations, it can be challenging for the patient to know if that's the best course of action. Therefore, it is necessary to make sure that patients have access to telehealth so that some of these cases can be handled and care be provided to patients with less severe conditions. With the help of telehealth Urgent Care medicine can help patients in the following ways:

a. Primary Care Practices

Primary care offices can leverage telehealth technology to extend office hours, making it possible for patients to fill all of their needs within the practice, rather than turning to retail or online-only providers.

b. Exams for Respiratory Conditions

Several respiratory conditions, including colds, cases of flu, seasonal allergies, and cough, are among the most common reasons that compel patients to seek urgent care medicine. In most cases, they can be successfully diagnosed and treated effectively via telehealth, thereby reducing the risk of contracting more infections.

c. Ear, Nose, and Throat Ailments

Problems that are affecting the ear, nose, and throat, such as sinus symptoms, earache, and sore throat, are able to be treated with the help of telehealth and are remote video visits instead of in-person visits.

d. Conditions Affecting the Skin

The invention of hi-definition video capabilities has made it possible to diagnose and treat certain skin conditions such as insect bites, rashes, and skin infections effectively with the help of telehealth.

e. Other Urgent but Non-emergency Complaints

The variety of cases that can be addressed with telemedicine is vast. It includes many other complaints such as conjunctivitis, upset stomach, diarrhea, urinary tract problems and infections, urgent medication refills, etc. all of these are able to be treated with the help of telehealth.

Since telehealth is able to handle most cases of Urgent Care, it has eased the burden of unplanned medical treatment. Since the nature of Urgent Care appointments has amplified all of the costs and convenience benefits of telemedicine. Whenever a patient visits an

Urgent Care center, they tend to risk their exposure to infectious illness. While this cannot always be avoided, video visits help stops the spread of disease. With the help of telehealth, people only seek Urgent Care when unexpected symptoms arise, thus avoiding unplanned nerve-racking experiences. Each time a visit to the E.R. can be avoided through the use of telehealth, both the patient and the healthcare system wins.

If urgent care clinics do not adopt the technology in some form, they're likely to lose a portion of their client base by putting their lives at risk. There is a possibility that telemedicine could also put some urgent care clinics out of business. Nevertheless, there are many reasons why telemedicine should be embraced and not feared by urgent care providers.

Although telehealth is needed more than ever in these times, it is facing certain hurdles that may slow down its expansion. According to many, reimbursements from private insurers is one of the biggest obstacles that are slowing the expansion of telemedicine. However, with the help of buy-in from companies like United Healthcare and Blue Cross Blue Shield, which started ensuring up reimbursement for telehealth, this obstacle seems to be slowly shrinking. Instead of being seen as an emerging threat to the urgent care industry, here are some more reasons to consider telehealth as a growth opportunity for most immediate care facilities:

- Urgent care providers can help grow patient volume during the early months of operation, possibly even before the opening of the clinic doors.
- The patient pool for urgent care centers can be expanded from those who live within a 3-5-mile radius to a much larger geographic base with the help of telehealth.
- Providers can use telehealth for follow-up visits to create a stronger patient relationship and encourage customers to visit again.
- The technology can also help urgent care centers compete in the rapidly growing employer-based health and wellness-based service market.

Ultimately telemedicine might be able to help push urgent care higher on the perspicacity scale, thus positioning it just short of hospital emergency rooms in terms of depth and breadth of services being offered. In recent years, due to factors like flat-fee reimbursement and integration of nurse practitioners and physician assistants, there has been a degradation in the acuity of urgent care cases. Such that many centers now see a majority of their cases in sinusitis, upper respiratory infections, allergic rhinitis, and some other conditions that can be treated for lower cost in retail clinics or via telehealth.

Another important service that telehealth has impacted is ambulatory care or outpatient care, which is medical care provided on an outpatient basis. The services that Ambulatory care offers include diagnosis, observation, consultation, treatment, intervention, and rehabilitation services. This care also includes advanced medical technology and procedures that can be provided outside of hospitals[7]. In addition, Ambulatory care for sensitive conditions (ACSC) has also been introduced for the health conditions in which appropriate ambulatory care is able to prevent or reduce the need for hospital admissions, such as diabetes or chronic obstructive pulmonary disease. Various medical investigations and treatments for acute and chronic illnesses and preventive health care can also be performed on an ambulatory basis, including minor surgical and medical procedures, most types of dental services, dermatology services, and different types of diagnostic procedures, for instance, blood tests, X-rays, endoscopy and biopsy procedures of superficial organs. Other types of ambulatory care services typically include emergency visits, rehabilitation visits, and in some cases, telephone consultations.

Just like out-patient care, in-patient care has also been impacted by the use of telehealth. In-patient care is the care of patients whose condition requires admission to a hospital. Progress in modern medicine and the advent of comprehensive out-patient clinics ensure that patients are only admitted to a hospital when they are extremely ill or have severe physical trauma[2]. There are some important ways in which remote patient care can be used to improve outcomes for the patients who are admitted to any hospital.

a. Hospital Resources Can Be More Effectively Deployed

Realistically for many health systems, it is not possible to have every type of specialist available 24×7 in their hospitals. Telehealth makes sure that hospitals are able to conduct remote examinations and instruct on-site physicians even when the specialist is not physically present. This means that specialized care can be provided to patients without delay.

b. Support for Rural and Underserved Areas

In many places, there are general physician shortages or a lack of nearby specialists. With the help of Telehealth, the geographical reach of every resource is expanded, making sure that the right care is reaching more people. If a specialist is needed, doctors in the hospital can establish a remote connection with the respective provider on the mainland. This will reduce the expenses of moving patients to the providers or bringing providers to the patients.

c. Reducing Readmissions

The post-hospitalization period is undoubtedly a critical time to monitor patients, along with the hopes of reducing the chance of readmission. Telehealth, which includes follow-up visits and remote patient monitoring, has proven to have a substantial impact on hospital readmissions. When the Veterans Health Administration implemented telehealth for past heart attack patients, hospital readmissions because of heart failure dropped by almost 51%. A study on the Geisinger Health Plan also backed this up by showing that telehealth actually reduced 30-day hospital readmissions by as much as 44 percent.

d. Expansion of Services

Another way by which telemedicine can be used for the people in the hospital is to expand the services that they are able to receive. For example, people who will benefit from mental health services following discharge can start receiving those services while they are still in the hospital, even if the hospital does not have those resources on staff.

Telehealth promises to deliver care that is respectful and responsive to individual patients' preferences, needs, and values, including patients' values in clinical decision making. Telehealth applications, particularly virtual visits, also have great potential to meet patients' needs and respond to their preferences and values without having to see a healthcare provider in person. Virtual home visits are especially desirable for patients who live far from medical care or have limited mobility. They also permit the addition to the visit of remotely located relatives or caregivers, which could increase compliance with health care instructions and support more effective shared decision making. Many organizations now also allow patients to view their medical notes or results online, upload information, and share their records with other healthcare providers.

What needs to be noticed is that there is a theme that fuses the uses of telemedicine inside the hospital and out. In both cases, the use of telehealth has resulted in more efficient use of resources, improved patient outcomes, and a wider range of available services. Healthcare systems need to realize that the window to act is open now. The current crisis of COVID 19 has further demonstrated the relevance of telehealth and created an opening to modernize the present healthcare delivery system. This modernization will be achieved by cementing telehealth in the care continuum at scale. With a $3 billion revenue, the telehealth market has the potential to grow to $250 billion sooner than we think. The seeds for success were sown in the last few months during the COVID-19 crisis. Healthcare systems that will come out ahead after the pandemic ends will be those that have acted decisively, invested in building capabilities at scale, worked hard to rewire the care delivery model, and deliver distinctive, high-quality care to consumers in the now[8].

Improving Access to healthcare

CHAPTER 8

Post-Covid-19 Patient-providers' Landscape

The COVID 19 pandemic has brought with itself a plethora of changes. These changes have, in turn, compelled humankind to explore, adjust and devise means to make the most of the situation they are in. Moreover, these changes have also changed the operations, policies, and strategies of organizations. Now, most organizations are implementing new policies and practices, including work from home and extended sick leaves to ensure their employees' wellbeing. Among all industries, it is healthcare that has had to adapt rapidly to the prevailing situation.

The healthcare industry is known to be the fifth biggest in the United States. It contributes more than $1.2 trillion to the Gross Domestic Product (GDP) of the country along with ensuring maintenance of health. However, according to the Siegal+Gale Global Simplicity Index, the healthcare industry ranks dead last out of twenty-five industries in the United States due to the simplicity of experience. Whether it is the interminable wait times, never-ending stacks of paper forms to complete, confounding language, or the overly complicated insurance plans, the healthcare industry has become one that U.S. consumers have slowly developed a love-hate relationship with[1].Over the past years, quite many researchers have concluded that the key to changing the customer experience of individuals using healthcare is to see them as consumers instead of seeing them as patients. As customer experience continues to advance as the last real competitive differentiator in most industries, it stands to reason that these experiences must improve in healthcare in order for the existing players to survive.

According to the Consumerization of Healthcare Study by Econsultancy and Adobe, the healthcare industry in which both insurance companies and medical providers play a vital role is ranked second-lowest in terms of being fast to respond and offering choices for communications. This study also concluded that 75 percent of consumers want the same experience in healthcare that they are likely to receive from other industries[2].Some of the basic services that most people believe are lacking in health care include price transparency as well as consistency, the ability to comprehend the service coverage and its benefits, bill payments, and assistance with getting simple tasks done. Consumers of healthcare services are seeking highly personalized, simple, and well-connected experiences that place them directly in charge of their health and empowers them. All consumers want is to be heard, understood, and accompanied by friends, family, and healthcare experts as they traverse their health journey – all while receiving the highest levels of quality care.

The consumers of today have relatively greater selectivity, are more technologically savoir-faire, and have elevated expectations from anything they choose to invest money and effort in. They demand to have a say in the making of critical decisions, secure help when needed, and be able to formulate, dictate and apprehend their own consumer experience ultimately. This includes being able to explore and research before making a decision, having information available at their fingertips across various devices and channels that are current, authentic, and intellectually contextualized.

Thus, there is no doubt that nowadays, consumers are more knowledgeable than they were ever before and, as such, have little time for experiences that they are not sure about. Often organizations misjudge the worth of a consumer's time and fail to understand that along with money, time should be at the top of their priority list. The consumer needs to feel valued, and there is no better way to make one feel valued than valuing the time they are investing in your services.

The patient-doctor landscape has changed, especially because of the prevailing pandemic. The needs of both patients and doctors have evolved. The factors that did not seem important earlier are now vital for establishing a stable relationship between a doctor and a patient. They also impact a person's overall health can help health plans tailor their programs to address the evolving needs of their members in this rapidly evolving time. It's essential for people to have access to information and resources around services such as mental healthcare, coaching, and telemedicine, which can influence their social determinants of health. The factors include socioeconomic conditions, healthcare literacy, public safety, social norms, and attitudes, among many others.

The affordability of healthcare is getting challenging day by day. This is why socioeconomic conditions are one of the factors that mostly impacts the Doctor-Patient landscape along with access to healthcare services, which may pose a challenge to those who are living in rural areas or do not own devices that can help them gain access to healthcare services from the comfort of their homes. Similarly, access to educational, economic, and job opportunities and the quality of education and job training also affects the Doctor-Patient landscape as a well-trained doctor will be able to satisfy each patient's needs. Patients who have a sense of their conditions or possess healthcare literacy tend to make it easier for the doctor as well.

An essential social determinant for a successful doctor-patient relationship is culture fit. This includes knowledge of different languages, local food markets, community-based resources, transportation options, public safety, and neighborhood safety. These few factors may impact the patient-doctor landscape post COVID-19 and should be considered by the healthcare industry.

It has been a little more than 20 years since the infamous term "experience economy" was initially coined in a 1998 article by B. Joseph Pine II and James H. Gilmore. Today's concept of customer experience is relatively more immersive. It is intended to evoke a sensory or emotional connection with the service being offered. However, no two people have precisely the same experience because acquiring experience is an inherently personal and interactive process. This is why companies do not compete today only on products, pricing, and service delivery; they, in fact, fundamentally compete on the experience they provide, and those who create an emotional connection with consumers are the ones who win[3].

When it comes to the healthcare industry, it is necessary to divert attention to the term that is being used for the consumer and its impact as well. The word "patient" has historically evoked the picture of a person who is in some form of pain or is suffering silence. Etymologically this word has moved from its Latin roots to old French and Middle English in the late 1800s. However, it has carried the same meaning of accepting or tolerating delays, problems or suffering without becoming annoyed or anxious. Synonyms that are associated with the word patient are forbearing, uncomplaining, tolerant, and resigned.

This age-old understanding of the term "patient" seems inconsistent with today's efficient, technologically savvy, experience-elevated consumers. It also raises the question that to what extent have organizations that are responsible for delivering healthcare have inadvertently eroded or misconstrued the consumers' experience by making healthcare providers see an individual as a condition instead of a person – a patient, not a consumer? The debate over the label consumer vs patient has mostly resided within the academia for more than 20 years, with concerns tied to the patient relationship becoming an article of trade – considering individuals as either objects or goods, thereby reducing the compassion and care that needs to be extended to those who are unwell or are experiencing a distressing health event. It is about time we change the term and even our thinking to a consumer-centered mindset and divert actions in the same direction. The figure below entails some of the much-needed practices that will make sure that the wellbeing of the patient is at the center of each treatment (see figure 8.1). Patient centeredness can be defined as the treatment of a person with respect and dignity and making sure that the patient is involved in all decisions related to their health. Such care approach is also called person centered care and is associated with the healthcare rights of a person (Figure 8.1).

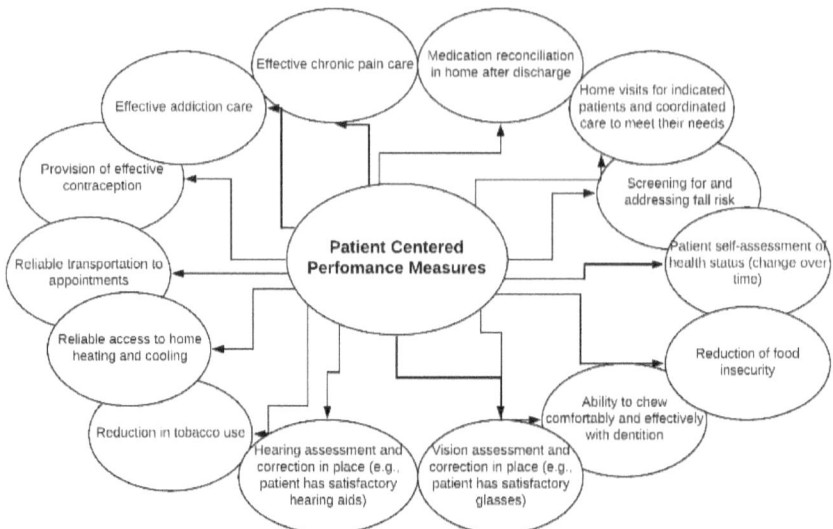

Figure 8.1: Patient Centered Performance Measures

Figure 8.1 represents the patient-centered performance measures that can improve the prospects of person-centered care. These include screening and addressing the fall risks, patient self-assessment of health status, reduction of food insecurity, ability to chew effectively with dentition, vision assessment and correction in place, hearing assessment and correction in place, reduction tobacco use, improvement in housing standards, reliable transportation to appointments, provision of effective contraception, effective addiction care, effective chronic pain care, medication reconciliation in the home after discharge, and home visits for indicated patients and coordinated care strategies. Following measures are depicted in figure 8.1 as measures for patient centered performance;

1. Home visits for indicated patients and coordinated care to meet their needs which can be achieved by registering indicated patients as critical ones. Home visits can help such patients to meet their routine medical needs.

2. Screening for and addressing fall risk; referring to the older age patients, obese, and individuals with mobility problems, balance disorders, chronic illnesses, and impaired vision.
3. Patient self-assessment of health status (change over time); involving changing the self-assessment strategies that can be applied easily.
4. Reduction of food insecurity; developing guidelines and policies that address threats of food shortage and food preservation practices.
5. Ability to chew comfortably and effectively with dentition; for the patients in dental care, must be provided adequate treatment and nutrition plan according to their oral health condition.
6. Vision assessment and correction in place (e.g., the patient has satisfactory glasses); visually impaired must be catered through referral to appropriate places.
7. Hearing assessment and correction in place (e.g., the patient has satisfactory hearing aid); hearing impairment is needed to be responded through the provision of effective hearing devices that are comfortable and easy to use.
8. Reduction in tobacco use; informing the patient regarding the haphazard effects of tobacco on the body, addressing social support referrals.
9. Reliable access to home heating and cooling; referring the patients to the social services agencies for the improvement of their living standards
10. Reliable transportation to appointments; providing accessible and cost-effective transport to the follow-up patients.
11. Provision of effective contraception; informing the likely effects of contraception, side effects and helping the service users in reaching a reliable decision.
12. Effective addiction care; providing rehabilitation services, informing the damaging effects of substance abuse on the body and overall life.
13. Effective chronic pain care; involves taking care of patients' medical, physiological, social and psychological needs and

management of pain and other symptoms that compromise the quality of life.
14. Medication reconciliation in home after discharge; Efficient medication reconciliation services provision and likely changes in the health modalities which patient can manage through self-care.

Healthcare prospects are improving at a rapid pace with the inclusion of innovation and technology. These improvements have led to the development and implementation of care models that support patient-centered care. Further improvement in patient-centered care can be ensured by using these effective patient-centered care reforms as identified in figure 8.1.

Today's consumer is directly in control and mandates to have their high expectations met or exceeded. Consumers outside of the healthcare industry largely have a better experience than the "patients" in the healthcare system today. This is mainly due to the alteration and focus, which was articulated by Gilmore and Pine toward the experience economy. Yet, the healthcare industry has not adopted this shift and still produces woefully lacking experiences and remains way behind other industries in terms of customer experience.

Most industries nowadays are focusing on enhancing customer experience, along with quality and pricing. They believe that giving attention to the consumer's feelings and opinions regarding a product or service is the key to success. As we observe the strides that other industries have made, the shift from a straight exchange of goods and services to a more profound and multifaceted relational experience with the consumers at the center is the key to success. Today, consumer expectations are just as high in other industries as the healthcare industry. However, those industries are much further, along with healthcare. For instance, in another highly regulated industry such as finance and retail banking – there has been an evolution of personalized banking, moving from transactional ATMs and teller services to digitized self-service and online banking experiences[4].There are various factors that affect the customer experience in the healthcare industry today. The foundational issue is the lack of trust and transparency between all the stakeholders. Patients, or let us say consumers, are increasingly unable to trust doctors or health insurers. They want to know that their treatment is being done by the best clinical hands possible and that their insurers will cover the costs for most if not all of their treatments. However, insurers are unable to trust doctors and providers to administer all the necessary treatments to the consumers and consequently place a colossal administrative burden on the providers to ensure that the proper quality controls are being implemented. Lastly, even doctors are unable to trust health insurers to reimburse them appropriately and pay them their dues on time.

Another issue that is quite common is the shortage of healthcare providers or clinicians, which includes both doctors and nurses. It has been observed that now a lot of doctors are dropping out of the profession at quite alarming rates due to burnout as they spend less time doing what they actually love the most, that is, spending time with consumers and helping them regain their health. Instead, they end up spending more time being bogged down in loads of administrative paperwork and convoluted in complicated reimbursement processes.

One of the reasons of shortage of clinicians in the absence of interoperability between each of the stakeholders, where systems, processes, and data do not talk to each other to create an integrated, fluid, and reliable workflow. This problem can be traced back to decades-old use of legacy systems and the fragmentation of use of electronic health records (EHRs), preventing portability as well as visibility between entities. The truth is that both consumers and doctors hardly ever have all of the needed data in one place.

On the other hand, outdated regulatory and compliance policies that differ in each state also tend to impose unnecessary administrative burdens on both providers and insurers. In addition to all of this, the growing number of seniors diagnosed with chronic conditions who are living longer are more socially isolated and have a more considerable wealth disparity among them. The industry is unable to meet the demands of this large portion of the population.

The rise in prices of lifesaving drugs is also one of the factors that have impacted anyone and everyone who is interacting with the healthcare industry. The COVID-19 pandemic has affected world economics, including the pharmaceutical sectors worldwide. While currently there has been no definitive treatment developed for this novel infectious disease, the pharmaceutical industry is assisting governments to address the unmet needs of COVID-19, with the help of research and development actions on potential treatment strategies to balance the medicines supply chain in the time of crisis. Along with this, pharmaceutical sectors are struggling to maintain natural market flow, as the recent pandemic affects access to essential medicines at an affordable price, which is the primary goal of every pharmaceutical system.

Since the development of a vaccine for COVID-19 is assumed to be more than a year away, the existing drugs, many of which are actually off-patent, have now become the first line of defense against the virus, and clinical trials are already taking place. Once the effectiveness of any of the available drugs is determined, the number one priority is going to be to make sure that they are accessible and affordable for all masses. An analysis, which was recently published by Andrew Hill and colleagues, estimated that the medications that are being studied are primarily drugs that are used to treat diseases like hepatitis C and HIV. The main reason behind analyzing and testing the existing drugs is to spend a minimum on the production costs as repurposed medications would be relatively inexpensive. For instance, production costs are estimated to be $0.28 per day for Lopinavir/ritonavir (a medicine used for treating HIV) and $0.28 per day for hydroxychloroquine (a medicine used for treating malaria and rheumatoid arthritis). Despite low manufacturing costs, these and similar drugs tend to retail for up to $510 per course of treatment in countries like India and Pakistan, where drug costs are strictly controlled -- and up to $18,610 per course in the U.S., where price controls are lacking[5].Big drug companies in the U.S. have raised prices on about 245 medicines. This includes the medications that are commonly used in intensive care units, lifesaving cancer drugs, blood pressure medications, and some more essential medicines that are being used to treat COVID-19 or are being tested for use to combat the illness. According to a report from Patients for Affordable Drugs, an advocacy group that has been campaigning for lower drug prices, this price increase began to occur since the first coronavirus case surfaced in the United States in January[6]. This report also found that out of the 245 drugs with price increases, 61 are being used to treat COVID-19 symptoms. In contrast, 30 of them are being used in coronavirus-related clinical trials, and 20 are commonly administered in most hospital ICUs. In addition, 22 mental health drugs had also had price increases since the start of the outbreak in the U.S., along with some over-the-counter medicines such as Tylenol and others that can be used to treat coronavirus symptoms at home. Some other drugs whose prices increased are:

1. Morphine, fentanyl, and ketamine are being used to treat the COVID patients who are sedated and on ventilators. These drugs have been listed by the Food and Drug Administration (FDA) as being in short supply. As a result, certain manufacturers have increased the price of drugs by about 10 percent.
2. Chlorpromazine, which is an antipsychotic drug, is suggested as an alternative in the ICU when some of the sedation medicines are in short supply. This drug is now being used in clinical trials for COVID-19. One manufacturer's 9.9 percent price increase can add $125 a day to the bill for an ICU patient.
3. Vasoscript is the brand-name version of vasopressin and is recommended for COVID-19 patients with unstable blood pressure. This drug's price has increased by 10 percent or $197 per vial.
4. Xarelto is one of the many blood thinners widely used by older Americans and has increased in price by nearly 5 percent. A 30-tablet bottle now costs $470.
5. Olumiant, a commonly used drug to treat rheumatoid arthritis, has recently been suggested to yield good results with COVID-19-related respiratory diseases. The cost of a 30-tablet bottle of

this drug has increased by almost 6 percent, thus bringing the price to about $2,265 a bottle.
6. Ativan, which is a drug used to treat depression and anxiety, has increased in price to nearly 8 percent and a 100-tablet bottle now costs $5,677.
7. Provenge, a widely used prostate cancer drug, observed a price increase of about 6 percent. One intravenous bottle of this chemotherapy drug now costs $62,602.

It is very important for the healthcare industry to prioritize means of getting really good at solving their consumer's problems and not just create another digital solution or renovate and decorate the hospital's waiting room with a fresh coat of paint and some abstract paintings. Real impact that is both efficient and engaging should be immersed in the consumer data and tackle all the problems through discovery and also via rapid experimentation. The healthcare industry must delve beyond the mere surface and put consumers squarely in charge of their own health.

What healthcare is actually in dire need of is focus on the customer experience that facilitates massive simplicity and starts with genuine customer empathy. The stakeholders of the healthcare industry need to see, feel, and think through the consumer problems meticulously and not just throw another digital solution into the mix. There is a multitude of siloed point solutions, including digital health apps, wearables, and devices that are constantly striving for the consumer's attention and could possibly just be adding more "noise" to an already excessively "noisy" industry[7].

The need should be to get better at interrogating the experience in healthcare and understanding consumer behavior so that the key jobs are done with efficiency and proper planning so that each practice moves beyond the norm of providing incremental solutions. Moreover, we need to divert attention to how each decision is made and explore the "why" behind them. This can be done by examining the data and information that are foremost on both consumers' and leaders' minds and is responsible for informing their decisions. Another aspect that is responsible for informing the decisions is the social determinants of Doctor-Patient Landscape post-COVID 19. It has been observed that there are a number of factors that will be contributing to the quality of healthcare after the pandemic is over, and life slowly returns back to its normal pace.

Changing face of patient-doctor relationship.

The Overreaching of Insurance Copanies

CHAPTER 9

Healthcare Insurance Post-COVID-19

The worldwide pandemic has transformed the way people view their health and that of their families. Given the gravity of the situation, people are concerned about not just managing their health but also being able to afford it, given the rising costs of healthcare. In the pyramid of hierarchy of needs, health has claimed a primary position as the control that we previously had over our health has been taken away by the unprecedented impacts of COVID 19.

The previous concept of insurance being the umbrella for a rainy day is no more. Despite eating well, exercising often, and making sure that you are taking all your supplements on time, there is no assurance that the virus will not impact us. To tackle the looming fear of uncertainty, behavior, and mindset regarding health insurance has undergone tectonic shifts.

The first shift is in the perception of health insurance. Now people perceive health insurance as a priority instead of the previous perception of it being a necessity. The second shift is from being a safety net to being a savior. The probability of falling ill from being a distant possibility to a distinct possibility is the third shift that has been witnessed.

The Centers for Medicare and Medicaid, commonly known as C.M.S., have devised plans that cover services that are considered as out-of-network facilities and charge enrollees that are affected by the emergency with no more than in-network rates. Similarly, drug plans also require enrollees to use preferred retail or opt for mail-order pharmacy networks. However, this may seem difficult given the limitations that are imposed due to the pandemic. Therefore, during the crisis, C.M.S. has permitted plans to relax these restrictions. This could be an essential transformation for many participants of Part D plans[1].

C.M.S. has also created two Healthcare Common Procedure Coding System (HCPCS) codes that are designed to report testing for coronavirus. Labs that test patients for the new coronavirus using the Centers for Disease Control and Prevention (C.D.C.) 2019 Novel Coronavirus Real-Time RT-PCR Diagnostic Test Panel may bill for that test using the new HCPCS code (U0001). This code is used specifically for C.D.C. testing laboratories in order to test patients for the SARS-CoV-2. The second HCPCS billing code (U0002) has allowed laboratories to bill for non-CDC laboratory tests for the SARS-CoV-2/2019-nCoV - COVID-19[2].

Food and Drug Administration (F.D.A.) issued a new, streamlined policy for specific laboratories to develop their own validated COVID-19 tests on February 29, 2020. The second HCPCS code may be used for tests developed by these additional laboratories when submitting claims to Medicare or health insurers. Diagnosis coding for coronavirus is also available.

Apart from relaxation in policies and additional testing services, C.M.S. has also expanded its telehealth coverage, which was previously rather tightly restricted. Telehealth services are being covered under Part B for traditional Medicare enrollees during the virus crisis of COVID 19. However, these services are just not limited to COVID-19 care. This has also helped in redefining telehealth and expanding its use. Furthermore, previously patients were required to connect from a health facility, such as an outpatient center, that must have approved video conferencing technology; now, patients are able to connect from home with the help of a video call on a smartphone or any other digital device.

The requirement that telehealth be provided by a doctor the patient had seen within the last three years has also been waived.

Even though the COVID has already brought with itself a plethora of changes in the policies and practices in the healthcare industry, further changes are being proposed as well. These changes are expected to help in expanding coverage or easing the cost burdens, either during the crisis or even permanently. These changes include waiving the Part A deductible for people who are hospitalized for COVID-19 and lack supplemental insurance, along with mandating Part D plans to allow enrollees to order extra supplies of prescriptions.

Advocates are also urging the authorities to cap the cost of prescription drugs under Part D as it does not cap the total amounts that enrollees must pay out of pocket each year, and high prices of specialty drugs have burdened enrollees. Another critical change that is being proposed could help a vast group of Americans who have disabilities and are younger than Medicare's eligibility age of sixty-five. Currently, people who are awarded Social Security Disability Insurance can enroll in Medicare but face a 24-month waiting period before their benefits kick in. This requirement is proposed to be waived off as, according to C.M.S. data, 8.2 million Medicare enrollees were younger than age 65 in 2018[3].

In order to better manage the health needs and requirements, Managed Healthcare Plans were introduced in the latter part of the 20th century. They are types of health insurance plans that can provide a health insurance policy to individual members of a group or an employer.

This group or employer is the plan sponsor of the managed care plan and helps beneficiaries who are members of the plan by getting them more favorable rates or medical insurance services at a discounted rate from their plan's health provider network. Managed health care plans also allow plan sponsors to negotiate reduced rates for their policyholders with the affiliated hospitals, medical service providers, and physicians by including them in the network.

Managed health care plans have proven to be a cost-effective substitute to traditional fee-for-service or health insurance plans as they share the medical cost financial risks between member individuals, their insurance plans, and members of the managed care network[4].

The H.M.O. Act was passed in 1973, and managed care plans became available to most Americans by the late '80s. They are among the most widespread and extensively used health insurance coverage plans in America. Managed health care plans tend to differ from traditional plans due to the fact that its affiliates usually must select a "primary care physician" from the network of doctors that is provided by the plan sponsor and the hospital. Being part of this network will provide plan members with access to services from network health service providers at set rates, thus reducing the costs of the plan.

Apart from providing reduced rates and guaranteed access to health care services, the managed health care plan offers other benefits for both plan members and sponsors. These benefits may include:

1. Members of the health network profit from having a secure stream of clients.
2. Plan Members have an easier time since working with providers in the networks helps in avoiding the paperwork. The filing is done by the network members and medical service providers with the help of billing systems. The H.M.O. plan makes this the easiest.

In the past years, managed health care plans have become a popular health insurance choice among the American population as healthcare costs have amplified. The kind of managed plan you have will edict your method of obtaining your medical services. The main types of network health plans are (see figure 9.1):

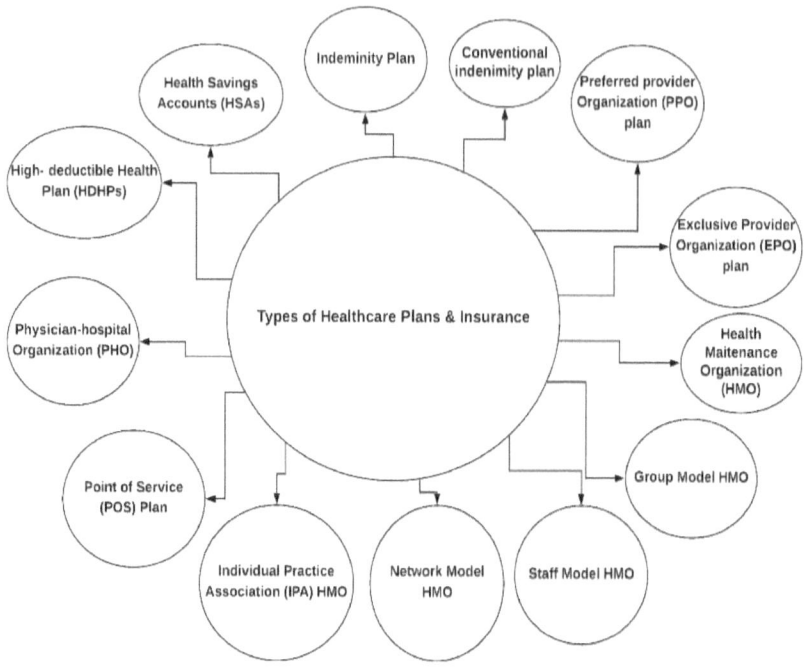

Figure 9.1: Types of Healthcare Plans & Insurance

Figure 9.1 represents the various types of healthcare plans and insurance. The prominent plans and insurance include Executive Provider Organization Plan (EPO), Health Maintenance Organization, Group Model HMO, Staff Model HMO, Network Model HMO, Individual Practice Association (IPA) HMO, Point of Service (POS) plan, Physical Hospital Organization, High-Deductible Health Plan, health saving accounts, indemnity plan, conventional indemnity plan, and Preferred Provider Organization (PPO).

Elaboration on types of health care plans and insurance depicted in Figure 9.1 is presented;

1. Indemnity plan; refer to the plan that allows the individual to direct their own healthcare and visit any hospital or doctor they want. A set portion of total charges is then paid by the insurance company.

2. Conventional indemnity plan; this traditional plan enables the service user choice of any healthcare service provider without impacting the reimbursement. Such plans reimburse the service providers or service users based on the expenses incurred as a part of the treatment process of a patient.
3. Preferred provider organization (PPO) plan; PPO plan contracts with the medical providers such as physicians and hospitals in order to create a network of participating providers. The user has to pay less if they use providers who belong to the plan's network.
4. Exclusive provider organization (EPO) plan; EPO plan requires the service users to use the hospitals and doctors within its own network, similar to HMO.
5. Health Maintenance Organization (HMO) plan; HMO plan limits coverage to care from physicians who generally work for or are in contract with HMO. Except in an emergency, it usually does not cover out-of-network care.
6. Group Model HMO; It is an HMO that provides care for HMO members by contracting with a single multi-specialty medical group.
7. Staff Model HMO; An HMO that provides medical care to the subscribers in a centralized medical operation on an exclusive basis.
8. Network Model HMO; An HMO that provides health services by contracting with more than one independent physician group.
9. Individual Practice Association (IPA) HMO; HMO patients enrolled in the HMO are seen by individual practitioners, but they also treat their own patients who are not enrolled in HMO. Compensation to the physician is based on either discounted fee schedule or a per-patient fee.
10. Point of Service (POS) Plan; POS plan helps and directs the members to select a primary care physician, like an HMO, from a list of participating providers. Such plans provide greater flexibility of freedom to see out-of-network providers.

11. Physician-hospital Organization (PHO); PHO serves as the legal entity formed by a group of physicians or hospital to achieve market objectives or further mutual interests.
12. High deductible Health Plan (HDHPs); HDHP is a higher deductible as compared to other conventional insurance plans. It has been defined as any plan with a deductible of at least $1,350 for an individual or $2,700 for a family.
13. Health Saving accounts (HSAs); HAS is a tax-advantaged account that helps people to save for their medical expenses, which are generally not reimbursed by HDHPs.

Healthcare plans and insurance ensure that the service users are accessing the services easily. Moreover, these plans and insurance policies also reduce the high cost associated with treatment and medications for the patients. Healthcare plans intend to improve the overall organizational framework of the healthcare institute and facilitate its alignment with regulatory reforms.

1. Health Maintenance Organization (H.M.O.)

A Health Maintenance Organization, or H.M.O., provides employers or groups with a method to take care of all employees' or members' healthcare needs with reduced costs by dealing with certain doctors, hospitals, and even clinics. The employee should use these specific providers for the reduced fees to be provided to their medical insurance plan. Despite being the least flexible, the H.M.O. plan offers the easiest claim experience as the network takes care in handling the claims for the members.

2. Preferred Provider Organization (P.P.O.)

Preferred Provider Organization, or P.P.O., offers reduced costs to members billed to their health insurance plan. Just like an H.M.O., the employees or members of this plan can select the physician they want to consult instead of being solely restricted to the H.M.O. providers. In addition, a member can also choose between a member or a nonmember provider.

3. Point of Service Plan (P.O.S.)

Point of Service plan or P.O.S., members can choose their physician that has previously agreed to provide services at a reduced fee. In a P.O.S., the member uses the chosen physician as a gateway before moving on to a specialist. Whenever the employee or member has a medical issue, the P.O.S. physician must be contacted first to attain the most benefit from the health insurance plan.

4. Exclusive Provider Organization (EPO)

In an Exclusive Provider Network or EPO, the employee or member of the plan is allowed to choose from the providers within the network and do not have to work with a primary care physician before moving on to the specialist. However, any service taken outside of the network may not be covered at all.

Managed-care plans are constantly pressured by a variety of marketplace forces which have been intensifying over the past years. These forces have compelled these plans to make significant shifts in their overall business strategy. Plans are being continually modified to offer less deterring managed care products and product features that respond to the consumers' and purchasers' demands for a wide range of choices and flexibility. Since consumers and purchasers prefer broad and stable networks that require plans to incorporate rather than eliminating providers, and plans are seeking less contentious contractual relationships with both physicians and hospitals. These changes, if not minimized, can erode their ability to control costs, plans are shifting from an emphasis only on increasing market share to a renewed emphasis on protecting profitability. Consequently, purchasers and consumers face escalating health care costs under these changing conditions.

On multiple fronts —consumer, purchaser, provider, and regulatory—managed care plans are facing mounting pressures to change. Consumers are becoming more active in health care participants. They are demanding more choice, greater flexibility, and fewer restrictions on access and service delivery. Employers (purchasers) are demanding less restrictive managed care to appease employees and at least so far have been willing to absorb most of the higher ensuing costs. Consumers' and purchasers' preferences for broad and stable networks give providers the upper hand in contract negotiations with plans. Also tipping the scales in favor of providers is consolidation among both physicians and hospitals and the reappearance of capacity constraints for many hospitals. With their new clout, these providers are pressuring plans to pay more and reduce the scope of risk in risk-contracting arrangements; others are pressuring plans to replace risk payment with fee-for-service (FFS) payments (for physicians) or per diem and case-rate payments (for hospitals). Federal and state regulations sought by consumers and providers in response to perceived problems with health maintenance organizations (H.M.O.s) are prompting additional changes. Also, declining H.M.O. enrollment is pressuring plans further.

The coronavirus continues to exert an inconsistent impact on the nation's minority communities, which are suffering from extreme levels of poverty and the health issues caused by it. As the most critical health insurer for people with low incomes, Medicaid is at the forefront of COVID-19 testing and treatment. Seventy percent of all Medicaid beneficiaries are enrolled in comprehensive care plans offered by managed care organizations (MCOs). These plans' performance is central to the accessibility, timeliness, and quality of COVID-19 care.

In May, C.M.S. issued an informational bulletin that described the actions that states could take to further strengthen managed care. The bulletin discusses state Medicaid options for advancing payment and care delivery. It identifies certain options particularly relevant during the pandemic: temporarily increasing monthly capitation payments in order to reflect unforeseen costs; increasing provider fees to better reflect the added pandemic response costs; and "retainer" payments to the network providers who deliver personal care and habilitation services, such as personal attendants or speech therapy, to keep these providers afloat as the pandemic causes a precipitous decline in the use of care.

Now healthcare consumerism and patient experience are modifying the healthcare industry one step at a time. As compared to the past, when a healthcare provider's reputation was primarily dependent on word-of-mouth recommendations from friends, family, or even their primary care provider, the present situation of healthcare reputation management is quite different. However, with the growth in online reviews on social media platforms and rating and review on websites, online reputation management today is no longer something hospitals, systems, or group practices can afford to overlook[5].

The reputation of any healthcare organization, either large or small, can be advanced or tarnished with a single comment, review, or news article that is posted online. Therefore, proactive management of a healthcare organization's online reputation is vital to its success in general. The progressively intense competition within the healthcare industry has also elevated the significance of online reputation for physicians and hospitals in catching the attention of new patients and building loyalty with existing patients. After spending years on building a strong reputation by traditional means, hospitals and healthcare organizations need to adapt their strategies to make sure that the same is reflected online.

Healthcare organizations have adopted an engagement strategy in addition to their social media policy, focusing on timely personalized responses to online comments, reviews, and inquiries. This helps them establish and maintain a sense of trust with their existing and potential patients. Patients need to see and feel that hospitals are willing to go above and beyond what is expected of them in order to provide the best standard of care. When patients feel their concerns or complaints are being heard and appropriate efforts are being made to resolve their issues, a hospital's reputation and credibility are reflected in online reviews. Patient feedback management can help accomplish timely service recovery by assisting organizations to uncover and act on negative online reviews quickly. It even creates an opportunity to engage with patients who left a positive review and help turn these consumers into brand advocates.

COVID has not only transformed the way we look at life and health; it has also changed the way we manage it. These changes are characterized by modifications in policies and practices in almost every sector. However, the most significant change has been observed in the healthcare sector. The health insurances and managed care models have also been altered, and new policies have been introduced in accordance with the new normal. These policies and practices have helped people of all ages maintain their health and seek treatment despite being isolated or quarantined. They have also helped in transforming what healthcare looks like by the increased use of telehealth which has bridged the gap between a doctor and a patient and has made it easier for all to consult a physician or a specialist without risking their lives. Once the pandemic ends, the changed policies and practices will pave the way for better policies that will improve healthcare by making it more affordable and less complicated for people.

Among several issues, healthcare was a dominant issue in the race between the incumbent President Donald J. Trump and Democratic Runner Vice President Joe Biden. To efficiently enact healthcare reform, Biden is preparing ways that can reduce costs, increase competition, and make the system less complex to navigate. Surprise billing, industry consolidation, and prescription drug pricing, in addition to COVID-19 response and Affordable Care Act (ACA) perseveration, are the areas that will be focused on by Biden in the next four years of his presidency[6]. However, challenges might be created by potentially split Congress for the Biden administration to execute the agenda and strategies for healthcare priorities and more. This may also subject healthcare management to complexities.

Changing role of Health Insurance companies

The role of health insurance companies has evolved significantly, driven by shifts in healthcare systems, technological advancements, regulatory frameworks, and societal expectations. These changes reflect broader transformations in the healthcare landscape, where the focus is increasingly on preventive care, patient-centered models, and cost management. Below are key factors that highlight the dynamic and expanding role of health insurance companies:

1. From Payers to Health Managers

Historically, health insurance companies primarily acted as payers, reimbursing medical expenses for their policyholders. Today, their role has expanded to that of health managers. This shift places greater emphasis on preventive care and overall wellness. Insurers now actively promote healthier lifestyles by offering wellness programs, fitness incentives, and chronic disease management tools, aiming to reduce long-term healthcare costs. By promoting healthy behaviors and early interventions, insurance companies can better manage risk, reduce hospital admissions, and improve population health outcomes.

2. Adoption of Value-Based Care Models

A major transformation in the healthcare insurance landscape is the shift from fee-for-service to value-based care models. Under traditional fee-for-service arrangements, healthcare providers were compensated based on the volume of services they delivered. In contrast, value-based care emphasizes outcomes, rewarding healthcare providers for improving patient health rather than for the number of procedures performed. This model fosters better care coordination, encourages higher-quality care, and seeks to control escalating healthcare costs by focusing on measurable improvements in patient outcomes.

3. Integration of Technology and Data Analytics

The integration of advanced technology has significantly reshaped the role of health insurers. Digital transformation, powered by big data analytics, artificial intelligence (AI), and machine learning, has enabled insurers to enhance risk assessment, detect fraud, and personalize healthcare plans. Digital health tools such as telemedicine, wearable devices, and mobile health applications allow insurers to monitor patient health in real time. These innovations lead to better patient engagement, timely interventions, and reduced reliance on expensive medical treatments, improving the overall efficiency of healthcare delivery.

4. Adapting to Regulatory and Policy Changes

Health insurance companies must continuously adapt to evolving regulatory and policy environments. In the U.S., significant legislation like the Affordable Care Act (ACA) introduced numerous regulations, such as prohibiting the denial of coverage for pre-existing conditions and mandating essential health benefits. These regulatory shifts have forced insurers to enhance access to care, lower costs, and improve pricing transparency. By ensuring compliance with government regulations, health insurers play a crucial role in shaping a more equitable and accessible healthcare system.

5. Addressing Healthcare Equity

Health equity is becoming a central focus for health insurers, particularly as disparities in healthcare access and outcomes become more visible. Insurers are actively engaging in efforts to reduce these disparities by designing insurance plans tailored to underserved and marginalized communities. Initiatives aimed at addressing social determinants of health, such as housing and food insecurity, are increasingly integrated into insurance offerings. Through partnerships with community health organizations and public health campaigns, insurers aim to close the healthcare gap and provide more equitable access to essential health services.

6. Managing Rising Healthcare Costs

The rising cost of healthcare services has prompted insurers to adopt more proactive cost management strategies. Insurers now negotiate payment rates with healthcare providers, promote the use of cost-effective treatment options, and implement cost-sharing mechanisms like higher deductibles and co-pays to share financial responsibility with consumers. In addition, insurers are encouraging the use of generic drugs and advocating for outpatient and home-based care when appropriate, which are often more cost-effective alternatives to traditional hospital-based care.

7. Expanding Role in Prescription Drug Management

Prescription drug costs are a significant driver of healthcare expenditures, and health insurers have taken on a critical role in managing these expenses. Pharmacy benefit managers (PBMs) work with insurers to negotiate drug prices with pharmaceutical companies, seeking to reduce costs for both insurers and patients. Additionally, insurers promote the use of generic drugs and biosimilars as alternatives to more expensive brand-name medications. This strategy helps lower the financial burden on consumers and improves the sustainability of the healthcare system.

8. Consumer-Centric Insurance Models

The rise of consumer-driven healthcare has pushed insurers to create more flexible and personalized insurance plans. High-deductible health plans (HDHPs), often paired with Health Savings Accounts (HSAs), empower consumers to take greater control of their healthcare spending. Insurers are also investing in tools that provide consumers with transparent information about healthcare costs and provider quality, enabling informed decision-making. As consumers demand more autonomy and clarity, health insurers are shifting towards models that cater to individual needs and preferences.

9. Telehealth and Remote Care Services

The COVID-19 pandemic accelerated the adoption of telehealth, which has now become a standard part of many insurance plans. Insurers are expanding coverage for virtual care services, allowing patients to consult healthcare providers remotely. This not only enhances access to care but also reduces the need for in-person visits, lowering healthcare costs. By integrating remote care options into standard coverage, insurers are contributing to more efficient and convenient healthcare delivery, especially for routine consultations and follow-ups.

10. Global Health Coverage and Cross-Border Care

As globalization increases, the demand for health coverage across borders has grown. Many insurers now offer plans that cater to international travelers, expatriates, and multinational businesses. These plans often include telemedicine services and coverage for care in multiple countries. By accommodating the healthcare needs of global populations, insurers are addressing the growing complexity of healthcare in an increasingly interconnected world.

Conclusion

The evolving role of health insurance companies mirrors the broader shifts taking place in healthcare, where technology, value-based care, preventive health, and patient-centered approaches are becoming the norm. No longer limited to being mere payers of claims, insurers are now partners in managing patient health, promoting wellness, and addressing systemic healthcare challenges such as rising costs and disparities in access to care. As healthcare continues to transform, health insurers will play an even more integral role in shaping the future of global healthcare delivery.

CHAPTER 10

Managing Patients Experience and Quality Improvement

The human body is encompassed by billions of cells that are programmed to die as they age. This means that as one ages, they become weaker and are more prone to developing health issues. Apart from causing a decline in physical and mental functioning, this natural process also brings about multimorbidity, which is now one of the most prevalent issues in the aging population.

Multimorbidity is the co-occurrence of two or more chronic conditions. It has been known to affect up to 95 percent of the primary care population aged 65 years and older. Even though the prevalence of multimorbidity tends to increase with age, it is not exclusively a condition that only affects the elderly. In fact, multiple studies have reported high rates of multimorbidity amongst working-age populations as well.

The amount of people affected by multiple chronic diseases or multimorbidity is increasing dramatically worldwide. Thus caring for them has placed considerable strain on many health systems around the world. Since individuals with multimorbidity have complex care needs and are some of the costliest and challenging patients to manage, many countries struggle to manage them. However, it has been repeatedly recognized that more sustainable models of care for individuals with multimorbidity need to be introduced as a matter of urgency. Policymakers and healthcare providers are in need of good quality evidence on which to build the case for change.

The risk factors for multimorbidity have not been well studied in the past. According to studies, aging is the most consistent and potent risk factor among many others (see figure 10.1).

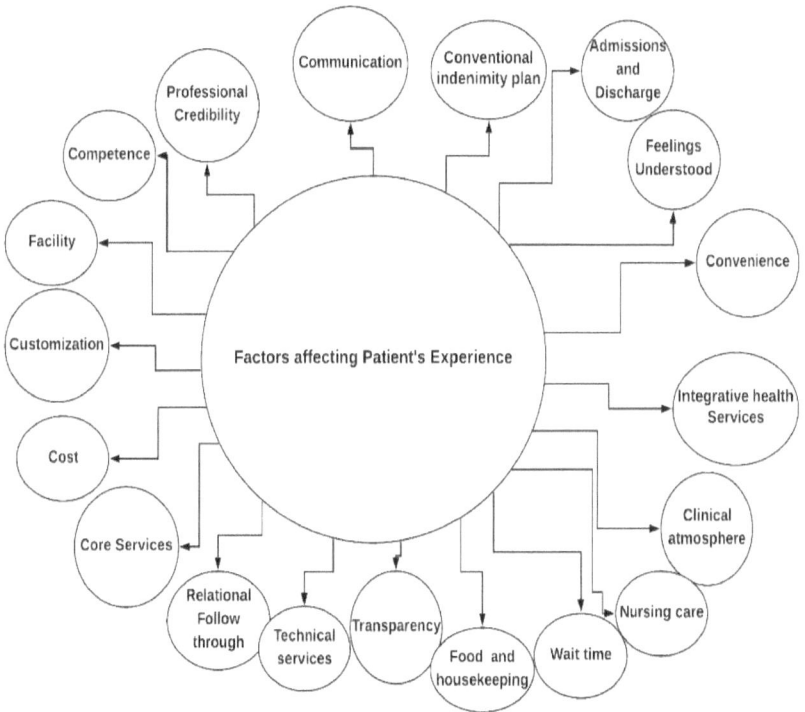

Figure 10.1: Factors Affecting Patient's Experience

Figure 10.1 highlights the factors affecting patient's experiences within healthcare. These include administration and discharge, feelings understood, convenience, integrative health services, clinical atmosphere, nursing care, wait time, food and housekeeping, transparency, technical services, relational follow through, cost services, cost, customization, facility, competence, professional credibility, communication, and conventional indemnity plan.

Explanation of these factors affecting patient experience is presented as follows;

1. Communication; Patient communicated effectively for their needs has positive experience and satisfaction as compared to poorly communicate patients.
2. Conventional Indemnity plan; Patients provided with appropriate reimbursements on a timely basis have better treatment plans scheduled which improve their experiences.
3. Admissions and discharge; Patients are needed to be informed of their discharge information and likely implications after discharge for improvement of their care experience.
4. Feelings understood; Psychological wellbeing of patients play an important role in affecting their overall health. Practitioners and nurses managing their psychological needs and understanding their feelings can improve patients' experience.
5. Convenience; Convenience of patients is more important than the quality of care. Patient experience is positive when their setting is convenient for mobility, communication, and other daily activities. Transport and accessibility convenience of healthcare also plays an important role.
6. Integrated health services; Integrated services are accustomed to providing quality-based, affordable, and reliable services that cover the majority of healthcare spectrums for patients.
7. Clinical atmosphere; Clinical atmosphere influences patient experiences such as communication protocols, convenience, accessibility to physicians, and attitudes and behavior of nurses and practitioners.
8. Nursing care; Holistic nursing care improves patient experiences and their satisfaction. Nursing care is an integral part of a healthcare system that promotes patient health and wellbeing at large.

9. Wait time; Service users of healthcare are the most critical entities, and extended wait time affects their satisfaction and experiences negatively.
10. Food and housekeeping; Hygienic conditions, healthy and clean food, and clean setting not only improves patient experience but also improves their mental and physical health and wellbeing.
11. Transparency; Informed decision-making practices in healthcare and shared decision making helps in sustaining transparency between patients, nurses and doctors.
12. Technical services; Sophisticated technology and maintenance of technical services such as healthcare equipment, instruments and infection control helps in improving patient experiences.
13. Relational follow-through; Patients must be informed regarding the importance of follow up for maintaining relationships and keeping pace with treatment and recovery. Relational follow through establishes a positive nurse-patient or physician patient-relationship, which improves the patient experience.
14. Core services; These involve diagnostic services and treatment protocols undertaken by the doctors. Evidence-based care supports treatment prospects and improves the patient recovery process.
15. Cost; Cost-effectiveness and accessibility to healthcare services affect patient experience and satisfaction. Affordable services help in sustaining patients' health and wellbeing.
16. Customization; Customization in healthcare facilitates professionals to understand their patients and in providing care that is more effective, personal and informative which improves their experience.
17. Facility; Location of the facility and the overall setting must be convenient for the patient to keep patients satisfied.
18. Competence; Competency in healthcare services enables professionals to deliver effective and continuous care for the patients. Competency framework in healthcare services helps to overcome the challenges in treatment processes which, in turn, improves the patient experience.

19. Professional credibility; Refers to education, performance, experience, and demonstrates professional development and helps to sustain patient trust in healthcare services.

Additionally, patient experiences are also affected when the prospects of service delivery do not align with standard practices. It is necessary to implement evidence-based care and identify the drawbacks in implemented healthcare services. Patient experiences can be improved by improving the quality of care, shared decision-making, and promoting access to treatments.

According to a study, multi-morbidity may be the result of a multisystem loss of reserve and function that leads to a low-grade pro-inflammatory state, multiple hormonal dysregulations, and increased susceptibility to chronic diseases[1]. In addition, women and individuals with a lower socioeconomic status appear especially prone to developing multimorbidity[2].

A 10-year follow-up study conducted in Finland found that smoking, physical inactivity, high body mass index with hypertension, and low level of education were predisposing factors for multimorbidity amongst a disease-free population[3]. Another study found a clear association between obesity and multimorbidity. It also revealed that accumulating an unhealthy lifestyle progressively increases the risk of multimorbidity[4]. Perhaps this is why the modern working-age population is also at the risk of developing multimorbidity.

Studies have discovered that the consequences of multimorbidity are not just wide-ranging, but they are also severe. One of the most common consequences of multimorbidity is premature death, accompanied by more frequent hospital admissions and more extended hospital stays. In addition, they are also known to make frequent visits to various specialists during the year[5]. An analysis of the direct costs of multimorbidity in the United States Veterans Affairs Health Care System revealed that, out of the 5% of the highest-cost patients in the system who actually account for 47% of total healthcare costs, about two-thirds had multiple chronic conditions[6].

Multimorbidity also severely affects an individual's overall wellbeing, quality of life, and ability to function normally. According to research, an inverse relationship between multimorbidity and overall quality of life was reported, with the closest association of multimorbidity being on the physical functioning of the individual[7]. A decrease in physical functioning may lead to depression and several affective disorders that only add to the medication burden that is associated with multimorbidity. One of the most common struggles that patients with multimorbidity face are managing the multiple medications prescribed to them, leading to difficulties with treatment adherence and a further reduction in the overall quality of their life[8].

Even though the number of patients with multimorbidity is continually increasing, clinical practice guidelines and delivery of healthcare are still primarily built around single diseases, which can have many undesirable effects. In order to deliver better and more cost-effective care for patients with multimorbidity, a shift in the paradigm from the present vertical monomorbid approaches to horizontal multimorbid ones needs to be implemented. Health-care services need to be reorganized to deliver individualized and more structured care, better care coordination and management, enhanced multi-disciplinary teamwork, and more generous support for patient education and self-management – optimizing the use of 21st-century technology solutions as per convenience. In addition, clinical practice guidelines also need to be developed in relevance to the needs of patients with multimorbidity. This will also help in making complex treatment decisions in the absence of high-quality or direct evidence.

However, during this time of considerable change, the extra investment will be required in the start so that the focus moves onto primary prevention, the management of younger patients with multimorbidity, and the development of healthcare systems that are better equipped to meet the needs of both older and younger patients. It is deemed that, within 20 or so years, this investment will reap the rewards, bringing tangible benefits to individuals, populations, and healthcare systems.

Even though most healthcare systems are traditionally disease-oriented and focus on curing or managing individual acute and chronic conditions, patients with multimorbidity are often in these systems. Most individuals with multimorbidity are affected by common conditions, including hypertension, ischaemic heart disease, and diabetes. None of these issues are rare and are individually treatable. This means that the problem originates from the failure to accommodate the interplay between them adequately.

Since a disease-oriented approach does not cater to the needs of patients with multimorbidity, fragmented, inefficient, and ineffective care is provided to the affected individuals. In order to improve the resilience and sustainability of health systems, a paradigm shift towards a more patient-centered model that addresses the needs of these individuals more holistically, focusing on multi-disciplinary, integrated, and coordinated care is needed. Moreover, innovation and reform at all levels of the political and health-care systems will also be required.

Almost one in every four people residing in the U.K. and USA face multimorbidity, which increases to at least two-thirds of those older than 65 years. It is associated with reduced quality of life, impaired functional status, worse physical and mental health, and increased mortality. The increasing prevalence of multimorbidity, driven by the aging population, represents a significant challenge to all healthcare systems since these patients are heavy users of services.

Attempts to advance the care of patients with chronic diseases have been focused on developing guidelines to implement standardized care for each disease. However, this approach does not suit individuals with multimorbidity, as recommendations based on disease-specific guidelines can be inappropriate for patients with co-existing conditions. Since each of these conditions is considered in isolation, patients with multimorbidity are prescribed numerous drugs along with lifestyle changes. They are expected to attend frequent healthcare appointments. This means that the treatment itself serves as an excessive burden for patients with multimorbidity, alongside their burden of illness. Additionally, the segmentation of care for multiple diseases means that health care for patients is often severely fragmented and poorly coordinated. Older adults have been known to seek one professional who can take continuing responsibility for their overall care and keep in mind their personal situation and preferences when advising about treatment decisions.

Recognizing these problems, organizations in England, the USA, Europe, and internationally have published guidance about improving the management of patients with multimorbidity. This increase incited The U.S. Department of Health and Human Services to call for a paradigm shift in how care is provided since, in the USA, people with multimorbidity account for more than two-thirds of total health spending. There is a broad consensus about the critical components of this approach, which reflect not only a patient-centered care model but also insights from the Chronic Care Model.

These components include a regular comprehensive review of patients' problems according to their individual circumstances, a focus on the quality of life and function as well as disease control, tailoring treatment recommendations to each individual's priorities and situation, balancing risks and benefits of treatment while seeking to reduce treatment burden (particularly inappropriate polypharmacy), promoting self-management, sharing decisions with patients, and agreeing to an individualized care plan. A multi-disciplinary team in the community should deliver services, but with one clearly defined professional responsible for coordinating care. These changes require system redesign facilitated by clinical information systems that provide decision support and allow sharing of information between care providers.

In order to tackle multimorbidity, in particular, a focus on planning in several key areas must be maintained. The U.S. Department of Health and Human Services (HHS) defines these quality improvement efforts as "systematic and continuous actions that lead to measurable improvement in health-care services and health status of targeted patient groups[9]." Whereas the Institute of Medicine states that healthcare quality is the degree to which health care services for individuals and populations increase the likelihood of desired health outcomes and are consistent with current professional knowledge[10].

There are concerns that need to be addressed in order to maintain healthcare quality for all patients and especially for the ones who have multimorbidity. The first issue is the recognition of the fact that both social deprivation and mental health problems tend to increase the risk of multimorbidity. Therefore, it is necessary to make a commitment to ensure that social and healthcare providers are working closely with the patients to address these issues effectively.

Those with mental health problems must receive treatment from a broad range of professionals. This includes psychiatrists, psychologists, and home nurses, who will serve to connect patients with hospital, community, and social care providers, in order to monitor the patient's condition and medications. Apart from receiving both acute and long-term treatments, patients with mental health conditions must also be engaged in group therapies and disease-prevention programs, acquire occupational therapy and participate in programs that promote rehabilitation, social inclusion, independence.

The second issue is the increase in the prevalence of multimorbidity that is continually rising across our population and within younger age groups. The solution to this challenge is the strengthening of prevention programs along with health promotion and education. The National Public Health Institute, in collaboration with its Centre for the Management of Prevention Programmes and Health Promotion designs, prepares and monitors national prevention and screening programs, including those targeted towards lifestyle interventions. Health promotion and education programs are also delivered at the primary care level by nurses and other healthcare professionals in health education centers within the community health centers.

In 2011, the concept of "model practices" was aimed at enhancing the role of primary care practices in the prevention of chronic conditions and the encouragement of lifestyle changes. These practices are mainly supported by registered nurses who work part-time in family medicine practices in order to educate patients with chronic diseases/multimorbidity on risk-factor management and self-care. The goal is to increase the time available for each of these activities within each model practice and expand the service across all primary care providers. Model practices play a crucial role in navigating patients between specialists, reducing duplication and omission, and improving service efficiency.

Lastly, the third issue that needs to be addressed is the growing needs of vulnerable population groups living with multiple risk factors and chronic conditions who do not attend services offered in primary health care. This can be done by strengthening community nursing in primary care and introducing protocols and practices that ensure cooperation between both primary and secondary care patients. With the help of social services, this aim will become even easier to achieve.

Since the passage of the Affordable Care Act (ACA), much attention has been drawn to ensuring healthcare quality improvement by payers, clinicians, as well as consumers alike. The importance of quality improvement efforts was highlighted by the level of buy-in across industry stakeholders. In addition, the escalating healthcare costs and higher-than-ever number of insured Americans have also heightened the need for a better quality of healthcare. This had led to an increase in research around patient outcomes and safety, care coordination, efficiency, and cost-cutting. Additionally, care redesign initiatives are being evaluated to guide future healthcare quality improvements.

Under the mandate by ACA, the National Strategy for Quality Improvement in Health Care (National Strategy) was created in 2011 by the Agency for Healthcare Research and Quality (AHRQ) in order to guide quality improvement efforts at local, state, and national levels through three key aims and six priorities. These aims are:

- Improving overall quality by making health-care even more patient-centered, reliable, accessible, and most importantly, safe
- Improving the health of the population by supporting proven interventions to address behavioral, social, and environmental determinants of health
- Reducing the cost of quality care for individuals, families, employers, and government

Furthermore, National Healthcare Quality and Disparities Report (NHQDR) evaluated more than 250 measures of healthcare processes, outcomes, and access yearly in a variety of settings, including hospitals, community health centers, and private practices. These insights led to the identification of essential patient-centered performance measures (see figure 8.1).

Over the years, the NHQDR has reported progress in all six priority areas established by the AHRQ.

1. Making care safer by decreasing the harm caused in the delivery of care

In 2013, the findings of a study published in the Journal of Patient Safety gained much attention. This study revealed that medical errors in hospitals resulted in more than 210,000 deaths per year. This report further strengthened the efforts to promote quality measures and reduce harm in healthcare.

According to the NHQDR, almost half of all patient safety measures significantly enhanced, with a median improvement of about 3.6 percent per year. In addition, there was a 17 percent reduction in hospital-acquired conditions, including pressure ulcers, falls, and infections. This resulted in approximately 50,000 fewer patient deaths and $12 billion in healthcare cost savings, along with a significant reduction in adverse drug reactions.

2. Ensuring each person and family are engaged in health-care

An essay in Health Affairs described patient-centered care as a means of enhancing quality and outcomes by helping them stay involved in their own care, building patient-provider relationships, and revolving care around patient needs. Literature shows that person-centered care reduces the length of stay, lowers maintenance and operating costs, enhances employee retention, and reduces unfavorable events.

It was also reported that nearly all person- and family-centered care measures in NHQDR improved. Patient-provider communication enhanced from 2005 to 2012, as the percentage of adults who reported poor contact with health providers continued to decrease. A significantly lower degree of poor communication was also reported between parents and their children's health providers. The AHRQ also established the Consumer Assessment of Healthcare Providers and Systems, which was a research organization that releases surveys allowing patients to evaluate their care and healthcare professionals to measure patient-centered care.

3. Promoting effective communication and coordination of care

According to the National Strategy, effective communication within healthcare delivery settings and care coordination across the healthcare system decreases errors and overutilization of services. It also helps patients move efficiently through a complex system involving different providers across multiple settings.

The NHQDR found that healthcare facilities experienced an improvement in discharge processes and care coordination facilitated by the adoption of health information technologies such as electronic medical records. This report also showed a significant increase in the percentage of patients with severe conditions who received complete, written discharge instructions. The rate of heart failure patients who received full discharge instructions increased by 35 percent. In an attempt to improve care coordination, the Centers for Medicare & Medicaid Services (CMS) adopted Medicare and Medicaid Electronic Health Record Incentive Programs that provided financial incentives to implement certified electronic health record technology.

4. Promoting efficient prevention and treatment practices for leading causes of mortality, beginning with cardiovascular diseases

One of the primary goals of the National Strategy is to target the diseases that are accountable for the number of American disabilities and deaths, such as cardiovascular disease, through intensive prevention and treatment programs. The NHQDR found that half of the effective treatment measures have improved life-threatening conditions. For instance, the percentage of heart attack sufferers treated within 90 minutes of their arrival to a hospital has significantly increased over time. The overall performance of other treatment measures has also improved, thus leading to better outcomes in not just cardiovascular disorders but also in cancer, pneumonia, and HIV care.

Additionally, even the Centers for Disease Control and Prevention have been continually pursuing prevention efforts in order to reduce various heart disease risk factors, including smoking, sodium intake, and, most importantly, high blood pressure. Multiple campaigns, including Million Hearts, Tips From Former Smokers, and Sodium Reduction in Communities, were initiated to target heart disease, obesity, diabetes, stroke, and health disparities.

5. Working with communities to promote extensive use of best practices to enable healthy living

The National Strategy maintained its commitment to work in communities by promoting healthy living, increasing preventive services, and enhancing evidence-based interventions to improve population health and wellness. The NHQDR found that with the help of this approach, almost half of the measures of healthy living were improved. Moreover, adolescent vaccines were among notable improvements, including increases in the percentage of adolescents receiving the meningococcal and tetanus-diphtheria-acellular-pertussis vaccines.

There are various programs that aim to promote healthy living, such as Let's Move, which is an initiative designed to enhance the health of children by guiding parents, nutritious meals in schools, along with various physical activity programs. Health Leads is another program that integrates patients' social needs into their medical care, with clinicians "prescribing" basic resources like food and heat as a part of treatment. Health Leads advocates are also known to connect patients to helpful social programs. In 2014 alone, these advocates connected more than 13,000 patients and their families to the resources they needed for the treatment.

6. Making quality care affordable for individuals, families, employers, and governments by developing new healthcare delivery models

Before the ACA, the NHQD report revealed that healthcare was becoming more expensive day by day. However, the recent reports showed that care affordability has "leveled off" or stopped worsening. This report also indicated that the percentage of people who specified a financial impediment due to the lack of primary care providers has not improved in the past two years. Moreover, access and cost barriers to health insurance are being targeted with the help of tax credits, coverage options in the Health Insurance Marketplace, and cost-sharing reductions.

The importance of managing a patient's experience and quality care in healthcare has been highlighted repeatedly over the past years. It has led to various practices and policies in order to ensure the same. In the present times, when the scope of healthcare is not just improving but is from shifting from one form to another, quality assurance is even more necessary.

One of the most important lessons that the prevailing pandemic of COVID-19 has taught us is that management of patient experience and delivery of healthcare is not just ensured with the help of human force. The use of technology and devices that can make processes and procedures easier for patients and healthcare professionals is one of the most imperative ways of making sure that seeking treatment is not a never-ending tiresome process. However, this does not mean that appropriate policies should not be implemented as they, too, play an essential role in enhancing the quality of care.

As the healthcare industry continues to progress, managing patient experiences and quality of care also needs to be enhanced in accordance with the changing needs of the patients. Therefore, it is necessary for healthcare professionals to observe the changes in needs of patients carefully and to make sure that the right care is being provided at all times.

The importance of managing a patient's experience and quality care in health care has been highlighted repeatedly over the past years. It has led to various practices and policies in order to ensure the same. In the present times, when the scope of health care is not just improving but is shifting from one form to another, quality assurance is even more necessary. Different strategies have been adopted for the improvement of the quality of services and patient experiences, which are largely relying on evidence-based practices.

Patient's voice matter

In modern healthcare, the patient's voice is a crucial element in ensuring effective, empathetic, and personalized care. Understanding the significance of listening to patients not only improves outcomes but also builds trust and enhances the quality of care. Below are key reasons why the patient's voice matters.

1. Patient-Centered Care

Healthcare today has shifted toward a patient-centered model, where the patient's experiences, needs, and preferences are central to all treatment decisions. When patients are encouraged to share their perspectives, it allows healthcare providers to gain insight into their unique situations. For example, a patient's cultural or personal values might influence how they perceive illness and treatment options. By listening, healthcare providers can tailor treatments to fit the patient's specific needs, ultimately leading to more personalized and effective care. This holistic approach ensures that care is not just about treating the disease but about caring for the person as a whole.

2. Improved Outcomes

When patients feel heard and valued, they are more likely to actively participate in their treatment plans, leading to improved health outcomes. Studies show that active patient engagement enhances treatment adherence. Patients are more likely to follow medical advice, attend follow-up appointments, and complete prescribed regimens when they feel their input is respected. This collaboration fosters a trusting relationship between healthcare providers and patients, where both parties work together to optimize health and well-being.

3. Informed Decision-Making

A key component of patient-centered care is shared decision-making. When patients can communicate openly with healthcare providers, they are more likely to fully understand their condition and treatment options. This process empowers patients to make decisions that align with their values, lifestyle, and goals. Rather than simply following a doctor's orders, patients become active participants in their own care, resulting in decisions that are more personalized and sustainable. Patients who are involved in decision-making are often more satisfied with their care, as they feel respected and empowered.

4. Patient Safety and Quality of Care

The patient's voice plays a critical role in ensuring patient safety and maintaining high-quality care. Patients are often the first to notice when something feels off, whether it's a side effect of medication, a new symptom, or an issue with the treatment environment. By paying attention to these observations, healthcare providers can identify potential safety risks early and prevent adverse events. Moreover, patient feedback can help healthcare organizations identify systemic issues, such as inefficient processes or communication gaps, ultimately leading to continuous improvements in the quality of care provided.

5. Building Trust and Empathy

Listening to patients fosters a sense of trust and empathy, which is the foundation of a strong patient-provider relationship. When healthcare professionals take the time to genuinely listen to a patient's concerns and show empathy, it creates an environment where patients feel valued, understood, and supported. This emotional connection is vital in healthcare, as patients are more likely to be forthcoming about their symptoms and challenges when they feel their provider truly cares. Furthermore, trust and empathy lead to greater patient satisfaction, which contributes to better overall care and cooperation.

Dealing with Non-Compliant Patients

Managing non-compliant patients can be one of the more challenging aspects of healthcare. However, understanding the reasons for non-compliance and employing strategies to engage and support patients can lead to improved adherence and health outcomes. Below are effective ways to address patient non-compliance.

1. Understand the Root Cause

Non-compliance often arises from various factors, including fear, misunderstanding, financial constraints, or cultural beliefs. It is crucial for healthcare providers to take the time to understand the specific reasons why a patient may not be following their treatment plan. For example, a patient may avoid medication due to cost concerns or may be hesitant to follow medical advice due to cultural practices. By identifying and addressing these barriers, healthcare providers can tailor interventions to the patient's specific situation.

2. Clear and Effective Communication

Patients may fail to adhere to treatment plans if they don't fully understand them. Healthcare providers must prioritize clear communication, using plain language and avoiding medical jargon. This ensures that patients comprehend the treatment plan, its benefits, and potential risks. Encouraging patients to ask questions and express concerns helps to reinforce understanding and clarify any misconceptions.

3. Building Trust and Rapport

Trust is central to encouraging patient compliance. When patients trust their healthcare provider, they are more likely to follow medical advice. Providers should show empathy, respect, and a genuine interest in the patient's well-being. Building a strong relationship encourages open dialogue, allowing patients to feel comfortable discussing their concerns or hesitations, which, in turn, can help resolve issues related to non-compliance.

4. Shared Decision-Making

Involving patients in the decision-making process can improve compliance. When patients feel a sense of ownership over their treatment plans, they are more likely to adhere to them. Shared decision-making encourages patients to voice their preferences and choose treatment options that align with their lifestyle and values, making them more invested in their own care.

5. Offer Alternatives and Flexibility

Rigid treatment plans can be a deterrent for some patients, especially if they conflict with their daily lives or personal beliefs. Offering flexibility and alternative options when possible can increase adherence. For instance, if a patient is unable to take medication at a certain time, exploring alternative dosing schedules or medications may improve compliance without compromising treatment effectiveness.

6. Education and Support

Patients who are non-compliant may need additional education and support to understand the importance of following through with their treatment plan. Providing patients with educational materials, access to support groups, or scheduling follow-up consultations can reinforce the need for adherence and give them the tools they need to succeed.

Addressing any misconceptions or fears through education can alleviate barriers to compliance.

7. Non-Judgmental Approach

Approaching non-compliance with a non-judgmental attitude is essential. Patients are more likely to respond positively when they feel understood rather than reprimanded. Healthcare providers should focus on finding solutions instead of placing blame, creating an environment of openness and collaboration. This compassionate approach encourages patients to be more honest about their struggles with compliance and to work toward a resolution.

By recognizing the importance of the patient's voice and adopting compassionate, solution-focused approaches to non-compliance, healthcare providers can foster better relationships and improve patient outcomes. These practices lead to more effective, personalized care and ensure that patients remain engaged and committed to their health journey.

CHAPTER 11

Leadership and Healthcare Productivity

Leadership and productivity are a primary concern in just about any industry. Organizations are continuously looking for individuals who have good leadership skills and are productive. In addition, they are also conducting training and facilitating short courses to equip their existing employees with the same skills.

The need for individuals with leadership and productivity skills is rapidly increasing in the healthcare industry as well. Doctors, nurses, and other healthcare workers are often overwhelmed by the sheer number of tasks they need to complete apart from attending to their needs. The healthcare industry's lack of productivity makes patients often feel they aren't getting proper attention and even sometimes complain about healthcare workers "doing nothing." Employees with good leadership skills are no less than assets for an organization. They help achieve the organization's goals while ensuring that both employees and consumers are happy and satisfied. A few ways in which leadership skills are important in healthcare are (see figure 11.1):

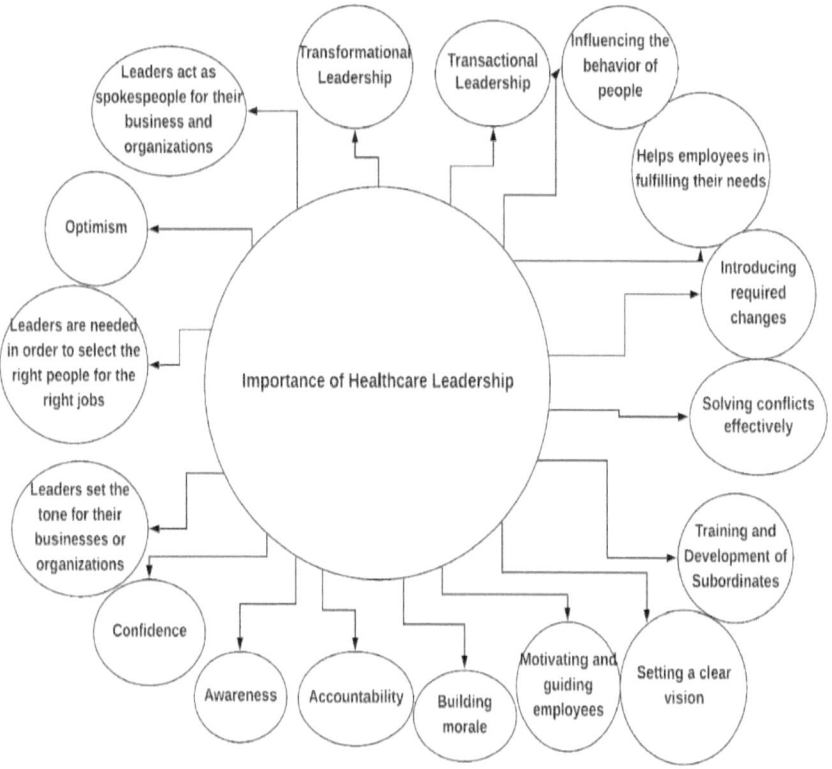

Figure 11.1: Importance of Healthcare Leadership

Figure 11.1 indicates the factors that represent the importance of healthcare leadership. These include the introduction of required changes, solving conflicts effectively, training and development of subordinates, setting a clear vision, motivating and guiding employees, building morale, accountability, awareness, confidence, leaders set the tone for their businesses and organizations, selection of right people for right jobs, optimism, transformational leadership implementation, transactional leadership implementation, influencing behavior of people, and helping employees in fulfilling their needs.

The importance of healthcare leadership can be explained under the light of the following representative factors:

1. Transformational Leadership

This theory of leadership is based on the involvement of leaders where they work with teams to identify required changes, create a vision for the team members to guide the change via inspiration, and execute the change efficiently with the dedicated and committed members of the group. Transformational leadership is the most widely adopted leadership model in different business sectors[1].

2. Transactional Leadership

Transactional leadership style refers to the leadership style that focuses on organization, supervision and performance. It is also called managerial leadership, in which the executives rely on punishments and rewards to achieve optimal job performance from their subordinates. The style is based on transaction or exchange. A reward is set for employees performing their tasks to specified standards while employees not working against their set standards are punished.

3. Influencing the Behavior of People

Influencing the behavior of people is not about certain hard skills rather, it depends on understanding oneself and the impact of a person on social dynamics at play in the organization. The ability to influence is an essential leadership skill. When a leader influences their people, they impact on the attitudes, behaviors, choices, and opinions of others. Here, influence is not to be confused with control or power. Rather, it involves noticing what factors motivate employees' commitment and using that understanding to create positive performance and results.

4. Helps Employees in Fulfilling Their Needs

Ideal leaders help employees in fulfilling their needs. A personal relationship is created by the leader with his subordinates and intends to meet their demands. A leader is followed by people when he provides them security, gives them the right to work, provides opportunities to earn wealth, and tries to understand their feelings. A leader helping their people can also improve the overall performance at an individual and collective level.

5. Introducing Required Changes

Ideal leaders are not afraid of changes in the organization; rather, they foresee the need for change and develop a protocol for their people to embrace change. Change management is the integral skill of ideal leaders, and healthcare sectors constantly require changes to correspond to the growing health needs of service users. It has also been learned that leadership is one of the leading factors that brings an affirmative change in the organization[2].

6. Solving Conflicts

Resolving conflicts requires sufficient information and a strategic mindset. Leaders respect the unique differences in the people and learn to visualize things from different points of view, rather than to impose their influence, rank or hierarchy. It makes them better understand how to avoid conflict in future. Ideal leaders develop a shared decision-making platform to resolve conflicts with the help of their followers and other leaders in the organization.

7. Training and Development Subordinates

The personal and professional development of subordinates in any firm is directly related to leadership style because this development is understood as maturation and growth of skills, knowledge, and attitudes. This growth and development of subordinates is acquired as a result of learning-at-work actions and via training. Further, the training and development of subordinates are directly linked with positive results.

8. Setting a Clear Vision

A clear picture refers to all the parts that make up the big picture and seeing the big picture to analyze the dilemma. A leader can make big decisions regarding how to move forward by understanding the way things work. A leaders' vision must also enable them to encourage their people to move towards their goals which sufficiently benefits the organization. Leaders in healthcare make decisions by visualizing the whole picture and setting work standards according to the challenging health needs of service users.

9. Motivating and Guiding Employees

An ideal leader understands the basic needs of their employees, his superiors, and peers. They use their leadership skills as a means of motivating and encouraging others. Being a role model also serves as a key motivator that influences people in reaching their set objectives. A good example must be set by the leaders to ensure their people to develop and grow and achieve their goals effectively. Ideal leaders guide their peers and encourage them to work with commitment in challenging times[3].

10. Building Morale

Leaders adopt different strategies to boost employee morale. They reward their employees for hard work, which motivates their commitment level within the workplace. Leaders recognize the special events of their employees, which makes the staff feel belonged and cherished on a personal plane. Leaders listen to their employees and use a shared decision-making process to promote employees' interest. These strategies build the morale of employees and make them value and respect the organizational prospects.

11. Accountability

If the leader takes accountability for something, they intend to take its full ownership. Accountability helps leaders in eliminating the effort and time a person spends on unproductive behavior and distracting activities. When a person is accountable for their activities, they teach others to value their work. Accountability helps the leaders to increase their team members' confidence and skills when done in the right manner[4].

12. Awareness

For a great leader, self-awareness is an essential trait. By knowing self-values, needs, personality, emotions and habits, they affect their own actions and the actions of others effectively. Awareness among leaders makes them better able to manage stress and make better decisions. Followers of self-aware leaders do the same and make a collective effort to sustain the competency within the organization.

13. Confidence

Confidence is an integral part of competent leaders. Confident leaders deal with the challenges and feel positive about their ability to lead their people. They project through a "can do" attitude and overcome whatever comes their way smartly. Team members of confident leaders are also competent enough and correspond to challenges confidently by following their leader's path. For healthcare leaders, self-confidence is really necessary to accomplish high goals. Such leaders avoid procrastination, passing problems to others or ignoring the problems.

14. Leaders Set the Tone for Their Businesses or Organizations

It is necessary for the leader to visualize problems and strategies for the organizations from each point of view. Leaders, with their prominence and skills, set the tone for the organization. Their people look forward to a confident, competent, empath and compassionate supervisor who they would love to work with each day. Ideal leadership skills enable leaders to establish a culture of success. They embed values, norms and culture by their actions, professional expertise, and interaction with the employees.

15. Leaders are Needed to Select the Right People for the Right Jobs

Some leaders have the potential to view hiring as a work of art. A combination of skills is required for making better decisions for hiring. The selection of the right people for the right job is a critical task that requires recruiters to assess the qualities, experiences and interests of candidates. Effective leadership skills are needed for the selection of competent employees whose expertise align with the job.

16. Optimism

Optimism is another ideal quality of leaders, and optimistic leaders have the potential to envision a better future for their employees. Such leaders are able to motivate and inspire people to work towards their shared vision of success and towards their goals. The best trait of optimistic leaders is that they do not allow their subordinates to wallow in the dark and difficult times. They portray the best of what their employees can get and guide them positively towards success.

17. Leaders Act as Spokespeople for Their Business and Organizations

Leaders benefit the business and organization by their skills and strategies. They are aware of potential issues and steer the organization in the right direction with their knowledge and experience. Leaders motivate their employees and make them more committed to the success of the organization. They act as the spokesperson for their business and the organization with the collective efforts of their employees.

Healthcare leadership helps the organization to reach its goals and overcome the challenges induced by the external environment. Moreover, effective healthcare leadership helps in predicting the risks and promotes compliance with statutory regulations of the state. Ideal leadership in healthcare promotes the education of their followers and advocates the rights of practitioners[5].

One of the most important reasons why the healthcare industry needs more individuals with leadership skills is because they set the tone for organizations by selecting the right people for the right job. They are confident, optimistic, and highly motivated. They know the value of accountability and are quick to resolve conflicts and maintaining unity. They are not afraid of bringing about the required changes and guide others in doing the same. Most importantly, they help others reach the same pinnacle of success and facilitate them as well.

Productivity is also as crucial as having leadership skills. Therefore, it is equally valued as leadership skills. Just like leadership skills, productivity can also be learned. This means that any individual can learn to be productive or improve their productivity using the right tools and methods. A few ways to improve productivity are:

1. Rethink Your Workflows

Repetitive or overlapping workflows can often hinder employee productivity. If your employees are doing the same task two or three times over, when they should just be sharing test results and other information about a patient, their productivity is bound to decrease. Similarly, inefficient workflows also hinder employee productivity if they have to wait for information that should be readily available and accessible such as Electronic health records. However, due to poor interfaces and poor structure, sometimes EHRs cause more problems than they solve.

2. Use Technology

While it's essential to ensure any technology you adopt supports your workflows and boosts productivity, there's often a benefit to using technology in a healthcare setting. Appropriate tech can reduce mistakes and resolve administrative issues apart from increasing employee productivity by allowing employees to complete their tasks faster than usual. They know they're getting the right information when needed, and they spend less time sorting out mistakes or correcting courses. Fewer errors also mean they spend less time administering inappropriate treatments—errors that cost your organization and decrease productivity.

3. Use A Communications Application

One of the most useful technologies available to those in the healthcare sector is a communications application. The application can travel with healthcare workers from site to site, and it's easily accessible through a smartphone. This means that they can be connected to each other and their patients no matter where they are. Communication is a massive part of any healthcare job[6]. Nurses, pharmacists, clinicians, and other healthcare workers need to communicate with each other about patients. They need to be able to do so quickly and easily. A communications application allows healthcare workers to coordinate with each other to get more work done in any given shift.

4. Offer Incentives and Rewards

If your employees seem to lack productivity, there is a high chance that they feel disengaged. Disengagement is a serious problem. As many as 70 percent of American employees report some degree of disengagement level with their jobs. It can cost organizations billions of dollars each year by decreasing productivity and increasing burnout levels. The WHO recommends that disengagement can be managed by offering rewards based on employee performance. These rewards don't strictly need to be cash-based or monetary. They can be as simple as social recognition, which increases the recipient's prestige among their peers. Moreover, individual rewards have also been shown to increase team productivity.

The Healthcare industry can function adequately if its employees work closely together as part of a cohesive team. In order to ensure that the team meets the high standards which are needed for patient care, administrators must implement quality control measures for both employees and equipment. The most talented and caring healthcare workers may fail patients if systems are not in place to keep things functioning smoothly. Various factors may impact the quality of medical services (see figure 11.2).

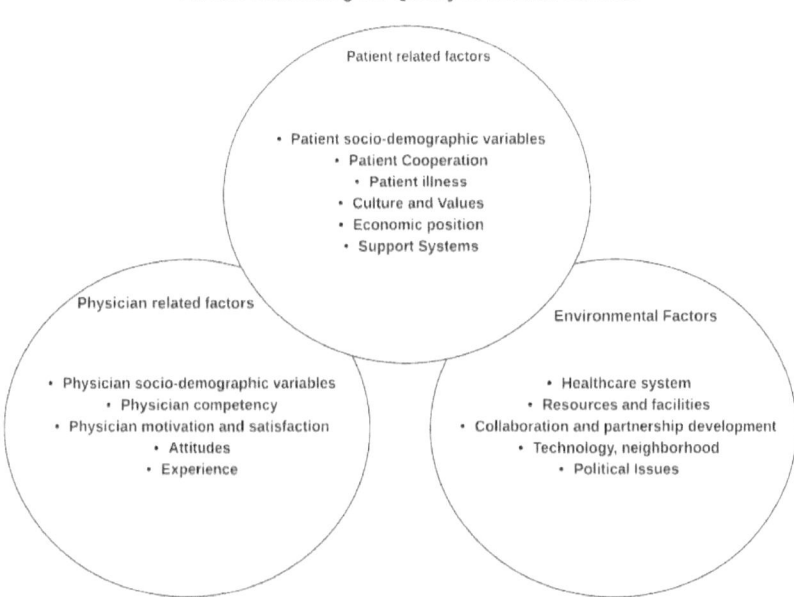

Figure 11.2: Factors Influencing the Quality of Medical Services

Figure 11.2 highlights the factors influencing the quality of medical services. These factors are divided into three domains; patient-related, physician-related, and environmental. Patient-related factors include patient illness, culture and values, patient cooperation, support systems, economic position, and patient socio-demographic variables.

Physician-related factors include physician competency, experience, attitudes, physician socio-demographic variables, physician motivation, and satisfaction. Environmental factors include political issues, resources and facilities, technology, neighborhood, and healthcare systems. These factors significantly affect the quality of services in healthcare organizations.

These factors have been further elaborated below;

Patient-related Factors

1. Patient socio-economic demographic variables; Healthcare quality, and outcomes are influenced by the socio-economic status of patients. Patients belonging to low socio-economic status receive poor preventative services, fewer indicated cardiac interventions and worse diabetes care. Elimination of disparities must be the top priority of healthcare practitioners.
2. Patient cooperation; It improves the quality of medical services by improving the treatment outcomes. The standards of quality in medical services can be achieved when patients cooperate in the treatment process and medication management.
3. Patient illness; Practitioners are required to assess likely comorbidities patient might have and which can act as an obstacle in the treatment process. Patient illness can compromise the quality of care.
4. Culture and values; The influence of values and culture on health is vast. It affects illness and death, perceptions of health, approaches to health promotion, beliefs about causes of disease, and how one experiences and expresses pain and illness. Culture and values of patient influence medical services and the experiences of patients within healthcare.
5. Economic position; Patient economic position is the predominant aspect that enables or disables them to reach the required medical facility and treatment. Low-income families lack access to advanced treatment protocols, and the type of services provided to them are generally substandard.
6. Support systems; Patient receiving support from carers, family members, or social support providers achieve a greater success rate. Therefore, support systems, such as health insurance plans, help improve the quality of services patient gets.

Environmental Factors

1. Healthcare systems; Healthcare systems considerably affect the quality of medical services. Improved quality of medical services requires coordination among members of different organizations and providers. Healthcare systems must develop on principles that promote coordination of highly complex therapeutic, diagnostic and logistic processes and practices to improve the quality of care. The bureaucratic and highly departmentalized structure of healthcare systems poses a significant obstacle for quality improvement in healthcare.
2. Collaboration and partnership development; The ability of the physicians and practitioners to effectively collaborate and communicate with other institutions and professional, is essential for the delivery of high-quality medical services. Teamwork and cooperation are important factors among healthcare providers and important component of quality care services.
3. Technology, neighborhood; Environmental factors like technological advancement in the healthcare facility help improving the standards of quality and care services provided to the patients.
4. Political issues; A direct impact is made on the quality of care services in the medical sector by political issues. Government guidelines and funding help healthcare organizations to function in a range of activities that improve their overall service measures.

Physician-related Factors

1. Physician socio-demographic variables; A physician's personality and character affects the quality of medical services. A link should be developed between the attitude of physician and communication with patients and their income. Physicians lack the motivation to improve their communication skills in a public hospital that demand medical services.

2. Physician competency; It evolves physicians' proficiencies in performing well and thus improving the overall work functions and quality of services provided in health care. Physician competency is the crucial factor in improving their professional development along with medical quality services.
3. Physician satisfaction and motivation; For improvement of quality of medical services, physicians' job satisfaction is very important. The factors in a healthcare organization that influence the job motivation of doctors include organizational policies, job identity, recognition, managerial leadership, working environment, chances for promotion, co-workers, and pay.
4. Attitudes; Physician's attitude help patients in feeling secure and belonged to the setting. The positive attitude of physicians helps in establishing and strengthening trust between their patients, thus improving the quality of medical services.
5. Experience; Professional expertise, and experiences of physician play a role in improving or reducing the quality of care in healthcare organizations. It directs their clinical practices and the team members involved in managing patients.

Each of these factors tends to impact the quality of services that a healthcare organization may provide. This means that the administrators need to look at all aspects of their organization to identify how and where quality control measures would be most effective. While every healthcare facility has its own unique needs and challenges, the basic principles of leadership, teamwork and procedural safeguards are common across all industries. Similarly, supporting staff and introducing policy measures to maintain quality is vital for all healthcare facilities as it helps create a safe workplace that is healthy for patients and workers alike. Here are a few ways to maintain healthcare quality:

1. Create Concrete Processes

Employee intuition and common sense are significant. Healthcare is a human profession by its very nature. No healthcare employee should feel trapped within strict rules that compromise sensitivity to patients. However, workers should use their discretion only within established processes so that caregivers and patients are protected by well-conceived procedures that ensure quality maintenance.

These procedures serve to provide a baseline of expected actions and activities within the healthcare setting. For example, ward staff might be required to do a thorough cleaning of equipment and rooms every few days. Test results may have to be double-checked by technicians and doctors before discussion with the patient. Depending on the healthcare setting, specific protocols can be established that go above and beyond the quality control processes required by the city or state to achieve excellence in patient care.

2. Maintain a Clean Work Environment

In addition to protocols regarding the sterilization of equipment and surgical rooms, workers should also be encouraged to keep all areas free of hazards. Healthcare settings usually have injury and illness prevention programs, which are required by state law. However, a healthcare environment that only meets minimal standards is not an optimal workplace.

Creating a culture that encourages employees at all levels to avoid spills, pick up equipment parts, and refrain from creating tripping hazards. An established procedure for cleaning up spills or removing hazards is an integral part of a safety program. Furthermore, reducing clutter also raises the level of professionalism in the workplace by boosting the quality of care.

3. Hold Impromptu Equipment Tests

Access to equipment poses unexpected hazards and risks to patients. Even someone who uses a machine daily may still misuse equipment or slip into bad habits that can compromise safety. Spot-checking equipment usage helps ensure that the equipment is working correctly and will not harm the patients or employees.

Do tests on small groups of employees at a time. This will also help in monitoring their hands-on use of the equipment in action. Make sure to note any deviation from safety protocols. Let employees know if they have made any errors so that they can correct themselves immediately.

4. Keep Inventory of Equipment Spare Parts

Healthcare organizations' equipment is so essential that lives will be at risk if it fails to function. Therefore, every quality control program should maintain an inventory of everything that is needed to help the equipment work at optimal capacity. Moreover, workers should know where spare parts are located if they are trained to replace them. If specialized maintenance is required, staff should know whom to contact on an emergency basis to repair equipment. It would be best if alternative protocols are established to maintain high patient care levels while the standard equipment is being fixed.

5. Properly Train Your Managers

Quality control measures mean little if not correctly implemented. The management team is responsible for creating these processes and introducing them to the healthcare organization. This requires great skill at all stages of the Quality Assurance process. Management training not only ensures the optimization of Quality Assurance but also raises the level of excellence of the healthcare team.

Proper management training systems help establish a solid footing for a healthcare organization—the knowledge, experience, and leadership capacities of a management team filtrates throughout the team. Strong management supports talented employees and those struggling to serve the overall objective of high-quality patient care.

In order to know the impact of certain actions, practices, or policies, quality measures are derived. These measures help keep up with the changing needs of the consumer and make sure that the service being provided is of optimum quality. In a classic formulation of the dimensions of quality of care almost 40 years ago, Avedis Donabedian described quality as including structure (viewed as the capacity to provide high-quality care), process (now often termed performance), and outcomes. The Agency for Healthcare Research and Quality (AHRQ) outlined the three types of quality measures being used today using the Donabedian classification model.

In general, either processes or outcomes may be valid measures of quality. For an outcome to be a valid measure of quality, it must be closely related to care processes that can be manipulated to affect the outcome. Similarly, for a process to be a valid measure of quality, it must be closely related to an outcome that people care about. The parts that each of these plays in quality measurement are described below.

a. **Structure Measures.**

Structural measures are the health care provider's overall ability to provide high-quality care: the institution's capacity, systems, and processes. These measures may include whether the organization uses more modern electronic medical records and medication order entry systems. Measures could also include how many board-certified physicians are on staff the ratio of providers to patients.

b. **Process Measures.**

Process measures are what the institution does to maintain or improve health. These measures can reflect both preventative measures or those already experiencing health issues. These measures should evaluate how the institution is meeting generally accepted standards of practice. Most publicly reported health care quality measures are process measures.

c. **Outcome Measures.**

Outcome measures reflect the impact of the institution's patient interventions and how they improved patients' health. Examples of outcome measures include rates for surgical mortality, surgical complications, and hospital-acquired infections.

Even though quality measures have the potential to improve healthcare, some healthcare professionals have warned that there is only limited evidence that many quality measures result in improved health outcomes. This includes those who are tied to incentives by insurers or governments. Despite this, quality measures and comparative quality ratings continue to increase in popularity. This is mainly because the measures are based on intermediate endpoints such as risk-factor control or care processes vulnerable to gaming, over-test, and over-treatment. Instead, quality measures should be based on patient-centered outcomes, with individualized approaches to clinical complexity.

Some observers question the relationship of structural measures or standards to either process or outcome measures because of little empirical evidence of direct connections. Structural standards may provide a baseline in terms of capacity, but compliance does not assure that high-quality care is provided. Nor does their use clearly mean that high-quality care cannot be provided unless these standards are met. However, continuing attention has been given to the importance of governance, financial structures, the health care workforce, and the capacity to provide accessible and coordinated care. Such standards have been combined with measures of performance and outcome to assess the quality of care.

Measures of the quality of care based on processes are well-developed in comparison to outcome measures. Nevertheless, they are good measures only if those processes can be linked to important outcomes for patients. Similarly, outcomes are good measures of quality of care only to the extent that they can be linked to actions on the part of the health care system that can be changed. Healthcare managers' actions should be aware that poor health outcomes are not always clear. However, the accountability of individual practitioners and healthcare systems for patient and population health outcomes is an issue that can often only partially be addressed by health care professionals as they may more accurately be understood as societal issues.

During the last decade, many healthcare systems have begun to apply a quality improvement model called continuous quality improvement or total quality management. One assumption of this model is that the health care organizations and systems within which professionals practice can always improve. One way to foster this improvement is to set up continuous monitoring systems. These systems alert the organization when performance in some areas is slipping and confirm that efforts at improving care are succeeding. For organizations that have embraced continuous quality improvement methods, measurement of performance and outcomes is integral to their operations. In such cases, the cost of measurement is part of the cost of doing business. Ideally, the collection of information is continuous and detailed, and external reporting of performance uses some of this information[7].

Leadership and productivity in the healthcare sector are being given the attention they need mainly because the patient is now being viewed as a consumer. This had also helped healthcare organizations improve their policies and practices, which in turn have decreased burnout levels in healthcare employees and dissatisfaction levels in the patients. With the help of a productive and well-managed workforce, the healthcare industry can overcome all its weaknesses and function together as a unit more efficiently.

Measures of the quality of care based on processes are well-developed in comparison to outcome measures. Nevertheless, they are good measures only if those processes can be linked to important outcomes for patients. Similarly, outcomes are good measures of quality of care only to the extent that they can be linked to actions on the part of the health care system that can be changed. Healthcare managers' actions should be aware that poor health outcomes are not always clear[10]. However, the accountability of individual practitioners and healthcare systems for patient and population health outcomes is an issue that can often only partially be addressed by health care professionals as they may more accurately be understood as societal issues.

The paradigm of healthcare productivity

The concept of productivity in healthcare has long been centered on the delivery of more care—more patients seen, more procedures completed, and more treatments administered—within the same amount of time or resources. As healthcare systems evolve in complexity, the definition of productivity is undergoing a significant transformation. Rather than merely focusing on throughput, the paradigm is shifting toward a more nuanced understanding that prioritizes quality, outcomes, patient satisfaction, and the integration of technology. In the near and distant future, healthcare productivity will no longer be a matter of quantity but one of efficiency, personalization, and sustainable impact.

The Traditional View of Healthcare Productivity

Historically, healthcare productivity has been viewed through the lens of operational efficiency—maximizing the number of patients seen per hour, the number of tests conducted per day, or the speed of surgical interventions. The underlying goal was to increase output, often driven by the pressures of a fee-for-service system. This perspective, while beneficial for scaling services, often overlooked other critical aspects such as quality of care, patient-centeredness, and long-term health outcomes.

This model has proven unsustainable for several reasons:

- **Burnout and Workforce Strain**: The emphasis on speed and volume has led to increased burnout among healthcare professionals, reducing their ability to provide compassionate, patient-centered care.

- **Quality Compromise**: In many cases, high throughput has been associated with a decrease in the quality of care, as less time is available to address complex, holistic patient needs.
- **Misaligned Incentives**: Fee-for-service models encourage more interventions, not necessarily better or more effective ones. This has led to increased healthcare costs without proportional improvements in patient outcomes.

Shifting the Productivity Paradigm: Value Over Volume

In the future, healthcare productivity will move from the traditional volume-based metrics to a value-based model. This shift is already underway with initiatives like value-based care (VBC), where the focus is on improving patient outcomes and experiences while controlling costs. Value-based models encourage healthcare systems to prioritize interventions that lead to long-term health benefits, reduce hospital readmissions, and enhance the patient experience. This shift will require healthcare systems to rethink how productivity is measured and achieved.

Key Components of Value-Based Healthcare Productivity:

1. **Patient Outcomes**: The ultimate goal of healthcare is improving health, not just providing treatments. Productivity will be measured by how well patients recover, how effectively chronic diseases are managed, and how health outcomes compare to cost inputs.
2. **Patient Satisfaction**: The patient experience will be a key metric for productivity. This includes not only satisfaction with care but also with access, communication, and the overall experience within the healthcare system.
3. **Efficiency of Resource Use**: Healthcare systems will need to manage resources—time, staff, equipment, and technology—more efficiently without compromising quality. The balance

of efficiency and quality will be critical to future productivity models.

The Role of Technology: AI, Automation, and Big Data

Technology will be at the forefront of this paradigm shift, transforming how care is delivered, measured, and optimized. Emerging technologies will enable healthcare providers to achieve productivity gains that are inconceivable within today's systems. These innovations will redefine healthcare productivity by enhancing precision, speed, and personalization.

1. **Artificial Intelligence (AI)**: AI-powered tools will enhance diagnostic accuracy, support decision-making, and automate routine tasks. From imaging analysis to predictive analytics for patient outcomes, AI will reduce the cognitive burden on physicians, allowing them to focus on complex, high-value tasks. AI will also help with optimizing workflows and scheduling, reducing bottlenecks in care delivery.
2. **Telemedicine and Virtual Care**: The expansion of telemedicine will redefine how productivity is measured. By reducing the need for physical visits, healthcare providers will be able to manage larger patient panels more effectively. In the future, productivity will include how well healthcare systems leverage virtual care models, combining in-person care with remote monitoring and AI-driven consultations.
3. **Automation and Robotics**: Automation in hospitals and clinics will streamline administrative tasks, freeing up healthcare workers to spend more time on direct patient care. Robotic-assisted surgeries, meanwhile, will enhance precision and reduce recovery times, improving overall productivity by minimizing complications and hospital stays.

4. **Big Data and Predictive Analytics**: The use of large datasets will enable healthcare systems to make more informed decisions about resource allocation, patient care strategies, and public health interventions. Predictive analytics will forecast patient needs and optimize workflows, ensuring that healthcare systems can anticipate demand and respond proactively.

Personalization and Preventive Care

Another fundamental shift in healthcare productivity will be the move from reactive to proactive and preventive care. Advances in genomics, wearable health devices, and personalized medicine will allow for highly individualized care plans that prevent illness before it occurs, or detect it early when interventions are most effective.

Key Innovations:

1. **Genomic Medicine**: The future of healthcare productivity will involve personalized treatments based on an individual's genetic makeup. This will allow healthcare providers to target therapies more precisely, improving outcomes while reducing unnecessary treatments.
2. **Wearable Technology and Remote Monitoring**: Wearable devices, from fitness trackers to sophisticated biosensors, will continuously monitor patients' vital signs and other health metrics. This data will feed into healthcare systems in real-time, allowing for early interventions and reducing the need for emergency care. The result will be a system that prioritizes wellness, with productivity measured by the ability to maintain health, not just treat disease.
3. **AI-Assisted Preventive Healthcare**: AI will continuously analyze health data to predict potential issues, allowing providers to engage in preventive care rather than reactive treatments. This will redefine healthcare productivity, as the

system becomes more efficient at keeping people healthy rather than simply treating the sick.

Reimagining the Healthcare Workforce

Healthcare productivity in the future will also require a rethinking of the workforce. Traditional roles and hierarchies will give way to more flexible, interdisciplinary teams supported by technology.

1. **Interdisciplinary Collaboration**: Teams will be made up of physicians, nurses, data scientists, AI specialists, and patient advocates working together. The emphasis will be on collaboration, with each member of the team contributing specialized knowledge to enhance care delivery. This will increase the overall productivity of the healthcare system, as tasks will be distributed based on expertise rather than rigid job descriptions.
2. **AI Augmentation, Not Replacement**: Rather than replacing healthcare workers, AI and robotics will augment their capabilities, allowing them to focus on more complex and creative problem-solving. The most productive systems will be those that effectively blend human expertise with technological support.
3. **Continuous Education and Adaptability**: The healthcare workforce of the future will need to be more adaptable and tech-savvy. Productivity will depend on the ability of workers to continuously learn and incorporate new technologies and practices into their daily routines.

Sustainability and the Future of Healthcare Productivity

As healthcare productivity moves into the future, sustainability will be a key focus. Efficient use of resources—both financial and environmental—will be critical for long-term success. This includes reducing waste, optimizing supply chains, and investing in green technologies to reduce the environmental impact of healthcare.

- **Green Healthcare**: The most productive healthcare systems of the future will not only provide better care but also operate in an environmentally responsible manner. Hospitals will use renewable energy, reduce waste through advanced recycling systems, and design facilities to minimize their carbon footprint.
- **Sustainable Healthcare Systems**: Efficiency will also mean addressing healthcare disparities. Systems that can effectively reduce inequities and provide access to underserved populations will be considered more productive, as they will contribute to overall societal health and economic stability.

Conclusion

The future paradigm of healthcare productivity will be about far more than just increasing throughput. It will involve a holistic view that considers the well-being of patients, the efficiency of resources, the integration of cutting-edge technology, and the sustainability of healthcare systems. Healthcare organizations will need to adapt to this new reality by embracing innovation, prioritizing value over volume, and investing in the workforce of the future. This shift promises to create a more effective, equitable, and sustainable healthcare system for all.

CHAPTER 12

Healthcare Providers Post-COVID-19 Readiness

Humans are born with innate abilities that are vital for their survival. Adaptability is one of the essential ones, as it helps us keep up with the changes around us. In the present times, the most significant changes that humans have been struggling to adapt to are the ones associated with COVID-19. The pandemic has not only brought changes in the way we live but also in our perceptions and approaches.

Since COVID has posed a significant threat to our health and well-being, the healthcare sector's practices and policies have changed. This transformation has taken place at a much faster pace than it had ever been. The direction of the change is apparent, and healthcare's future looks much better than before COVID. Some of the major changes that need to be taken into account are:

a. **From Healthcare to Health.**

A significant change in healthcare due to the pandemic is the shifting of focus. The healthcare industry is now focused on lifestyle, prevention, and early diagnosis from being solely concentrated on treatment. More resources such as time, money, and attention have been allocated from the end of the health chain (treatment and aftercare) to the start. This means that now there is a greater focus on promoting a healthy lifestyle, vitality, and wellness on primary and secondary prevention and early diagnosis instead of treatment and aftercare.

b. Virtual and Patient-centered Healthcare.

The second shift is from a logistical supply-driven model of healthcare at a hospital location to Virtual Healthcare. This means that healthcare is going to become more patient-centered, with a 'digital first' motto. Before COVID, the healthcare system favored the healthcare professional, not the patient. However, due to the pandemic, the focus has shifted on the patient. Their needs are being catered to with diligence. Logistics has been a major component of the patient healthcare journey: they need to make calls, arrange appointments, travel to and from the hospital, and spend time in the waiting room. Now that most appointments and consultations are being made online, logistics has ceased playing its role before. The present system is a more flexible system, where patients are more empowered and have more input. Patients can monitor and regulate far more at home, only visiting the hospital when absolutely necessary.

c. Data-driven and Personalized Health Insights and Interventions.

The third shift is from treatment based on standard protocols to personalized treatment based on data-driven insights and interventions. A new value chain will emerge around health data. Individuals have been experiencing a data explosion through wearables and growing numbers of 'always on' sensors in the home, work, and the medical environment. This data is being used for personalized insights and interventions primarily aimed at vitality, prevention, and early diagnosis. Not just that, this data is also creating a new data value chain that offers exciting opportunities for existing and even new healthcare practices. These value creation opportunities will be in data collection, for example, through sensor technology and the Internet of Things (IoT). Moreover, data analysis (through AI and machine learning), translating analyses to personalized insights and interventions for patients, and accessing these insights through user-friendly visual interface applications are also possible because of this data. However, since these data value creation opportunities are based on combining different datasets, we need to ensure data interchangeability through secure data platforms.

d. Future of Work in Healthcare.

COVID has redefined the future of work in healthcare and has introduced a new 'what, where, and how' for healthcare professionals. Healthcare professionals' roles will change dramatically in terms of the kind of work they do, where they do it, and how they do it. A fundamental change is how healthcare professionals are now supported by robotization, cognitive automation, and AI. Healthcare professionals can now spend considerably less time on data collection and administrative processes, freeing them up for a more personal approach, quality, and safety. They are less likely to be associated with a specific institution but work more from their own homes or a central location. Permanent contracts will be less common, with health professionals working more in networks or district teams, perhaps under their local municipal authority.

e. New Funding and Business Models.

The last shift is an increased focus on promoting population health. Funding will also need to change in this new health ecosystem. Silo budgeting, with separate funds for primary healthcare, hospitals, and healthcare, is not consistent with integrated patient health management. A 'fee for service' payment model has no place in a world of data-driven prevention. The new funding will also produce new business models for traditional and contemporary players in the health ecosystem.

The policies and practices of health administration have also changed due to the pandemic. Most, if not all, departments have revised their policies according to the pandemic protocols and procedures. One of the most significant changes that have occurred is the increase in quality of care. It needs to be noted that during the time of crisis, quality takes on a new definition. This is true in any form of national disaster, but especially true in these unprecedented times of a global pandemic.

Typically, quality conversations center around patients' health outcomes and their safety, their experience, and the processes that care delivery teams implement. Even though these are all essential considerations in evaluating care delivery, they have likely taken a back seat to the consideration of capacity. Now it does not matter if a healthcare provider is able to give patients the highest quality of care to meet their needs and preferences. It is about whether they can see patients in need of care at all.

This does not suggest that poor quality of care is being delivered by any means. It means that at this moment, each person must have access to the care they need. For the last 20 years, the entire U.S. health care system has been orienting care delivery towards patients and their families' needs and preferences. We can only hope that those lessons of compassion, patient-centeredness, and evidence-based practice guide our healthcare providers at this point in history.

That being said, there is cause to be concerned about the long-term effects of this crisis on a keystone workforce in health care – nurses. It is widely known in the health care quality world that nurses are the cornerstone of delivering high-quality health care in hospitals. Before this crisis, there was concern about the impending effects of a longstanding shortage of nurses globally. Prior to COVID, the question was whether we could continue to deliver high-quality care with an increasing nursing shortage due to aging Baby Boomers who would undoubtedly need more medical care as they age. In a shortage, the concern is mainly that nurses are likely to work longer hours and more shifts when short-staffed. The effects of being overworked can have implications for nurses, hospitals, and, ultimately, patients. Nurses can become burned out, leading to leaving either their position or, in many cases, even their profession. But, nursing burnout is not only felt by the nurses. Hospitals have higher turnover levels when nurses are burned out, and nurses who are burned out are more likely to make medical errors that can endanger patients. All of this was already a concern before the coronavirus (COVID-19) pandemic.

Based on reports of the working conditions at the front lines and the high-stress situation that healthcare professionals find themselves in right now, these issues will only be exacerbated in the immediate future. Without an intervention to increase the nursing workforce over the next decade, the healthcare industry will see similar capacity issues that it is witnessing now. This will not happen because there are not enough hospital beds, but because we do not have enough nurses. Hospitals will have to redouble their efforts to recruit and retain high-quality nurses to provide high-quality care for their patients and communities.

Over the last several decades, health care has always been an industry of rapid change and growth, thus requiring its clinical professionals to follow suit. During the COVID-19 pandemic, there has been an immediate demand for our clinical staff to perform work in different nursing areas or slightly different roles. For instance, surgical nurses are reassigned to work in departments treating COVID-19 patients, which requires nursing skills but within different processes and in a different capacity. Furthermore, a nurse or hospital professional may often be reassigned to work a different shift than they have routinely worked.

These hospital staffing adjustments help alleviate the nursing or hospital staffing demand; however, it also leads to an increase in staffing costs due to possible overtime hours and necessary training. The most expensive line item of a health care organization is its personnel costs. While healthcare professionals are ready to meet their patients' demands, their own needs are often neglected. Hospitals can help their employees with the help of peer-to-peer counseling to provide emotional support to their hospital staff due to the increased demands in their schedules. In addition, a food pantry for the staff to meet their physical needs, once they step away from the bedside and refocus their attention on their individual and family needs, can also help take care of the employees. Healthcare organizations meeting their staff's physical and emotional needs helps to reduce their stress levels, thus enabling them to focus while at the bedside.

Treatment plans and the use of insurance have also changed due to the pandemic. On March 12, Vice President Mike Pence announced that insurance companies, including private insurance, Medicare, and Medicaid, will cover the cost of testing for their beneficiaries[1]. Health care providers submit claims to insurance companies for reimbursement for COVID-19 testing, just as they do for other diagnostic testing types. Insurance companies determine the amount of reimbursement for the providers.

The federal government pays for COVID-19 testing as an insurer through reimbursement of claims submitted for Medicare patients. Patients with Medicare Part B do not have to pay out of pocket for a coronavirus test that is ordered by their physician or other health care provider. Individuals with Medicare Advantage plans have the same benefits. The Center for Medicare and Medicaid Services (CMS) also has a web page dedicated to keeping Medicare recipients informed on Coronavirus.

Individuals without health insurance have faced significantly more challenges in the face of COVID-19. The Emergency Medicine Treatment and Labor Act (EMTALA) requires hospitals to screen and stabilize patients with emergent conditions. However, it does not require hospitals to provide care at no cost for patients who cannot pay. They are not required to provide treatment for non-emergent conditions. The Families First Coronavirus Response Act (FFCRA), signed into law on March 18, 2020, stated the option to expand Medicaid coverage to uninsured individuals to provide coverage for COVID-19 diagnosis and testing with 100% federal financing. The coverage is limited to testing services free of charge to the individual. The legislation does not address coverage for COVID-19 treatment costs for uninsured people. Alabama is one of the states that has not yet expanded Medicaid coverage. It is unknown whether the state will take advantage of this new opportunity to provide coverage for COVID-19 testing for uninsured individuals. House Bill 447, introduced on March 12, 2020, seeks to expand Medicaid and is currently pending review by the House Ways and Means General Fund Committee[2].

The COVID-19 pandemic has also raised a host of ethical challenges. However, the key among these has been the possibility that health care systems might need to ration scarce critical care resources. Rationing policies for pandemics differ by institution, health system, and applicable law. Most people agree that a patient's ability to benefit from treatment and survive are first-order considerations. However, there is debate about what clinical measures should be used to make that determination and about other factors that might be ethically appropriate to consider.

The lack of measures presents real ethical challenges that arise when health systems reach the end of their capacity to handle patients' influx during a pandemic. As COVID-19 has spread globally, bioethicists have been working with physicians and other health professionals to create or revise policies, engage in clinical consultation, and help develop appropriate criteria for allocation decisions[3].

The transaction volume in the healthcare industry has reached all-time highs in recent years. However, the sudden and unanticipated cash flow and operational disruptions resulting from the COVID-19 pandemic have slowed most M&A and other transactional efforts for both strategic and financial investors. Parties have struggled to agree on valuation adjustments for the pandemic impact, and sellers have been reticent to bring new platforms to market.

Nevertheless, robust investor appetite still persists, particularly among private equity funds sitting on considerable dry powder for new investment even before the pandemic. Credit markets also remain favorable for leveraged buy-outs. Current monetary policies are promising low-interest rates for debt financing in the near term. Already investors are exploring ways to beat the curve by underwriting some uncertainty in their valuation assumptions and correspondingly exploring options to hedge that risk. However, smart investors are not merely assuming a "return to normal" but are somewhat willing to evaluate and explore what "new normal" will emerge for the target business.

The pandemic has exposed gaps in the process of healthcare delivery and opened new opportunities that can be addressed when participants across health, life sciences technology, and other subsectors join forces. Many investors are already exploring business combinations, joint ventures, and other innovative transactions to capitalize on these opportunities and address the new set of challenges facing providers and patients to deliver and receive care safely and effectively[4].

It is guaranteed that life after COVID will not be the same, and the new normal may just become a long-term change. This means that both healthcare providers and patients need to be ready for the change for their health and that of others. Healthcare workers' readiness will help make sure that the organization is achieving its goals and is not lagging behind, especially when it comes to the use of technologies and practices to make healthcare delivery smoother and safer. In addition, it will also make sure that the healthcare industry keeps up with the changes that occur post-COVID.

Pandemic has affected healthcare leadership and management, and these challenges have made healthcare managerial frameworks and practices more competitive and resilient. Post pandemic trends in healthcare management are shifted more towards the improvement of quality of medical services and enhancing the patient-centered care approach[5].

Since COVID has posed a significant threat to our health and well-being, the healthcare sector's practices and policies have changed. This transformation has taken place at a much faster pace than it had ever been. The pandemic has exposed gaps in the process of healthcare delivery and opened new opportunities that can be addressed when participants across health, life sciences technology, and other subsectors join forces. Many investors are already exploring business combinations, joint ventures, and other innovative transactions to capitalize on these opportunities and address the new set of challenges facing providers and patients to deliver and receive care safely and effectively.

Shrinking Primary care provider (Can PA and NP do the job/)

CHAPTER 13

Healthcare Organizational Leadership Post-COVID-19

For the first time in history, the entire global economy was shut down because of a health crisis. In March 2020, the global outbreak of SARS-CoV-2 (severe acute respiratory syndrome coronavirus-2) infection was declared a global pandemic, and the entire world was immediately under lockdown (World Health Organization, 2020). With the help of simulations of outbreak responses, it was predicted that, without an intervention, 7 billion infections and 40 million deaths from COVID-19 would occur worldwide this year[1].

The pandemic painfully demonstrated that healthcare is a vital part of our life and hence inseparable from other aspects. It severely affected most countries worldwide and drove their healthcare system to the point of exhaustion. However, amid the chaos and the rising human toll, healthcare services have been continually undergoing decentralization and fragmentation in many severely affected countries. It has also exposed the global healthcare system's vulnerabilities in both developed and underdeveloped countries. An avalanche of cases has overburdened healthcare structures due to long-neglections and underfunding of public health sectors and unorganized policies, practices, and leadership. So much so that experts fear that if its spread is not curtailed by taking bold steps and consistent management choices, the virus may cause an unprecedented human catastrophe.

Before the pandemic, our healthcare systems across the globe were not designed to deal with a crisis like such. This unpredictable, large-scale health challenge required an urgent mobilization of resources and changes in practices. In many ways, the COVID pandemic is wholly opposed to the direction that healthcare systems, particularly in developed countries, have been taking over the past years. Nevertheless, there is no doubt that this change was for the better, and healthcare systems are now more efficient than before.

Healthcare systems are composed of numerous professional groups, departments, and specialties with intricate and nonlinear interactions. Such systems' complexity is often unparalleled due to constraints relating to different disease areas, multidirectional goals, and multidisciplinary staff. Within large organizations such as healthcare systems, the numerous groups with associated subcultures might support or conflict with each other. To capitalize on the organization's diversity as a whole and efficiently utilize resources when designing management processes, efficient leadership is direly needed. At the same time, it is also necessary to encourage personnel to work towards common goals. Since no leader is the same, multiple leadership approaches can be adapted to the healthcare setting to optimize management in this highly complex environment.

A clinician's challenges when leading within the complex setting of modern healthcare services include diverse and changing needs, increasing patient expectations, and the high cost of new interventions and treatments. This requires clinicians to consider the needs of the wider patient population, to make decisions that make the best use of resources, deliver clinical quality, and implement clinically-led service improvements that are likely to succeed. A result-oriented leadership style best meets these challenges.

The functional results-oriented leadership style focuses on an organization's process implying leadership as having the specific role and skills necessary to deliver the group's desired results based on and meeting the needs of three areas, namely, individuals, teams, and tasks.

It emphasizes on establishing the leadership role that facilitates effective and efficient healthcare provision.

Leadership in uncertain times requires adaptability. A typical example is the temporary destabilization of doctors' professional security when the staff is redeployed to unfamiliar clinical specialties. Furthermore, trainees have also witnessed an abrupt suspension of training opportunities, including canceled clinical rotations and exams. However, practices encouraging sharing and flexibility in roles will likely lead to a deeper appreciation for adaptive teamwork and mutual encouragement. Formal training is replaced by novel experiential learning, providing proficiency in managing emerging complexity and adapting to unorthodox service delivery.

Leadership in decision-making has also faced a new challenge. With changing national guidance on anticipated healthcare demands, many non-essential processes have been postponed and phased responses to what procedures and on which patients have been implemented. On a scale not encountered before, clinicians undertake difficult conversations about escalated care's suitability, as those most affected by and vulnerable to COVID-19 are often elderly and have comorbidities.

In recent months, healthcare experts have been in the news more often than usual due to the global pandemic, COVID-19. Nurses and doctors have been asked to meet higher than usual demands to help with the growing number of patients who have fallen victim to the coronavirus pandemic. With the growing need to properly support our frontline workers during this global crisis, one element to consider is our healthcare leaders' capability to handle such a shift.

Based on a Huron Consulting Group study, 21% of healthcare leaders stated that their organization lacks a specific leadership strategy. Furthermore, 67% of respondents viewed innovation as more than new technology. Successful healthcare leaders need clinical skills, business competencies, and interpersonal or soft skills to guide their organizations to success. The essential components of a healthcare organization's leadership are:

1. Empathy

To explain what empathy is, it is necessary first to know the difference between empathy and sympathy. Sympathy is showing shared feelings of pity or compassion for another person. On the other hand, empathy is the ability to put yourself in someone's shoes and walk alongside them during times of sorrow. It's not to say that sympathy isn't a valuable trait, but empathy is a useful tool in helping others feel genuinely understood and appreciated.

For healthcare leaders who want to connect with their employees, empathy is necessary to be practiced on many levels. Healthcare leaders should practice empathy on an individual level, and they should also encourage others within their organizations to do so. Some ways to practice empathy are:

- Modeling the desired behaviors in front of your teams and encouraging others to do so.
- Preaching values with both words and actions by taking a detailed look at common roadblocks or stressors and offering guidance or support helps employees overcome obstacles.
- Create 'comfort zones' for emerging Gen Z or other generations who may feel under-represented in a new work environment.

2. Communication

There are many ways we all communicate with coworkers or supervisors. Whether it's an email, a video chat, or texting, it is best to choose your circumstances' right delivery method. By choosing an appropriate way to communicate, a leader exhibits a willingness to solve problems expeditiously and appropriately. It also shows one's ability to empathize with another. While the conversation may not be a positive one, it's necessary to work through issues and come to a mutual place of understanding. A leader's overall goal is to act as a coach, mentor, and problem solver—all of which require excellent communication skills.

3. Strategic Decision-Making

A successful leader should be able to handle making various decisions daily. Many of these decisions could impact their employees. For instance, solving any employee problems within their teams without escalating the issue demonstrates a leader's ability to be a strategic decision-maker. This is an incredibly important skill for healthcare leaders to have as they navigate a high-consequence industry[2].

Being a strategic decision-maker requires weighing potential outcomes on the workforce while still balancing the organizations' needs. Individuals who hold these positions must be ready to gather and analyze statistical data, information from others in the organization, and even third-party consultants. Each of us makes choices throughout our day, but making a strategic decision requires forethought and excellent communication skills.

4. Self-Awareness

Self-awareness is touted as one of the capabilities most necessary for outstanding leadership. It can either mean success or failure for healthcare leaders. In addition to being fast-based and demanding daily, healthcare is also a constantly and rapidly evolving industry. This is why healthcare leaders must be sufficiently agile enough to quickly grasp and devise strategies to manage change or solve problems. Moreover, by being aware of their strengths and weaknesses, leaders can also identify gaps in their abilities and compensate by leveraging new tools or processes.

Furthermore, being self-aware can also mean leaders are better equipped to develop future successors. By identifying similar strengths in an employee they are considering for a promotion, the self-aware leader can seek out those who have the capabilities necessary yet lack themselves. Finally, healthcare leaders should be open to continuous learning programs for themselves and their employees.

5. Customer-First Oriented

Healthcare is a fast-paced, high-risk industry. Every decision healthcare practitioner make at work affects the patient's well-being and, potentially, their life. A good leader can navigate a stressful environment without creating additional stress by reacting impulsively. Leaders who take a customer-first approach should also encourage employees to do the same and share ideas, information, reactions, and perspectives—while actively listening. This investment signals respect and open-mindedness, and a commitment to continuous growth. It engages employees in their work, their teams, and the organization as a whole[3].

Most importantly, it demonstrates that leaders value employee contributions and input on strategies. By sustaining employee engagement over time, great leaders elevate their organizations, lower turnover, and improve patient experience, quality of care, and health outcomes. Adopting this 'outside-in' viewpoint means healthcare leaders should design solutions to meet customers on their terms.

Today, healthcare organizations are subject to rapid and fundamental changes to enhance service quality, patient satisfaction, and productivity. With these changes, healthcare professionals also face a heavy workload, increased patient awareness, various problems related to staff skills, lack of resources, low occupational and life quality, and workplace violence. However, there is the expectation that healthcare professionals should ethically treat patients and put ethics first in their professional performance. Across the world, healthcare professionals are guided to use professional codes that emphasize their obligation to respect, protect, and defend the fundamental rights of the people involved in nursing and health care.

One of the most powerful methods to promote ethics in health care is to role model ethical performance on the managerial level. Individuals in formal leadership positions should promote ethics, which means they should implement ethical leadership, an approach that has attracted much attention in recent years. This leadership style involves developing appropriate normal behavior through personal actions and interpersonal interactions and promoting such behaviors in subordinates through bilateral exchanges and strengthening of decision-making. Ethical leaders must also strive to model and support ethical performance and, at the same time, be sensitive to moral issues and enhance performance by fostering respect for human dignity, thereby playing an essential role in promoting patient safety, increasing the capacity to discuss and act upon ethics in daily activities, and supporting the ethical competence of healthcare professionals.

Some studies in this field have indicated that ethical leadership leads to reduced work leave and increased job satisfaction in nurses through decreasing moral distress and creating an ethical milieu. Furthermore, this leadership style also boosts confidence in the leader, organizational commitment, and psychological empowerment. It exerts considerable effects on the staff's creativity and energetic feeling. Disappointment and lack of confidence, commitment, and motivation are among the side effects of leaders' unethical behavior that negatively influence both patients and organizational efficacy. Some studies have also demonstrated that the leaders' supportive behavior and confidence in management are essential for stabilizing nursing values. These behaviors include empowering nurses to express their concerns and worries and providing recommendations for improving their work environment and nursing care.

Many healthcare managers are working to utilize social media to engage patients and consumers effectively. Through effective marketing and communication tactics, organizations can move away from traditional advertising techniques and use the internet to connect with consumers in the healthcare field. Consumers heavily rely on information found online and use the internet to gather healthcare information and connect with other patients to garner support and learn about similar conditions. Others utilize these resources for research or to share experiences with healthcare providers and other related organizations. Patients also tend to seek information via social media to select doctors, specialists, and hospitals to make informed decisions on the best practices to seek care. Individuals also use social media to post reviews or other comments that support or possibly deter others from choosing that type of healthcare in the future. Providers need to be active on social media and provide accurate information, connect with readers, and implement marketing techniques where applicable. Here are a few reasons why healthcare professionals use social media:

1. Share Information

Social media is intended to provide individuals the ability to access information quickly and communicate with others. Healthcare organizations utilize these tools and websites to share information with consumers in various ways, such as sharing general information about flu shots and tips to avoid a cold. Sharing news regarding outbreaks or health hazards is an effective way for healthcare facilities to provide accurate information to patients. However, it is important to note that all patient-specific information requires permission, along with a signed release. Other forms of sharing information through social media include:

- Provide updates on new technologies
- Introduce new doctors in practice on social networks
- Answer questions on various topics (e.g., how to reach doctors or hours of operation)
- Deliver generic pre-operative and post-operative care information
- Offer patients any updates that relate to the practice itself

2. Compare and Improve Quality

Another effective way healthcare managers utilize social media is by evaluating their competitors to get an insight into the services they offer and overall patient satisfaction. By looking into different practices and their social media involvement, professionals can mimic them to enhance their own. Some organizations will do better through social media; providers can quickly determine whether they need to take more appropriate action to respond to patient requests and improve customer service.

To gather feedback and improve quality, social media interaction can provide doctors and physicians with immediate responses from individuals to understand common reactions to medications and overall consensus from patients on new techniques in the industry. Using this information that is readily available on social media allows healthcare organizations to learn from patient reactions and adjust accordingly. By the following feedback on these sites, healthcare professionals also have the opportunity to evaluate the possibility of additional services in the industry.

3. Train Medical Personnel

Some healthcare organizations have begun to utilize social media channels as part of their training process. During presentations, trainees are encouraged to use specific hashtags on Twitter, Instagram, and Facebook or join other groups to engage one another to make training processes more enjoyable and interactive. These training techniques provide trainees a central location to ask questions and quickly receive answers. Social media gives participants the power to provide the presenters with immediate feedback on training sessions.

Trainees are not the only people who benefit from this social media technique. Organizations can use training videos and pictures from training sessions to engage audiences and enhance their social media channels by marketing their facilities and exemplifying their innovative training processes.

4. Live Updates During Procedures

Although somewhat controversial, there has been an increase in doctors and surgeons providing updates from the operating room. Through Twitter and other social media outlets, healthcare professionals can deliver up-to-date information during procedures to fellow doctors, medical students, or simply curious individuals. Some say these updates are a distraction in the operating room, while others argue that it is an innovation and provides educational value that should be embraced.

The use of social media during operations also provides healthcare facilities the ability to gain attention from industry-specific outlets and mainstream media. As a marketing approach, organizations create a buzz on social media with these updates, creating excitement and enhancing public awareness of an individual organization to attract patients and medical personnel.

5. Communicate in Times of Crisis

In times of crisis, the use of social media has increased to provide minute-by-minute information to consumers. Through social media, hospitals and other organizations can deliver real-time updates on hospital capacity, operation status, and emergency room access. Having an active social media presence allows healthcare professionals to pass along information shared by organizations such as the Red Cross and the Centers for Disease Control or communicate with news outlets[4].

As social media continues to become a valuable asset to healthcare organizations and new methods of use are implemented, the industry requires administrators to set guidelines and procedures for effectively managing these channels. To provide the best customer service and accurate information while adhering to HIPAA regulations, organizations need individuals versed in healthcare administration. For those interested in pursuing an online Master of Health Administration, The University of Scranton provides the most effective tools and resources to advance a healthcare career[5].

In a crisis-stricken world gripped by challenges, it is really hard for healthcare professionals to keep up with the changing practices and policies and the increasing burden of work. These changes may disrupt the workplace and also bring about ethical issues. All healthcare organizations need an efficient leader to make sure that healthcare professionals can do their job without worrying about the direction they are headed in. Moreover, an efficient leader's presence also ensures that the performance standards are being met and all the while helping professionals attain their personal goals.

COVID-19 has affected the future of healthcare leadership, which can be seen from the impact on frontline healthcare workers. Healthcare leaders and frontline employees are challenged with an ongoing lack of staff and supplies while efficiently trying to manage the tremendous surge in patient volumes for months. Many frontline workers have been asked to work in roles and departments that have been previously unfamiliar to them. Due to this pandemic, healthcare leaders have learned how to cope with emergency conditions that require constant work in the setting. A great shift has been observed in the organizational thinking that begins with executive leadership and governing body. This shift has also managed to develop and implement policies that align across the organizations, and sustain agreement at all leadership levels and avoid unacceptable medical errors. Leaders in future might be aware of ensuring that it is easy for the frontline what to do. They are aware of the importance of equipping the managers in order to effectively facilitate change by understanding and applying principles based on human factors. Post pandemic conditions have strengthened the competencies of healthcare leaders that will direct their future practices[6].

Before the pandemic, our healthcare systems across the globe were not designed to deal with a crisis like such. This unpredictable, large-scale health challenge required an urgent mobilization of resources and changes in practices. In many ways, the COVID pandemic is wholly opposed to the direction that healthcare systems, particularly in developed countries, have been taking over the past years[7]. Nevertheless, there is no doubt that this change was for the better, and healthcare systems are now more efficient than before.

Politics and Policies of HMOs

CHAPTER 14

Natural Disasters, Pandemics, and Public Health Administration

The United States primarily has a third-party payer system of healthcare. This means that a health insurance plan or a third party reimburses doctors for the bulk of the cost of healthcare services provided to patients. The nation used a mixed system of public and private insurance. The two major public programs are Medicaid, which helps low-income people and individuals with disabilities, and Medicare that helps people 65 or older or younger people with specific disabilities or kidney disease. Around 48 percent of Americans are enrolled in private health insurance through their employers[1]. The remainder of insured people either purchase private insurance through the individual market or receive insurance through a different publicly-funded program, like the military's TRICARE.

In 2010, President Barack Obama signed the Affordable Care Act into law. The law aimed to expand health insurance coverage to all Americans and to curb healthcare spending and costs. The reforms primarily affect the insurance industry and have been implemented incrementally beginning in the year of the law's passage in 2010.

Proponents of the reforms have said they will lower costs and improve access to healthcare, while opponents have said the legislation will increase costs and decrease the quality of healthcare delivery. The law has faced a number of legal challenges, and a July 2015 poll by the Kaiser Family Foundation showed 78 percent of Americans believe the law will continue to be challenged in the future[2]. Due to the complexity and size of the healthcare industry, which accounts for one-sixth of all spending in the nation, and the political disputes surrounding the law, the effects of its reforms are uncertain and will be watched closely over the next several years.

A number of routes could be taken that could impact federal healthcare policy. Primarily, healthcare laws can be changed by the legislative process, through which Congress passes a law and the president signs it. In this way, the federal government can alter some of the Affordable Care Act provisions or repeal them entirely. Healthcare policy could be changed through the regulatory process, whereby federal agencies write rules for how laws are implemented. Moreover, healthcare could also be impacted by administrative action. For example, the Republican Administration may be more likely to approve state proposals to expand Medicaid using an alternative method that the Obama administration had rejected. Finally, healthcare could be impacted by the court system via lawsuits. For instance, the federal government could withdraw its appeal in House v. Burwell, which would end reimbursements to insurers for reducing costs for low-income consumers.

Beginning in the mid-20th century, the federal government took an increasing role in regulating the healthcare industry. In that time, the National Institutes of Health and the Centers for Disease Control, the Food and Drug Administration, and the Department of Health and Human Services were established. Toward the end of expanding insurance coverage and controlling costs, the federal government also enacted a number of pieces of legislation during the second half of the century:

- Lyndon Johnson signing the Medicare bill, July 30, 1965
- Social Security Amendments of 1965, which established Medicare and Medicaid

- Health Maintenance Organization Act of 1973, which promoted prepaid group practice service plans known as health maintenance organizations (HMOs) as an alternative to fee-for-service plans
- Consolidated Omnibus Budget Reconciliation Act of 1985, which allowed employees to continue healthcare coverage if they would otherwise lose it (due to job loss, medical leave, etc.)
- Health Insurance Portability and Accountability Act of 1996, which limited the extent to which insurance companies could exclude people with preexisting conditions
- Patient Protection and Affordable Care Act of 2010, known as Obamacare, which established health insurance exchanges and required all citizens to obtain health insurance

Though there have been steady calls for a national health insurance program since the early 1900s, no such measure has been adopted in the United States. The United States Public Health Service includes:

1. Centers for Disease Control
2. National Institutes of Health
3. Food and Drug Administration
4. Health Resources and Services Administration
5. Alcohol, Drug Abuse, and Mental Health Administration
6. Agency for Toxic Substances and Disease Registry.

Additionally, several offices relating directly to the Assistant Secretary for Health deal with public health issues, such as the Office of Health Promotion and Disease Prevention and the Office of Planning and Evaluation. These offices are concerned with management, health policy, research, statistics; planning and evaluation; intergovernmental affairs; health promotion; and other special concerns.

The Centers for Disease Control is the main assessment and epidemiologic unit for the nation. It directly serves the population and provides technical assistance to states and localities. The National Center for Health Statistics within the Centers for Disease Control is the main authority for collecting, analyzing, and disseminating health data. The Agency for Toxic Substances and Disease Registry, also an assessment unit, focuses on environmentally related diseases. The National Institutes of Health, the government's primary research arm, both conduct research and support research projects across the nation. The Food and Drug Administration directly tests and assesses the safety of food, drugs, and a wide variety of consumer goods and sets standards for the safe use of these items. The Health Resources and Services Administration is primarily concerned with resource development and the health workforce. The Alcohol, Drug Abuse, and Mental Health Administration concentrate on developing programs and setting standards in these areas. Both the Health Resources and Services Administration and the Alcohol, Drug Abuse, and Mental Health Administration establish and support health services through grants and contracts to state and local government agencies, private health care institutions, and individuals. They also act as coordinators and technical assistants to recipients of contracts and grants. Sometimes these agencies provide services, such as the Indian Health Service in the Health Resources and Services Administration. The government provides health care services to Native Americans and Eskimos.

The other major division of the Department of Health and Human Services concerned with public health activities is the Health Care Financing Administration, which operates the Medicare and Medicaid programs. The federal government directly finances health services for elderly Americans through the Medicare program and provides grants to the states through the Medicaid program to assist them in financing health services for poor Americans. A large portion of Medicaid money also goes to finance long-term care for the elderly.

Other operating divisions of the Department of Health and Human Services are primarily oriented toward human and social services. These offices, although not designated specifically for health, conduct many health-related activities. For example, the Office of Human Development Services houses the Administration on Aging and the Administration on Developmental Disabilities, both of which are involved in long-term health care issues.

On the Business Side of Healthcare

The Department of Health and Human Services also operates regional offices in Boston, New York, Philadelphia, Atlanta, Chicago, Dallas, Kansas City, Denver, San Francisco, and Seattle. These offices are involved in program development and provide technical assistance to states and local areas within their region. They also oversee programs contracted from the federal government to the states.

Numerous activities occur throughout the Public Health Service and the Health Care Financing Administration branches, as well as in related government agencies. For instance, even though assessment is a significant responsibility of the Centers for Disease Control and the National Center for Health Statistics, it also takes place in the Health Resources Administration, which collects data on health manpower; the Food and Drug Administration, which inspects foods, drugs, and other products; the Office of Disease Prevention and Health Promotion, which collects statistics on prevention activities and the population's health status; the National Institute of Mental Health, which collects data on inpatient and outpatient mental health services; and the Health Care Financing Administration, which collects information on the use of health services.

Biological research is mainly the National Institutes of Health's task, and epidemiologic research is primarily the Centers for Disease Control's task. Whereas the National Center for Health Services Research, under the Office of the Assistant Secretary for Health, is the main authority for policy and health services research. But policy research and health services research can be sponsored by any of the many offices. The Health Care Financing Administration has an office of research and development. Policy-setting and providing technical assistance take place in nearly all federally conducted programs.

Financing personal and public health services are mainly the task of the Health Care Financing Administration's Medicare and Medicaid offices; however, grants for specific services are administered throughout the Department of Health and Human Services. The federal government directly delivers personal health services under the Health Resources and Services Administration's auspices in the Indian

Health Service and the Veteran's Administration, and the Department of Defense in military clinics and hospitals.

Overall, federal activities fall into two major categories: those that are conducted directly by the federal government—assessment, policy-making, resources development, knowledge transfer, financing, and some delivery of personal health care—and those that are contracted by the federal government to states, localities, and private organizations—the majority of direct service programs.

The federal government's health business's significant portion is conducted through contracts and grants to states, localities, and private providers and organizations. The federal government acts through financing intergovernmental and inter-organizational contracts to encourage various public health initiatives, convening participants around an issue, coordinating activities, and developing state and local provider contracts. In return for federal funds, states, localities, and private organizations must follow the federal standards and policies set in the agreement. Thus in many programs, the federal government takes an oversight, policy-setting, and technical assistance role rather than a direct provider role. Federal contracts can take the form of seed money for researching and development of new programs, such as Community Mental Health Centers, or support for ongoing activities, such as the Early Periodic Screening, Detection, and Treatment Program. Contracts can be made with agencies to operate specific public health programs or to support general agency activities. Contracts can also be made with health care providers, such as nursing homes or home health agencies, for directly delivering personal health services. Contracts with local areas and providers may be operated through the states or made directly with the local and private sectors.

Most contracts to states and localities were initially offered as "categorical" grants, focusing on particular health issues or populations. For instance, research training grants for education, nutrition information programs, substance abuse, mental health programs, and family planning programs. In the early 1980s, the federal Administration grouped numerous categorical grants to states into four major "block" grants: preventive health, maternal and child health, primary care, and alcohol, drug abuse, and mental health. However, a number of categorical aid programs remain, both as grants to states, localities, and private providers.

The Federal Emergency Management Agency (FEMA) is responsible for coordinating the federal government's response to natural and manmade disasters. FEMA is charged with providing immediate and long-term assistance to local and state governments and individuals. Throughout its almost 30-year history, FEMA has been synonymous with the word "disaster" because of its mission to assist in crisis times. Due to its long record of mistakes and, in some cases, failures that have exacerbated suffering caused by storms, fires, or earthquakes.

The federal government has provided disaster relief in one form or another since the early 19th century. The Congressional Act of 1803 is considered the first piece of disaster legislation in U.S. history, providing assistance to a New Hampshire town following an extensive fire. Over the next century, ad hoc legislation was passed more than 100 times in response to hurricanes, earthquakes, floods, and other natural disasters. Laws unique to each disaster authorized financial assistance to victims and both personnel and equipment to assist in recovery and clean up.

FEMA has played an important role during the current pandemic of COVID 19. President Trump has placed FEMA in charge of coordinating the federal response to the outbreak. While U.S. health authorities remain in the lead on the medical front of dealing with the virus, FEMA has been tasked with handling almost everything else. Pandemics are large-scale outbreaks of infectious diseases that can significantly increase morbidity and mortality over a wide geographic area[3]. They can cause significant economic, social, and political disruption. Evidence suggests that the likelihood of pandemics being needed during certain events has increased over the past century due to an increase in global travel and integration, urbanization, changes in land use, and greater exploitation of the natural environment. These trends will likely continue and intensify. Significant policy attention has focused on identifying and limiting emerging outbreaks that might lead to pandemics and expand and sustain investment to build preparedness and health capacity. Preparedness can be ensured by providing individuals with necessities that they might need during the pandemic. This may include:

Before a Pandemic

- Store additional supplies of food and water.
- Periodically check your regular prescription drugs to ensure a continuous supply in your home.
- Have any nonprescription drugs and other health supplies on hand, including pain relievers, stomach remedies, cough, and cold medicines, fluids with electrolytes, and vitamins.
- Get copies and maintain electronic versions of health records from doctors, hospitals, pharmacies, and other sources and store them for personal reference. Get help accessing electronic health records.
- Talk with family members and loved ones about how they would be cared for if they got sick or what will be needed to care for them in your home.

During a Pandemic

- Limit the spread of germs and prevent infection
- Americans can continue to use and drink tap water as usual during the COVID-19 pandemic. Please be sure to follow public health guidance as the situation develops.
- Avoid close contact with people who are sick.
- When you are sick, keep your distance from others to protect them from getting sick too.
- Cover your mouth and nose with a tissue when coughing or sneezing. It may prevent those around you from getting sick.
- Washing your hands often will help protect you from germs.
- Avoid touching your eyes, nose, or mouth.
- Practice other good health habits. Get plenty of sleep, be physically active, manage your stress, drink plenty of fluids, and eat nutritious food.

Health capacity can be ensured with the help of prophylactic measures, which are measures designed to prevent the occurrence of an adverse event, disease, or its dissemination. This includes standard protocols, procedures, or actions such as compression stockings during surgery to prevent post-operative blood clots. Prophylaxis is a good thing in health care. It prevents an unintended problem by addressing the potential issue before it actually becomes problematic. The prevention of harm or disease is often far more manageable, faster, less expensive, and less painful than treating the disease when it is allowed to occur[4].

Preventative care takes many forms and continues even after a disease process has been identified. Prophylaxis doesn't just mean preventing disease. It can also prevent a worsening of the disease, minimize disease severity, and prevent over-treatment. The types of prophylactic measures are:

a. **Primary Prophylaxis**

Preventing or increasing resistance to disease that has not occurred. This may include routine medical checkups and vaccinations. Pap smears, screening colonoscopies, and mammograms are often done as primary Prophylaxis when the patient is well, and there are no signs of disease. Once a disease is known to be present, screening is no longer considered primary Prophylaxis.

b. **Secondary Prophylaxis**

Measures that are taken to prevent the recurrence of a medical problem or injury that has already occurred. This includes changing the work environment to prevent re-injury or taking a statin to prevent recurrent heart attacks.

c. **Tertiary Prophylaxis**

Measures that are taken to reduce the impact of a chronic, ongoing disease or injury that is likely to produce long-lasting effects, such

d. Quaternary Prophylaxis

Quaternary Prophylaxis is the idea that excessive medical treatment should be prevented. Patients who will not benefit from further medical treatment should not be subjected to it. For example, suppose a patient does not respond to the first round of chemotherapy. In that case, there is no logical reason to do a second round of chemotherapy with the same medication.

Despite these measures, not everyone has access to healthcare in the U.S. It has been observed that the rural population is consistently less well-off than the urban population concerning health. However, the differences between the two populations are not always substantial. The rural population is more likely to engage in risky health-related behaviors and experience higher rates of chronic conditions and activity limitations. Rural residents are also more likely to be uninsured for longer periods of time. They are also less likely than urban residents to receive health care, including tests for various chronic conditions. Limited access to health care in rural areas is generally associated with the fact that there are fewer providers.

One-third of adults in rural areas, compared to less than one-quarter of adults in urban areas, report that they are limited in performing major activities such as paid work, housework, or school. Among people aging 18 and older, larger proportions of rural residents than urban residents also report limitations related to social, recreational, or family activities. Adults in rural areas are also more likely to report physical limitations. Approximately 14 percent compared to 9 percent in urban areas say that they have a physical limitation. This includes difficulty walking ten steps, three blocks, or 1 mile, lifting 10 pounds, standing for 20 minutes, bending or stooping, reaching over their head, or using their fingers to grasp[5]. Among the population under age 65, some 19 percent of rural residents and 16 percent of urban residents are uninsured[6]. Rural residents tend to stay uninsured for longer periods of time than urban residents.

Factors that may contribute to this disparity include the higher percentage of self-employed persons, small businesses, and agricultural enterprises in rural areas. Over one-third of rural residents, compared to about one-quarter of urban residents, have been uninsured for more than three years. A larger proportion of urban residents have never been insured.

Less than 11 percent of physicians in the U.S. practice in rural areas, yet about 20 percent reside in rural areas. Provider recruitment and retention problems in rural areas are related to several factors, including lower salaries, geographic isolation from peers and educational opportunities, and fewer amenities such as schools and recreation. The Department of Health and Human Services recommends a provider-to-patient ratio of one primary care physician to every 2,000 individuals. Over 20 million rural Americans live in areas with a provider-to-patient ratio of 1 to 3,500 or more. They are federally designated as health professional shortage areas (HPSAs). More than 2,200 physicians are needed to remove the HPSA designation from all rural areas. Yet, more than twice that number is needed to achieve the recommended ratio of 1 to 2,000 in these areas[7]. The shortage of mental health professionals in rural areas is even more severe. More than three-quarters of the counties designated as federal mental HPSAs are rural.

Even though weather forecasters can predict a natural disaster's arrival, one can never be prepared for its intensity. This means that the healthcare sector always needs to be prepared for the worst-case scenario and jump right into action in case of an emergency. Many agencies have been set up by the federal government to help the citizens residing in both rural and urban areas in times of need[8]. However, this does not mean that citizens should not take preventive measures. In fact, each individual must keep up with what is happening around them, be aware of what needs to be done, and be approached for help in crisis times.

Climate Smart Public Health Policies
Climate Smart Healthcare Leadership

CHAPTER 15

Environment, Sustainability, and Healthcare Management

Earth's surface has undergone unprecedented warming over the last century, and especially in this century. Every single year since 1977 has been warmer than the 20th century average, with 16 of the 17 warmest years on record occurring since 2001 and 2016 being the warmest year recorded in history. A study from 2016 found that there is very little likelihood that 13 out of the 15 warmest years on record would all have happened without the emissions from burning coal and oil[1].

The health of our bodies depends significantly on the environment we live in. This includes the air we breathe, the food we eat, and most importantly, the changes in the environment. Even though the human body is designed to regulate its internal temperature according to the external temperature, the drastic changes in the present world's environment are posing a great threat to human health.

However, the root of this threat lies in the actions of humankind itself. It is only because of the harmful actions of humans that the climate of the world is rapidly changing, thereby bringing about a detrimental impact on the health and overall lives of all living things.

These actions include heat-trapping emissions from burning coal, gas, and oil in power plants and cars; cutting down and burning forests; tiny pollution particles (aerosols); black carbon pollution, more commonly referred to as soot; and changes in land use that also affects the Earth's albedo.

The science on the human contribution to present-day global warming is quite clear. Human emissions and activities have caused around 100% of the warming observed since 1950, according to the Intergovernmental Panel on Climate Change's (IPCC) fifth assessment report in 2013[2]. The report also stated that it is extremely likely that more than half of the observed increase in global average surface temperature from 1951 to 2010 was caused by human activity. By 'extremely likely,' it meant that there was between a 95% and 100% probability that more than half of modern warming was due to humans. Similarly, the US fourth national climate assessment found that between 93% to 123% of observed 1951-2010, warming was due to human activities[3]. Furthermore, a 2016 study also found that almost two-thirds of the impacts related to atmospheric and ocean temperature can be confidently attributed to anthropogenic forces or human-caused drivers[4].

This means humans themselves have put their health at risk. A risk that is not only adversely impacting the overall quality of life but is also causing premature aging and age-related health issues associated with the same. The health effects of climatic disruptions include increased respiratory and cardiovascular disease, injuries and premature deaths related to extreme weather events, changes in the prevalence and geographical distribution of food- and water-borne illnesses and other infectious diseases, and threats to mental health. The chart presented below in figure 15.1 demonstrates the diverse impacts of climate change resulting in a rise in temperature, increasing CO_2 levels, rising sea level, and more extreme weather on environmental and human health. Moreover, the chart also demonstrates the implications of climate change on demographic transformations.

Figure 15.1: Impacts of Climate Change

Figure 15.1 indicates the impacts of climate change on the environment and public health. Human health is strongly linked with environmental or climatic changes and is affected by climate modulations. Increasing CO_2 level has led to environmental degradation and impacts on water and food supply. These changes have caused forced migration, mental and physical health impacts. Rising temperature has led to several mental and physical health severities due to severe weather and extreme heat. Moreover, more extreme weather has compromised the air quality and led to changes in vector ecology, enhancing the risk of respiratory and infectious diseases. Rising sea level has impacted the surface and groundwater quality and increased the allergens, thereby increasing a threat to the respiratory health of humans.

The health effects of global environmental change tend to vary between countries and are primarily based on their economic status. This means that developing countries are more impacted by climate change as compared to well-developed countries. For instance, loss of healthy life years in low-income African countries is predicted to be 500 times that in Europe. The fourth assessment report of the Intergovernmental Panel on Climate Change concluded that adverse health effects are much more likely in low-income countries and vulnerable subpopulations[5]. These disparities may well increase in coming decades, not only because of regional differences in the intensity of environmental changes, such as water shortages and soil erosion, but also because of exacerbations of differentials in economic conditions, levels of social and human capital, political power, and local environmental dependency.

These differential health risks also reflect the broader issue of access to global and local 'public goods.' Most of the world's arable land has now been privatized; stocks of wild species (fish, animals, and wild plants) are declining as population pressures and commercial activities intensify. In addition, fresh water is increasingly becoming subject to market pricing as well. Therefore, social policies should pay particular attention to the health inequalities that flow from unequal access to environmental fundamentals.

Availability of safe drinking water illustrates access to what, historically, was common property: 1.1 billion people lack safe drinking water, and 2.6 billion lack basic sanitation. The lack of safe drinking water can be attributed to the lack of water in general due to Earth's increasing temperature. Beyond diarrheal disease, water-related health risks also arise from chemical contamination—such as arsenic as a cause of skin pigmentation, hyperkeratosis, cardiovascular disease, neuropathy, and cancer.

Human-induced global climate change is now an acknowledged reality. Humankind took a long time to recognize the resultant health risks, current and future, and their unequal effects around the world, but the topic is now attracting much attention. Health risks are arising from the direct and indirect pathways and are reflected by changes in both average climate conditions and climatic variability. The main risks are:

- Effects of heatwaves and other extreme events (cyclones, floods, storms, wildfires)
- Changes in patterns of infectious disease
- Effects on food yields
- Effects on freshwater supplies
- Impaired functioning of ecosystems (for example, wetlands as water filters)
- Displacement of vulnerable populations (for example, low lying island and coastal populations)
- Loss of livelihoods

Extreme weather events, infection, and malnutrition have the greatest health effects in poor and vulnerable populations. In sub-Saharan Africa, over 110 million people currently live in regions prone to malaria epidemics. Climate change could add 20-70 million to this figure by the 2080s, assuming no population increase and including forecast malaria reductions in West Africa from drying[6]. Any such increase would exacerbate poverty and make it harder to achieve and sustain health improvements.

According to WHO, an estimated 12.6 million deaths could be attributed to deteriorating environmental conditions or 23 percent of the total[7]. The highest proportion of deaths attributable to the environment occurs in South-East Asia and the Western Pacific (respectively 28 percent and 27 percent of the total burden). The number of deaths attributable to the environment is 23 percent in sub-Saharan Africa, 22 percent in the Eastern Mediterranean region, 11 percent, and 15 percent in the Organization for Economic Co-Operation and Development (OECD) non-OECD countries of the Americas region, and 15 percent in Europe[8].

Deaths related to non-communicable diseases are rising in all regions: three-quarters of people who died from non-communicable diseases in 2012 lived in low and middle-income countries. The report also points to the drivers of the environmental health-related impacts - including ecosystem disruption, climate change, inequality, unplanned urbanization, unhealthy and wasteful lifestyles, and unsustainable consumption and production patterns - and outlines the massive health and economic benefits that action would bring.

Climate change is exacerbating the scale and intensity of environment-related health risks. Estimates from the WHO indicate that 250,000 additional deaths could occur each year between 2030 and 2050, mostly from malnutrition, malaria, diarrhea, and heat stress, resulting from climate change. The key environmental factors highlighted in the report include:

1. Air pollution, which kills 7 million people across the world each year. Of these, 4.3 million are down to household air pollution, particularly among women and young children in developing countries.
2. Lack of access to clean water and sanitation that results in 842,000 people dying from diarrheal diseases every year, 97 percent of which are in developing countries. Diarrheal diseases are the 3rd leading cause of death in children younger than 5, representing 20 percent of all deaths in children under 5 years.
3. Chemical exposure: Some 107,000 people die annually from asbestos exposure, and 654,000 died from exposure to lead in 2010.
4. Natural disasters: Since the first UN Climate Change Conference in 1995, there has been a loss of 606,000 lives, and 4.1 billion people have been injured, left homeless, or in need of emergency assistance as a result of weather-related disasters.

The spectrum of potential strategies to reduce health risks is wide, commensurate with the diversity of threats to health posed by climate change and other global environmental changes. Local policies and actions, both to mitigate environmental change at source and adapt to existing and unavoidable risks to health, will often need support from health attuned policies at provincial, national, and international levels. For example, community programs to mosquito-proof houses will need to be reinforced by improvements in the national surveillance of infectious diseases and outbreak warning systems.

In the present scenario, doctors and other health professionals have particular knowledge, opportunity, and, often, political leverage that can help ensure—through advocacy or direct participation—those preventive actions are taken. These actions include promoting public understanding, monitoring and reporting environmental change's health effects, and proposing and advocating local adaptive responses. In addition to these actions, health professionals can also promote adaptive strategies such as:

- Public education, primarily through healthcare settings such as doctors' waiting rooms and hospital clinics.
- Preventive programs—e.g., vaccines, mosquito control, food hygiene and inspection, nutritional supplementation.
- Health care (especially mental health and primary care) for communities affected by environmental adversity.
- Surveillance of disease (especially infectious disease) and key risk factors.
- Forecasting future health risks from projected climate change.
- Forecasting future health risks and gains from mitigation and adaptation strategies.
- Health sector workforce training and in-career development.

Many local actions can be taken to reduce the vulnerability of communities and populations. These will vary considerably between different regions of the world and prevailing socioeconomic conditions and available resources. During Australia's recent prolonged drought (2001-7), some rural health doctors reported that fostering and supporting communal activities (community choirs, social gatherings, financial advisory networks, etc.) increased local resilience against depression associated with loss of livelihood.

Climate change and other large-scale environmental changes are unlikely to cause entirely new diseases; however, they may contribute to the emergence of new strains of viruses and other microbes that can infect humans and alter the incidence, range, and seasonality of many existing health disorders. Hence, existing healthcare and public health systems should provide an appropriate starting point for adaptive strategies to lessen health effects.

Although adaptive strategies will minimize the effects of climate change, the more significant public health preventive challenge lies in stopping the process of climate change. This requires bold and far-sighted policy decisions at national and international levels, entailing much greater emission cuts than were being proposed a decade ago.

Scientists have concluded that we need to prevent atmospheric carbon dioxide concentrations exceeding 450-500 ppm to avoid the serious, perhaps irreversible, damage to many natural systems and ecological processes that a global average temperature increase of 2-3oC would cause. This requires early radical action as today's concentrations are approaching 390 ppm compared with 280 ppm before industrialization.

Health professionals, acting through citizens' or professional organizations, have both the opportunity and responsibility to contribute to resolving this momentous issue. Improving awareness of the problem is the first step. Since 1993, doctors from 14 countries (including six low-income countries) have played a central role in the Intergovernmental Panel on Climate Change's assessment of climate change's health effects. The health sector, meanwhile, must minimize greenhouse gas emissions from its own infrastructure, especially hospitals. The problem of climate change and declining public health can be solved with the help of investments in a healthy environment that aims to bring multiple benefits. These include:

- The successful phase-out of nearly 100 ozone-depleting substances (ODS) means that up to 2 million skin cancer cases and many millions of eye cataracts may be prevented each year by 2030 thanks to the healing ozone layer.
- Benefits from eliminating lead in gasoline on a global scale have been estimated at $2.45 trillion per year, or 4 percent of global Gross Domestic Product (GDP), saving an estimated 1 million premature deaths per year.
- Implementing proven, cost-effective measures to reduce emissions of short-lived climate pollutants such as black carbon

and methane could reduce global warming by 0.5°C by the middle of the century and save 2.4 million lives a year from reduced air pollution by 2030.
- Investments in preventative workplace health programs of around $18-60/worker can reduce sick leave absences by 27 percent. At the same time, the return on investment in water and sanitation services is between $5 and $28 per dollar.

In order to achieve these benefits, four integrated approaches have been recommended:

1. DETOXIFY: Remove harmful substances from and mitigate their impact on the environment in which people live and work.
2. DECARBONIZE: Reduce the use of carbon fuels and, thereby, emissions of carbon dioxide (CO_2) through renewables. Over their life-cycle, the pollution-related human health and environmental impacts of solar, wind, and hydropower are 3 to 10 times lower than fossil-fuel power plants.
3. DECOUPLE RESOURCE USE AND CHANGE LIFESTYLES: Generate the necessary economic activity and value to sustain the world's population with lower resource use, less waste, less pollution, and less environmental destruction.
4. ENHANCE ECOSYSTEM RESILIENCE AND PROTECTION OF THE PLANET'S NATURAL SYSTEMS: Build the capacity of the environment, economies, and societies to anticipate, respond to and recover from disturbances and shocks through protection and conservation of genetic diversity and terrestrial, coastal, and marine biodiversity; strengthening ecosystem restoration; and reducing pressures from livestock production and logging on natural ecosystems.

Health professionals all over the world are playing a critical role in promoting the public understanding of the harmful impact of actions that lead to climatic change. Several reports have highlighted the potentially great damage to the world's economic system from unconstrained climate change. However, the greater risk is to the vitality and health of all species, including humans, if current climatic trends continue to weaken the Earth's life support systems. This means that strategies and plans need to be devised to deal with the impact of climatic changes on public health, and these strategies need to be put in action at the earliest to prevent further damage. In addition, humans also need to make changes in their lifestyles and opt for eco-friendly methods and means.

The climatic change is adversely impacting all living beings. Natural resources are becoming scarce and are, therefore, becoming pricier as well. Due to this, it is becoming challenging for people to afford the basic necessities of life and maintain their health. Now is the time to bring about the change that can help reverse years of damage. Every time you choose an eco-friendly alternative, you are helping the environment and making the world a better place to live not just for yourself but for others as well.

The importance of a sustainable environment can be identified from the strong link between a sustainable environment and health. Various aspects of a sustainable environment positively affect human health upon different parameters. Sustained outdoor air quality is associated with zero threats of respiratory health issues such as asthma and chronic obstructive pulmonary diseases. It also reduces the susceptibility to infection and sensitivity to allergens.

Well-sustained environmental health ensures surface and groundwater quality and reduces the risks and threats of waterborne diseases such as cholera. Toxic substances and hazardous waste accumulation is currently a significant threat to human health. It can lead to genetic mutations, behavioral abnormalities, physical deformations, physiological malfunctions, cancer, and birth defects[9]. Sustainable environmental health with low levels of toxic substances and hazardous waste promises sustainability of human health and their generations. Good quality of environment reduces the risk of exposure to hazardous substances in the air, water, soil, and food. Sustainable communities and environment are important for the improvement and sustainability of mental health and wellbeing. It is also associated with a reduced risk of mental health disorders[10].

A strong link has been found between a sustainable environment, leading to quality infrastructure and surveillance, and human health[11]. Quality infrastructure enhances competitiveness and productivity, facilitating international trade and employment. It also reduces the risk of structural problems and strengthens green environment building. Furthermore, a well-sustained environment promises the quality of surveillance systems. These implications have a diverse impact on public health and reduce the threat of epidemics and pandemics. Sustainability of the environment ensures human health via positive impacts on global environmental health, encompassing the elements of the natural world. There is a significant need for proper urban planning to reduce economic and environmental impacts that accompany technological and natural disasters. Environmental sustainability can, in turn, reduce the risk of natural and technological disasters providing quality infrastructure for communities, ensuring long-term positive effects on the public health. Environmental sustainability has a direct influence on climatic changes via environment-friendly development activities, good air and water quality, and reduced carbon emission. Consequentially, these are positive health indicators for the public. Environmental sustainability reduces the risk of occupational hazards, thereby ensuring the sustainability of the physical and mental health of the public.

With changes in climate, indoor air pollution has been recognized as a threat to human health. Environmental sustainability, however, reduces the risk of indoor air pollution such as by using improved cooking stoves. Poor sanitation and inadequate heating are associated with negative impacts on physical health. Well-sustained sanitation not only ensures physical health but also reduces the risk of water-borne diseases. Green infrastructure is known to promote human health by avoiding electrical and fire hazards such as in the workplace environment. Quality infrastructure thus reduces occupational hazards and promotes the health and wellbeing of the public. Lead-based health hazards are a significant risk, particularly due to the wide use of deteriorating lead-based paint on windows, window sills, doors, and door frames. Titanium white paint is a great alternative that is less toxic and is considered safe enough to use[12]. Environmental sustainability ensures an improved public health surveillance system and promotes disease prevention, detection, and treatment. Environment protection agencies are emphasizing the electronic industry to make new and safer alternatives that pose less threat to human health. Industrial development is also shifting towards the use of renewable energy resources and environment-friendly development activities. This might affect public health to a significant extent by improving air quality and community infrastructure. Transformation towards green energy resources has been ensured after environmental risk assessment activities[13]. Environmental risk assessment helps in assessing the likely risk of harm that can be caused to the environment by the business. It includes activities that describe potential hazards and impacts of these activities before taking precautions to reduce the risks to the environment and health. Environmental sustainability benefits human health by sustaining the quality of elements of the ecosystem. It encourages human activities that benefit the overall ecosystem, water, and public health on a large scale.

Global warming has affected public health on a significantly large scale. Increasing temperature has damaged people's lung tissues which is caused by increasing ozone concentration. Due to severe negative impacts on the lungs, it can create further complications for asthma patients and patients with lung diseases. Due to ozone depletion, the human skin has become in direct contact with sunlight that has ultraviolet rays. This direct contact with UV rays is the major cause of various skin health-related disorders. Increasing global warming is also affecting various habitats and endangering various edible plant species. This, in turn, poses a threat to food security and malnutrition among certain countries that rely on plants for their food.

The climatic change is adversely impacting all living beings. Natural resources are becoming scarce and are, therefore, becoming pricier as well. Due to this, it is becoming challenging for people to afford the basic necessities of life and maintain their health. Now is the time to bring about the change that can help reverse years of damage. Every time you choose an eco-friendly alternative, you are helping the environment and making the world a better place to live not just for yourself but for others as well. There is a significant need for proper urban planning to reduce economic and environmental impacts that accompany technological and natural disasters. Environmental sustainability can, in turn, reduce the risk of natural and technological disasters providing quality infrastructure for communities, ensuring long term positive effects on the public health.

Climate Smart Resourcefulness

The concept of productivity in healthcare has long been centered on the delivery of more care—more patients seen, more procedures completed, and more treatments administered—within the same amount of time or resources. As healthcare systems evolve in complexity, the definition of productivity is undergoing a significant transformation. Rather than merely focusing on throughput, the paradigm is shifting toward a more nuanced understanding that prioritizes quality, outcomes, patient satisfaction, and the integration of technology. In the near and distant future, healthcare productivity will no longer be a matter of quantity but one of efficiency, personalization, and sustainable impact.

The Traditional View of Healthcare Productivity

Historically, healthcare productivity has been viewed through the lens of operational efficiency—maximizing the number of patients seen per hour, the number of tests conducted per day, or the speed of surgical interventions. The underlying goal was to increase output, often driven by the pressures of a fee-for-service system. This perspective, while beneficial for scaling services, often overlooked other critical aspects such as quality of care, patient-centeredness, and long-term health outcomes.

This model has proven unsustainable for several reasons:

- **Burnout and Workforce Strain**: The emphasis on speed and volume has led to increased burnout among healthcare professionals, reducing their ability to provide compassionate, patient-centered care.
- **Quality Compromise**: In many cases, high throughput has been associated with a decrease in the quality of care, as less time is available to address complex, holistic patient needs.
- **Misaligned Incentives**: Fee-for-service models encourage more interventions, not necessarily better or more effective ones. This has led to increased healthcare costs without proportional improvements in patient outcomes.

Shifting the Productivity Paradigm: Value Over Volume

In the future, healthcare productivity will move from the traditional volume-based metrics to a value-based model. This shift is already underway with initiatives like value-based care (VBC), where the focus is on improving patient outcomes and experiences while controlling costs. Value-based models encourage healthcare systems to prioritize interventions that lead to long-term health benefits, reduce hospital readmissions, and enhance the patient experience. This shift will require healthcare systems to rethink how productivity is measured and achieved.

Key Components of Value-Based Healthcare Productivity:

1. **Patient Outcomes**: The ultimate goal of healthcare is improving health, not just providing treatments. Productivity will be measured by how well patients recover, how effectively chronic diseases are managed, and how health outcomes compare to cost inputs.

2. **Patient Satisfaction**: The patient experience will be a key metric for productivity. This includes not only satisfaction with care but also with access, communication, and the overall experience within the healthcare system.
3. **Efficiency of Resource Use**: Healthcare systems will need to manage resources—time, staff, equipment, and technology—more efficiently without compromising quality. The balance of efficiency and quality will be critical to future productivity models.

The Role of Technology: AI, Automation, and Big Data

Technology will be at the forefront of this paradigm shift, transforming how care is delivered, measured, and optimized. Emerging technologies will enable healthcare providers to achieve productivity gains that are inconceivable within today's systems. These innovations will redefine healthcare productivity by enhancing precision, speed, and personalization.

1. **Artificial Intelligence (AI)**: AI-powered tools will enhance diagnostic accuracy, support decision-making, and automate routine tasks. From imaging analysis to predictive analytics for patient outcomes, AI will reduce the cognitive burden on physicians, allowing them to focus on complex, high-value tasks. AI will also help with optimizing workflows and scheduling, reducing bottlenecks in care delivery.
2. **Telemedicine and Virtual Care**: The expansion of telemedicine will redefine how productivity is measured. By reducing the need for physical visits, healthcare providers will be able to manage larger patient panels more effectively. In the future, productivity will include how well healthcare systems leverage virtual care models, combining in-person care with remote monitoring and AI-driven consultations.

3. **Automation and Robotics**: Automation in hospitals and clinics will streamline administrative tasks, freeing up healthcare workers to spend more time on direct patient care. Robotic-assisted surgeries, meanwhile, will enhance precision and reduce recovery times, improving overall productivity by minimizing complications and hospital stays.
4. **Big Data and Predictive Analytics**: The use of large datasets will enable healthcare systems to make more informed decisions about resource allocation, patient care strategies, and public health interventions. Predictive analytics will forecast patient needs and optimize workflows, ensuring that healthcare systems can anticipate demand and respond proactively.

Personalization and Preventive Care

Another fundamental shift in healthcare productivity will be the move from reactive to proactive and preventive care. Advances in genomics, wearable health devices, and personalized medicine will allow for highly individualized care plans that prevent illness before it occurs, or detect it early when interventions are most effective.

Key Innovations:

1. **Genomic Medicine**: The future of healthcare productivity will involve personalized treatments based on an individual's genetic makeup. This will allow healthcare providers to target therapies more precisely, improving outcomes while reducing unnecessary treatments.
2. **Wearable Technology and Remote Monitoring**: Wearable devices, from fitness trackers to sophisticated biosensors, will continuously monitor patients' vital signs and other health metrics. This data will feed into healthcare systems in real-time, allowing for early interventions and reducing the need for emergency care. The result will be a system that prioritizes

wellness, with productivity measured by the ability to maintain health, not just treat disease.
3. **AI-Assisted Preventive Healthcare**: AI will continuously analyze health data to predict potential issues, allowing providers to engage in preventive care rather than reactive treatments. This will redefine healthcare productivity, as the system becomes more efficient at keeping people healthy rather than simply treating the sick.

Reimagining the Healthcare Workforce

Healthcare productivity in the future will also require a rethinking of the workforce. Traditional roles and hierarchies will give way to more flexible, interdisciplinary teams supported by technology.

1. **Interdisciplinary Collaboration**: Teams will be made up of physicians, nurses, data scientists, AI specialists, and patient advocates working together. The emphasis will be on collaboration, with each member of the team contributing specialized knowledge to enhance care delivery. This will increase the overall productivity of the healthcare system, as tasks will be distributed based on expertise rather than rigid job descriptions.
2. **AI Augmentation, Not Replacement**: Rather than replacing healthcare workers, AI and robotics will augment their capabilities, allowing them to focus on more complex and creative problem-solving. The most productive systems will be those that effectively blend human expertise with technological support.
3. **Continuous Education and Adaptability**: The healthcare workforce of the future will need to be more adaptable and tech-savvy. Productivity will depend on the ability of workers to continuously learn and incorporate new technologies and practices into their daily routines.

Sustainability and the Future of Healthcare Productivity

As healthcare productivity moves into the future, sustainability will be a key focus. Efficient use of resources—both financial and environmental—will be critical for long-term success. This includes reducing waste, optimizing supply chains, and investing in green technologies to reduce the environmental impact of healthcare.

- **Green Healthcare**: The most productive healthcare systems of the future will not only provide better care but also operate in an environmentally responsible manner. Hospitals will use renewable energy, reduce waste through advanced recycling systems, and design facilities to minimize their carbon footprint.
- **Sustainable Healthcare Systems**: Efficiency will also mean addressing healthcare disparities. Systems that can effectively reduce inequities and provide access to underserved populations will be considered more productive, as they will contribute to overall societal health and economic stability.

Conclusion: A Holistic Vision of Productivity

The future paradigm of healthcare productivity will be about far more than just increasing throughput. It will involve a holistic view that considers the well-being of patients, the efficiency of resources, the integration of cutting-edge technology, and the sustainability of healthcare systems. Healthcare organizations will need to adapt to this new reality by embracing innovation, prioritizing value over volume, and investing in the workforce of the future. This shift promises to create a more effective, equitable, and sustainable healthcare system for all.

REFERENCES

Chapter 1

[1] The Common wealth fund, (2020). International Health Care System Profiles; United States. https://www.commonwealthfund.org/international-health-policy-center/countries/united-states

[2] Markit, I. H. S. (2017). The complexities of physician supply and demand: Projections from 2015 to 2030. *Assoc. Amer. Med. Colleges.*

[3] ACOG., (2018). The Late-Career Obstetrician–Gynecologist. https://www.acog.org/clinical/clinical-guidance/committee-opinion/articles/2018/06/the-late-career-obstetrician-gynecologist.

[4] Ibid 3

[5] Tolbert, J., Orgera, K., and Damico, A., (2020). Key Facts about the Uninsured Population. https://www.kff.org/uninsured/issue-brief/key-facts-about-the-uninsured-population/

[6] Knebel, E., & Greiner, A. C. (Eds.). (2003). Health professions education: A bridge to quality.

[7] Ibid 6

Chapter 2

[1] Healthy people, (2020). Global Health. https://www.healthypeople.gov/2020/topics-objectives/topic/global-health

[2] Schneider, E. C., Sarnak, D. O., Squires, D., & Shah, A. (2017). Mirror, Mirror 2017: international Comparison Reflects flaws and Opportunities for Better U.S. Heath Care.

[3] Morra, D., Nicholson, S., Levinson, W., Gans, D. N., Hammons, T., & Casalino, L. P. (2011). US physician practices versus Canadians: spending nearly four times as much money interacting with payers. *Health Affairs*, *30*(8), 1443-1450.

[4] McCoy, D., & Brikci, N. (2010). Taskforce on innovative international financing for health systems: what next?. *Bulletin of the World Health Organization, 88,* 478-480.

[5] Requejo, J. H., Bryce, J., Victora, C., Deixel, A., Wardlaw, T., Dwivedi, A., ... & Zimmerman, S. (2013). Accountability for maternal, newborn and child survival: The 2013 Update. *Geneva: World Health Organization and UNICEF.*

[6] Etienne, C., Asamoa-Baah, A., & Evans, D. B. (2010). *Health systems financing: the path to universal coverage.* World Health Organization.

[7] Bang, A., Chatterjee, M., Dasgupta, J., Garg, A., Jain, Y., Kumar, A. K., ... & Varkey, L. C. (2011). High level expert group report on universal health coverage for India.

[8] Lu, C., Chin, B., Lewandowski, J. L., Basinga, P., Hirschhorn, L. R., Hill, K., ... & Binagwaho, A. (2012). Towards universal health coverage: an evaluation of Rwanda Mutuelles in its first eight years. *PloS one, 7*(6), e39282.

[9] Abiiro, G. A., & McIntyre, D. (2013). Universal financial protection through National Health Insurance: a stakeholder analysis of the proposed one-time premium payment policy in Ghana. *Health policy and planning, 28*(3), 263-278.

Chapter 3

[1] Chung, M., (2017). Health Care Reform: Learning from Other Major Health Care Systems. https://pphr.princeton.edu/2017/12/02/unhealthy-health-care-a-cursory-overview-of-major-health-care-systems/

[2] Census.gov. (2016). Health Insurance Coverage in the United States: 2015. https://www.census.gov/library/publications/2016/demo/p60-257.html

[3] Ginter, P. M., Duncan, W. J., & Swayne, L. E. (2018). *The strategic management of health care organizations.* John Wiley & Sons.

[4] SHSMD., (2017). Four Reasons Why Strategic Management is Essential to Healthcare Organizations. https://my.shsmd.org/blogs/the-shsmd-team/2017/05/24/four-reasons-why-strategic-management-is-essential-to-healthcare-organizations

[5] Sfantou, D. F., Laliotis, A., Patelarou, A. E., Sifaki-Pistolla, D., Matalliotakis, M., & Patelarou, E. (2017, December). Importance of leadership style towards quality of care measures in healthcare settings: a systematic review. In *Healthcare* (Vol. 5, No. 4, p. 73). Multidisciplinary Digital Publishing Institute.

[6] Abbas, W., & Asghar, I. (2010). The role of leadership in organizatinal change: relating the successful organizational change with visionary and innovative leadership.

Chapter 4

[1] Fox, S. (2006). Most Internet users start at a search engine when looking for health information online. Very few check the source and date of the information they find. *PEW/Internet and American Life Project.*

[2] research2guidance., (n.d.). 325,000 mobile health apps available in 2017 – Android now the leading mHealth platform. https://research2guidance.com/325000-mobile-health-apps-available-in-2017/

[3] Heath, S., (2016). How Patient Portals Improve Patient Engagement. https://patientengagementhit.com/features/how-patient-portals-improve-patient-engagement

[4] Prescott, R., (2013). Mhealth: 2.8 million patients remotely monitored worldwide in 2012. https://www.rcrwireless.com/20130116/wireless/2-8-m-patients-remotely-monitored-worldwide-2012

Chapter 5

[1] Dieleman, J. L., Squires, E., Bui, A. L., Campbell, M., Chapin, A., Hamavid, H., ... & Murray, C. J. (2017). Factors associated with increases in US health care spending, 1996-2013. *Jama, 318*(17), 1668-1678. .

[2] California Health Care Almanac, (n.d.) https://www.chcf.org/wp-content/uploads/2019/05/HealthCareCostsAlmanac2019.pdf

[3] Ibid – 1

[4] Claxton, G., Levitt, L., Rae, M., & Sawyer, B. (2018). Increases in cost-sharing payments continue to outpace wage growth. *Peterson-Kaiser Health System Tracker, 15.*

Chapter 6

[1] CDC. (2021). Symptoms of COVID-19. https://www.cdc.gov/coronavirus/2019-ncov/symptoms-testing/symptoms.html

[2] WHO. (2021). Coronavirus disease (COVID-19) advice for the public. https://www.who.int/emergencies/diseases/novel-coronavirus-2019/advice-for-public

[3] Clift, K., (2020). How are companies responding to the coronavirus crisis? https://www.weforum.org/agenda/2020/03/how-are-companies-responding-to-the-coronavirus-crisis-d15bed6137/

[4] Priya, R., (2020). Survival strategies for businesses during COVID-19 lockdown. https://economictimes.indiatimes.com/small-biz/hr-leadership/leadership/survival-strategies-for-businesses-during-covid-19-lockdown/articleshow/75371157.cms?from=mdr

[5] Monaghesh, E., & Hajizadeh, A. (2020). The role of telehealth during COVID-19 outbreak: a systematic review based on current evidence. *BMC Public Health, 20*(1), 1-9.

[6] World Health Organization. (2020). *Mask use in the context of COVID-19: interim guidance, 1 December 2020* (No. WHO/2019-nCoV/IPC_Masks/2020.5). World Health Organization.

[7] World Health Organization. (2021). *COVID-19 vaccination: supply and logistics guidance: interim guidance, 12 February 2021* (No. WHO/2019-nCoV/vaccine_deployment/logistics/2021.1). World Health Organization.

Chapter 7

[1] Foley, (2014). 2014 Telemedicine Survey Executive Summary. https://www.foley.com/en/insights/publications/2014/11/2014-telemedicine-survey-executive-summary

[2] Williams, S. J., & Calnan, M. (Eds.). (2013). *Modern medicine: lay perspectives and experiences*. Routledge.

[3] McKinsey, (2020). COVID-19 Consumer Healthcare Insights: What 2021 may hold. https://www.mckinsey.com/industries/healthcare-systems-and-services/our-insights/covid-19-consumer-healthcare-insights-what-2021-may-hold

[4] Bestsennyy, O., Gilbert, G., Harris, A., & Rost, J. (2020). Telehealth: a quarter-trillion-dollar post-COVID-19 reality. *McKinsey and Company, 29*.

[5] American Medical Association. (2020). 50-state survey: Establishment of a patient-physician relationship via telemedicine. *2018 Accessed on October, 11*, 2018-10.

[6] Appleman, E. R., O'Connor, M. K., Rockefeller, W., Morin, P., & Moo, L. R. (2020). Using video telehealth to deliver patient-centered collaborative care: The G-IMPACT pilot. *Clinical gerontologist*, 1-10.

[7] Pallipedia. (2016). Ambulatory care. https://pallipedia.org/ambulatory-care/

[8] Bestsennyy, O., Gilbert, G., Harris, A., & Rost, J., (2021). Telehealth: A quarter-trillion-dollar post-COVID-19 reality? https://www.mckinsey.com/industries/healthcare-systems-and-services/our-insights/telehealth-a-quarter-trillion-dollar-post-covid-19-reality#

Chapter 8

[1] WHO, (2019). Global Spending on Health: A World in Transition. https://www.who.int/health_financing/documents/health-expenditure-report-2019.pdf?ua=1

[2] Gingiss, D., (2019). Why Treating Patients As Consumers Can Improve The Healthcare Experience. https://www.forbes.com/sites/dangingiss/2019/07/09/why-treating-patients-as-consumers-can-improve-the-healthcare-experience/?sh=174b48963a14

[3] O'Hara, M. (2017). Appearing Live: Spectatorship, Affect, and Liveness in Contemporary British Performance.

[4] Toma Kulbytė, T., (2021). 7 CUSTOMER EXPERIENCE STATISTICS YOU NEED TO KNOW FOR 2022. https://www.superoffice.com/blog/customer-experience-statistics/

[5] Nash, D., (2020). COVID-19 Drug Pricing: A Pivotal Point for Pharma. https://www.medpagetoday.com/infectiousdisease/covid19/86196

[6] Bikales, J., (2020). Companies have raised prices on 245 drugs during pandemic, advocacy group says. https://thehill.com/policy/healthcare/505115-companies-hiked-prices-on-245-drugs-during-pandemic-advocacy-group-says

[7] Erickson, S. M., Rockwern, B., Koltov, M., & McLean, R. M. (2017). Putting patients first by reducing administrative tasks in health care: a position paper of the American College of Physicians. *Annals of internal medicine*, *166*(9), 659-661.

Chapter 9

[1] KAGAN, J., (2021). Centers for Medicare & Medicaid Services (CMS). https://www.investopedia.com/terms/u/us-centers-medicare-and-medicaid-services-cms.asp

[2] ASCO. (2021). COVID-19 Coding and Reporting Information. New CPT ®, HCPCS, and ICD-10 CM Codes. https://www.asco.org/sites/new-www.asco.org/files/content-files/advocacy-and-policy/documents/2020-COVID19-Billing-and-Coding-Resource.pdf

[3] Miller, M., (2020). Medicare Is Updating Coverage to Help in the Coronavirus Crisis. https://www.nytimes.com/2020/03/24/business/coronavirus-medicare-elderly.html

[4] Araujo, M., (2020). Health and Medical Insurance Differences: HMO, PPO, POS, EPO. https://www.thebalance.com/health-and-medical-insurance-2645378

[5] HEALTHCARE REFORM, (n.d.). Healthcare Consumerism: The Disconnect Between Knowing What Needs to Change and Putting a Strategy in Place to Get There. https://www.medirevv.com/blog/healthcare-consumerism-the-disconnect-between-knowing-what-needs-to-change-and-putting-a-strategy-in-place-to-get-there

[6] Lambrew, J. M. (2018). *Getting ready for health reform 2020: What past presidential campaigns can teach us*. New York (NY): Commonwealth Fund.

Chapter 10

[1] Fabbri, E., An, Y., Zoli, M., Simonsick, E. M., Guralnik, J. M., Bandinelli, S., ... & Ferrucci, L. (2015). Aging and the burden of multimorbidity: associations with inflammatory and anabolic hormonal biomarkers. *Journals of Gerontology Series A: Biomedical Sciences and Medical Sciences*, *70*(1), 63-70.

[2] Violan, C., Foguet-Boreu, Q., Flores-Mateo, G., Salisbury, C., Blom, J., Freitag, M., ... & Valderas, J. M. (2014). Prevalence, determinants and patterns of multimorbidity in primary care: a systematic review of observational studies. *PloS one*, 9(7), e102149.

[3] Wikström, K., Lindström, J., Harald, K., Peltonen, M., & Laatikainen, T. (2015). Clinical and lifestyle-related risk factors for incident multimorbidity: 10-year follow-up of Finnish population-based cohorts 1982–2012. *European journal of internal medicine*, 26(3), 211-216.

[4] Nagel, G., Peter, R., Braig, S., Hermann, S., Rohrmann, S., & Linseisen, J. (2008). The impact of education on risk factors and the occurrence of multimorbidity in the EPIC-Heidelberg cohort. *BMC public health*, 8(1), 384.

[5] Vogeli, C., Shields, A. E., Lee, T. A., Gibson, T. B., Marder, W. D., Weiss, K. B., & Blumenthal, D. (2007). Multiple chronic conditions: prevalence, health consequences, and implications for quality, care management, and costs. *Journal of general internal medicine*, 22(3), 391-395.

[6] Zulman, D. M., Chee, C. P., Wagner, T. H., Yoon, J., Cohen, D. M., Holmes, T. H., ... & Asch, S. M. (2015). Multimorbidity and healthcare utilisation among high-cost patients in the US Veterans Affairs Health Care System. *BMJ open*, 5(4).

[7] Fortin, M., Lapointe, L., Hudon, C., Vanasse, A., Ntetu, A. L., & Maltais, D. (2004). Multimorbidity and quality of life in primary care: a systematic review. *Health and Quality of life Outcomes*, 2(1), 51.

[8] Townsend, A., Hunt, K., & Wyke, S. (2003). Managing multiple morbidity in mid-life: a qualitative study of attitudes to drug use. *Bmj*, 327(7419), 837.

[9] Improvement, Q. (2011). US department of health and human services health resources and services administration.

[10] https://www.ahrq.gov/patient-safety/quality resources/tools/chtoolbx/ understand

Chapter 11

[1] ElKordy, M. (2013). Transformational leadership and organizational culture as predictors of employees attitudinal outcomes. *Business Management Dynamics*, *3*(5), 15.

[2] Abbas, W., & Asghar, I. (2010). The role of leadership in organizatinal change: relating the successful organizational change with visionary and innovative leadership.

[3] Kouzes, J. M., & Posner, B. Z. (2007). The five practices of exemplary leadership. *The Jossey-Bass reader on educational leadership*, 63-74.

[4] Thompson, P. A. (2009). Creating leaders for the future. *AJN The American Journal of Nursing*, *109*(11), 50-52.

[5] Trastek, V. F., Hamilton, N. W., & Niles, E. E. (2014, March). Leadership models in health care—a case for servant leadership. In *Mayo Clinic Proceedings* (Vol. 89, No. 3, pp. 374-381). Elsevier.
[6] Healthcarecomm, (2011). Impact of Communication in Healthcare. https://healthcarecomm.org/about-us/impact-of-communication-in-healthcare/
[7] Hughes, R. (Ed.). (2008). Patient safety and quality: An evidence-based handbook for nurses.
[8] Ghiasipour, M., Mosadeghrad, A. M., Arab, M., & Jaafaripooyan, E. (2017). Leadership challenges in health care organizations: The case of Iranian hospitals. *Medical journal of the Islamic Republic of Iran*, *31*, 96.

Chapter 12

[1] Coombs, B., & Feuer, W., (2020). The coronavirus test will be covered by Medicaid, Medicare and private insurance, Pence says. https://www.cnbc.com/2020/03/04/pence-announces-coronavirus-test-will-be-covered-by-medicaid-medicare.html
[2] OCM., (2020). Health Administration professors discuss effects of COVID-19 on country's health care system. http://ocm.auburn.edu/experts/2020/04/1171200-healthcare-system.php?ref=coronavirus&cat=medical
[3] McGuire, A. L., Aulisio, M. P., Davis, F. D., Erwin, C., Harter, T. D., Jagsi, R., ... & COVID-19 Task Force of the Association of Bioethics Program Directors (ABPD). (2020). Ethical challenges arising in the COVID-19 pandemic: an overview from the association of bioethics program directors (ABPD) Task force. *The American Journal of Bioethics*, *20*(7), 15-27.
[4] Dwivedi, Y. K., Hughes, D. L., Coombs, C., Constantiou, I., Duan, Y., Edwards, J. S., ... & Upadhyay, N. (2020). Impact of COVID-19 pandemic on information management research and practice: Transforming education, work and life. *International Journal of Information Management*, *55*, 102211.
[5] Caligiuri, P., De Cieri, H., Minbaeva, D., Verbeke, A., & Zimmermann, A. (2020). International HRM insights for navigating the COVID-19 pandemic: Implications for future research and practice.

Chapter 13

[1] Walker, P. G., Whittaker, C., Watson, O. J., Baguelin, M., Winskill, P., Hamlet, A., ... & Ghani, A. C. (2020). The impact of COVID-19 and strategies for mitigation and suppression in low-and middle-income countries. *Science*, *369*(6502), 413-422.
[2] Chai, J. (2015). Strategic Decision Making in Health Care.
[3] Rosli, N., & Nayan, S. M. (2020). Why Customer First?. *Journal of Undergraduate Social Science and Technology*, *2*(2).

[4] Häyry, M. (2021). The COVID-19 pandemic: Healthcare crisis leadership as ethics communication. *Cambridge Quarterly of Healthcare Ethics, 30*(1), 42-50.
[5] Ibid – 4
[6] Shaukat, N., Ali, D. M., & Razzak, J. (2020). Physical and mental health impacts of COVID-19 on healthcare workers: a scoping review. *International Journal of Emergency Medicine, 13*(1), 1-8.
[7] El Bcheraoui, C., Weishaar, H., Pozo-Martin, F., & Hanefeld, J. (2020). Assessing COVID-19 through the lens of health systems' preparedness: time for a change. *Globalization and Health, 16*(1), 1-5.

Chapter 14

[1] Ehealthinsurance., (2021). Around 48 percent of Americans are enrolled in private health insurance through their employers. https://www.ehealthinsurance.com/resources/small-business/how-many-americans-get-health-insurance-from-their-employer
[2] Hamel, L., Firth, J., and Brodie, M., (2015). Kaiser Health Tracking Poll: Late June 2015 - A Special Focus On The Supreme Court Decision. kff.org/health-reform/poll-finding/kaiser-health-tracking-poll-late-june-2015-a-special-focus-on-the-supreme-court-decision/
[3] MeyerGregg, S., BlanchfieldBonnie, B., BohmerRichard, M. J., & Craig, V. (2020). Alternative care sites for the Covid-19 pandemic: The early US and UK experience. *NEJM Catalyst Innovations in Care Delivery*.
[4] World Health Organization. (2006). The safety of medicines in public health programmes: pharmacovigilance, an essential tool.
[5] HPI., (n.d.) Rural and Urban Health. https://hpi.georgetown.edu/rural/
[6] Ibid – 5
[7] Ibid – 5
[8] Khalid, A., & Ali, S. (2020). COVID-19 and its Challenges for the Healthcare System in Pakistan. *Asian bioethics review, 12*(4), 551-564.

Chapter 15

[1] Mann, M. E., Rahmstorf, S., Steinman, B. A., Tingley, M., & Miller, S. K. (2016). The likelihood of recent record warmth. *Scientific Reports, 6*(1), 1-7.
[2] Stocker, T. F., Qin, D., Plattner, G. K., Alexander, L. V., Allen, S. K., Bindoff, N. L., ... & Xie, S. P. (2013). Technical summary. In *Climate change 2013: the physical science basis. Contribution of Working Group I to the Fifth Assessment Report of the Intergovernmental Panel on Climate Change* (pp. 33-115). Cambridge University Press.
[3] Wuebbles, D. J., Fahey, D. W., & Hibbard, K. A. (2017). Climate science special report: fourth national climate assessment, volume I.

[4] Hansen, G., & Stone, D. (2016). Assessing the observed impact of anthropogenic climate change. *Nature Climate Change*, *6*(5), 532-537.

[5] Intergovernmental Panel on Climate Change. Climate change 2006: impacts, adaptation and vulnerability Cambridge: Cambridge University Press, 2007.

[6] Hulme, M., Doherty, R., Ngara, T., New, M., & Lister, D. (2001). African climate change: 1900-2100. *Climate research*, *17*(2), 145-168.

[7] World Health Organization. (2016). An estimated 12.6 million deaths each year are attributable to unhealthy environments. *WHO. March*, *15*, 2016.

[8] Ibid – 7

[9] Ishchenko, V., Pohrebennyk, V., Borowik, B., Falat, P., & Shaikhanova, A. (2018). Toxic substances in hazardous household waste.

[10] Srinivasan, S.,O'fallon, L. R., & Dearry, A. (2003). Creating healthy communities, healthy homes, healthy people: initiating a research agenda on the built environment and public health. *American journal of public health*, *93*(9), 1446-1450.

[11] Coutts, C., & Hahn, M. (2015). Green infrastructure, ecosystem services, and human health. *International journal of environmental research and public health*, *12*(8), 9768-9798.

[12] Skocaj, M., Filipic, M., Petkovic, J., & Novak, S. (2011). Titanium dioxide in our everyday life; is it safe? *Radiology and oncology*, *45*(4), 227-247.

[13] Calza, F., Parmentola, A., & Tutore, I. (2017). Types of green innovations: Ways of implementation in a non-green industry. *Sustainability*, *9*(8), 1301.

"We should enhance solidarity and get through this together. We should follow the guidance of science, give full play to the leading role of the World Health Organization and launch a joint international response ... Any attempt of politicizing the issue, or stigmatization, must be rejected."
- President Xi Jinping

www.ingramcontent.com/pod-product-compliance
Lightning Source LLC
Chambersburg PA
CBHW020635220526
45464CB00001B/161